THE BROOKLYN CYCLONES

THE BROOKLYN CYCLONES

Hardball Dreams and the New Coney Island

BEN OSBORNE

New York University Press

NEW YORK AND LONDON

NEW YORK UNIVERSITY PRESS
New York and London
www.nyupress.org

Library of Congress Cataloging-in-Publication Data
Osborne, Ben, 1974–
The Brooklyn Cyclones : hardball dreams and
the new Coney Island / Ben Osborne.
p. cm.
ISBN 0–8147–6205–0 (cloth : alk. paper)
1. Brooklyn Cyclones (Baseball team)
2. Coney Island (New York, N. Y.) I. Title.
GV875.B69O82 2004
796.357'64'0974723—dc22   2003023700

New York University Press books are printed on acid-free paper,
and their binding materials are chosen for strength and durability.

Manufactured in the United States of America

10 9 8 7 6 5 4 3 2 1

Contents

Preface   vii

Prologue: June 2, 2001   1

1   Opening Day   5

2   The First Few Brooklyn "Home Stands"   29

3   Kay and the Cyclones Become Celebrities   53

4   Coney Island's Team Begins Its Own Rivalry—The "Ferry Series"   76

5   Kay and the Cyclones Take the New York–Penn League by Storm   113

6   Brett Kay Moves to the BIG City, Anthony Stays in Coney Island   128

7   The Last Home Game of the Regular Season   149

8   The Postseason   168

9   Epilogue: September 15, 2003   181

2001 Statistics and Standings   194

Acknowledgments   196

About the Author   198

All illustrations appear as an insert following p. 102.

Preface

When I realized, as the hype started to build at the beginning of 2001, that there was really going to be a professional baseball team in Brooklyn, I was ecstatic. A lifelong baseball fan and, more specifically, a Los Angeles Dodger fan, I'd harbored a pride in Brooklyn baseball my whole life. The truth was, however, that my connection to Brooklyn baseball felt pretty faint. Now there was more than talk. The Brooklyn Cyclones were about to become reality.

My grandfather, Ashton Osborne, was born in Brooklyn in 1914 and lived in the Flatbush area until 1933, when he left to attend Wesleyan University in Connecticut. At that point his family moved to Plainfield, New Jersey, and his Brooklyn days were over. His passion for the Dodgers, however, had been ingrained.

Even though he moved to Chicago in 1946, my grandfather stayed devoted to the Dodgers. And when my father, Jeffrey, was born there the following year, Tommy Lasorda's metaphorical "Dodger Blue blood" was apparently injected into his veins. By the time my grandfather allowed my father to stay home from school to watch Game 7 of the 1955 World Series between the Brooklyn Dodgers and New York Yankees (which the Dodgers actually won!), my dad was as hooked on his team as a young fan could be. Surely there was some sadness in the Osborne household when the Dodgers left Brooklyn for Los Angeles in 1957, but the family ties to Brooklyn were no longer strong. My father and grandfather were

Dodger fans at that point, and a pride in the team's Brooklyn heritage remained without the pain felt by folks who no longer had Duke Snider as a neighbor.

My father married my mother (another Chicagoland native) and they moved to California, where I was born, and then they moved to suburban New York, where my sisters and I were raised. Through it all, including the death of my grandfather when I was just two years old, my father remained a die-hard, stay-up-late-for-the-scores, curse-the-TV type of Dodger fan. Needless to say, I became that same type of Dodger fan as well. The Dodger love was never because they had some great teams in the '70s or because we lived briefly in their adopted home state of California. The love was always because—and who knows how many *thousands* of times, from grammar school to high school to college to the Yankee Stadium bleachers, I've explained this—my grandfather had passed it on.

So, with my somewhat unrealized Brooklyn baseball history, and three years of living in the borough under my belt (a fact my grandfather is said to smile about from above), I was thrilled about this new team, the Brooklyn Cyclones. I was not the only one. Coney Island–raised Michael Fabricant, a published author and the head of the Ph.D. program at the Hunter College School of Social Work, as well as a mentor to my wife, introduced me to his friend, the literary agent Lane Zachary. Lane wanted to sell a book about baseball returning to Brooklyn—Coney Island, no less—and I wanted to write one.

Once I'd made a couple trips to Coney Island with notebook in hand, it became clear that the ups, downs, and predicted ups again of Coney Island were nearly as big a part of the story as was the baseball. Various politicians had been talking about rehabilitating this magical amusement area for the last forty years, and now something new was indeed coming to the neighborhood. I also learned that the book should be given some historical context. *Some,* that is, because I quickly found out that the history of Coney Island—especially the amusement parks that have dominated its land—is worthy of entire books, and of course, plenty already exist.

Besides, as fascinating as the neighborhood is, I needed to tell the story of the Cyclones' first season through *people,* not just amusement park rides or new stadiums. During the summer of 2001, I spoke to lots of interesting characters in Coney Island, from bartenders to local residents, Major League hopefuls to retired players. From the many good stories I discovered, two stood out that would best allow me to tell the tale of the 2001 season.

One main character is Anthony Otero, a teen with Puerto Rican roots who lives in the Coney Island Houses, part of the ugly clump of New York City housing projects located at the desolate western end of Coney Island. Directly countering the basketball-centric expectations I had when I first strolled onto the project grounds, Anthony is a baseball fanatic. He's not so into basketball and doesn't care much about football. He just loves baseball, as if he were a kid out of the 1950s. He loves to play the game, in whatever form he can, and when I met him, though he'd never actually been to a professional game in person, he watched baseball on TV every night.

At that time, Anthony was preparing to enter his freshman year at neighborhood Abraham Lincoln High School, a former gem of the New York City school system that is now just another one of the city's chronically overcrowded and understaffed "places of learning." For financial and scholastic reasons, even Anthony's parents would say the odds of his going to college out of Lincoln were small. But Anthony's dreams didn't involve college anyway. Without having anyone in his life who could actually tell him if they were realistic or not, he had dreams of playing professional baseball. The same dreams I had when I was a kid. The same dreams my father had. Probably the same dreams my grandfather had. Anthony had to be one of my stories.

Getting to know the players on the Cyclones was a little harder than meeting kids in the neighborhood who are used to being ignored. The individuals that made up the Cyclone team, at least for the summer of 2001, were celebrities. They played in front of loud, sellout, 7,500–person crowds at just about every home game, a sensation that contradicted the fact that these young men were at just the second rung on the seemingly interminable six-rung ladder to the big leagues. With the help of the Cyclones' media relations staff, I eventually learned the stories of most of the players—what they were like off the field and where they came from.

One story, one personality, stood out from the others. It belongs to Brett Kay, a cool Californian with a rich sports background. Thanks to his late father, as well as family, friends, and coaches who taught him the game, Brett has been around professional sports his entire life. This fact could have made Brett one of the least likely players to think he'd make the big time—after all, he knows how difficult it is. And, unlike Anthony, Brett had been exposed to so many aspects of professional life that he could have envisioned himself chasing any number of dreams. Besides his father, who had played professional football, Brett's older brother works for the Anaheim Angels and his "father figure," who coached him as a kid, is a major figure in southern California banking. What's more, Brett attended Mater Dei High School, a private school in Orange County with outstanding athletic teams and a respected college-preparatory curriculum. But Brett wasn't too worried about the real world. Brett knew he had an athletic body. And didn't he get from home to first awfully fast for a catcher? Maybe Brett had every reason to dream of a Major League career. Certainly more reason than Anthony Otero had. Brett was an obvious choice to be my other story.

Over the course of the inaugural season of the Brooklyn Cyclones, and for a good many months after it ended, Anthony and Brett took me through their respective pasts and into their futures. Through their words and actions—their *stories,* as it were—Anthony and Brett more than justified, in conjunction with a review of Brooklyn's baseball past and Coney Island's wild history, a long look at present-day Brooklyn baseball and all that went into making it happen.

And as much as Anthony's and Brett's experiences revolved around the modern-day Cyclones, references and ties to the old Dodgers abounded. The Brooklyn Cyclones were creating dreams just like the ones that the Brooklyn Dodgers had created for my father, grandfather, and literally millions of other baseball fans. This book honors their stories just as it honors those of today's players and fans.

Prologue June 2, 2001

It is less than four weeks before the Brooklyn Cyclones—the new Single-A farm team of the New York Mets—will play the first professional game of baseball to take place in Brooklyn since the Brooklyn Dodgers' last game there in 1957, and few people have any idea what to expect, including many who will be intimately involved in this historic season. Among the many people unsure of what the Brooklyn Cyclones will mean are Brett Kay, a native Californian who will soon play for the team, and Anthony Otero, a young boy who lives fifteen blocks from the Cyclones' not-quite-finished stadium in the Coney Island section of Brooklyn.

On this exact day, Kay, a college junior, is helping his Cal State–Fullerton team to a 9–3 victory over Mississippi State in a game that clinches a spot for his team in the College World Series. Even though he could come back for his senior season, Kay knows he wants to turn pro after next week's draft. However, he does not know what Major League team will take him, where it will send him, or how much money it will pay him. "Even though I'm thinking about [next week's draft], and some of my teammates are also, it's not hard to focus on what the team is trying to accomplish. Now I'm so excited because this is my first trip to Omaha—the team went my freshman year, but I got sick and couldn't go. We've got a good squad, with a bunch of good guys," Kay says. "I should get drafted, but it won't really affect how I play. Getting drafted is no big thing in this program—a bunch of my buddies have been drafted, and we've talked about it. For now we just want to go to the World Series and win, and I think we have the best team to do that."

Kay has never been to New York before, and he's never heard of the Brooklyn Cyclones.

Young Anthony Otero is winding down his eighth-grade school year at "Cavallaro" (short for Joseph B. Cavallaro Intermediate School #281), on 24th Avenue in the Coney Island section of Brooklyn. There is no middle-school baseball team—and Anthony admits that his grades are too poor to allow him to do much extracurricular stuff anyway—but he still likes to both play and watch the game of baseball. He watches Yankee games with his mother on a nightly basis and often plays the sport outside his apartment building, which is located within the Coney Island Houses complex buried deep along Surf Avenue. He and his family have heard on the news about the stadium being built fifteen blocks away, and his bus takes a left past the construction site whenever he goes to school. "I see it every day," Anthony says. "I didn't know what it was for a while, but then they put up a sign that said, 'Brooklyn Cyclones Baseball Stadium.' I don't really know who they are, but it seems exciting to have a baseball stadium nearby."

Not exactly a Web surfer or chatroom user (while there are some Internet stations at libraries in Brooklyn, neither his school nor his home affords him the opportunity to regularly go online), Anthony knows little about these "Brooklyn Cyclones." The Internet is relevant because it is there that the Cyclones are already alive and well. And, while the example of Anthony and many of his Coney Island brethren speaks to America's "digital divide," the modern, ticket-buying public is ably represented online, and that's as good a place as any to measure popularity these days. Even with the season more than three weeks away and the Cyclone roster still lacking actual players, there is a busy, fan-organized chatroom on www.yahoo.com. Furthermore, the official website of the team, www.brooklyncyclones.com, is dutifully recording the enthusiastic messages of current and former Brooklyn residents who are extremely excited about the team.

The hunger for baseball is so strong that most of the tickets have already been scooped up, about a third through season-ticket plans and most of the rest on the first day single-game tickets went on sale, April 28, at the nearby King's Plaza Mall. One message board on the Cyclones' site, titled "Brooklyn Baseball Memories," is flooded with posts that speak to the appeal of the Cyclones. One fan, Horace DeBussy Jones, writes: "The Dodgers, walks in Prospect Park, a special day at Coney, stickball, Louie's Sweet Shop, sitting on stoops at night, the Duke going long, egg creams and pretzels . . . all of that and so much more about Brooklyn summers—welcome back baseball, we missed you."

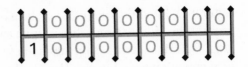

Opening Day

Monday, June 25, 2001, is a beautiful and stunning day in Coney Island, Brooklyn. The temperature is approaching ninety, and the ocean is glistening as the bright sun shines down on it. By 3:30 in the afternoon, Surf Avenue is teeming with people who have come to the neighborhood for the Brooklyn Cyclones' first home game, which will be the first professional baseball game played on Brooklyn soil in forty-four years. Appropriately, the Cyclones are a Class-A farm team of the New York Mets, the team that ostensibly replaced the Dodgers as New York's National League entry when they were birthed in 1962. The crowds are lining Surf Avenue from the Stillwell Avenue subway station through West 20th Street, with KeySpan Park taking up two whole blocks from 16th to 19th (there's no 18th street, and the official address is 1904 Surf Avenue), where Steeplechase Park once stood.

Fifteen blocks west, however, it's just another day at the Coney Island Houses. Between the shiny new stadium and the Houses are fifteen blocks that are so gray they seem incapable of reflecting the day's beauty. Nearly every building in this stretch, such as the Jewish Geriatric Center and the Surf Manor home for the mentally ill, is devoted to housing or "caring for" the poor, the old, or the handicapped. The massive stretch of New York City Housing Authority buildings (a.k.a. the projects) begins just west of KeySpan Park with the O'Dwyer Houses on the north side of Surf. The Coney Island Houses complex begins on the south side of Surf at West 29th and ends at West 32nd, with only the boardwalk and the water to the south of them. As you turn off Surf into project property, you see that the Houses property sports an awfully cheery sign welcoming visitors, featuring a cruise ship and palm trees in a bright beach motif. It's a nice enough image, but the Houses do not exactly conjure memories of peaceful, relaxing days in the sun. The Coney Island Houses are nothing if not drab, five red brick buildings standing an identical fourteen stories high that were built between 1955 and 1957 by the New York City Housing Authority. In total, the complex includes 535 apartment units. And it isn't just the Coney Island Houses that are drab. The projects on the blocks before it on the east, and those as far as one can see around the curve to the west, are also a picture of brutal architecture that had just one goal in mind—to "house" those who have nowhere else to live.

From WASPy Americans to Jewish, Italian, and Greek immigrants, to Latino and black Americans, to Russian Jews, the actual residential neighborhood of Coney Island has been home to a wide variety of ethnic groups. Economically, it has also changed drastically. Once it was basically a vacation spot for the very rich, while the local residents ran businesses that catered to the rich. It was then a lower-middle-class immigrant enclave for many years. The novelist Joseph Heller, of *Catch-22* fame, grew up in Coney Island in the 1930s and '40s. As he once wrote in *Show Magazine,* "There were apartment houses on every block in my section of Coney Island . . . none had elevators and one of the painful memories I have now is of old men and women laboring up the steep staircases. . . . Everyone's father had a job, but incomes were low."

The growth of the automobile's popularity and the birth of suburbs meant that people generally started to leave Coney Island when they could afford to. This was a phenomenon that took place in urban centers across America, but the exodus was even more pronounced in Coney Island. With the decline of the area's amusement parks, there was little reason to live out there, where daily life is very much removed from the bustle of rest of the city. New York City officials sped up the changes in the neighborhood when, in the late 1950s and into the '60s, they began knocking down multifamily homes throughout the western part of Coney Island and replaced them with towering project buildings that could house the people that greater New York City didn't quite want to deal with. Increasingly, this meant poor blacks, with a few Latinos sprinkled in. Unlike residents of neighborhoods such as Bedford-Stuyvesant in Brooklyn and Harlem in Manhattan, the black residents who made up the neighborhood through the '60s and '70s didn't really choose to be part of this community. Now that the forced migration of folks into this neighborhood is a couple of generations deep, some of the transplants have put down roots and established community organizations, such as the Astella Development Corporation, a nonprofit organization that was founded in 1975 by Coney Island residents who were concerned about the deterioration of their community. Still, services in the neighborhood are few and far between, and any feeling of the area's history is sorely lacking among the canyons of its housing projects.

Coney's depressing recent history, coupled with its magnificent, relatively ancient history, has meant that "revitalizing Coney Island" has been talked about for years, with many a politician promising to do just that. For as many years, the occasional book, magazine, or newspaper writer has been venturing down to the beach, chronicling the likelihood (or lack thereof) of just such a turnaround.

Maybe the turnaround is finally coming.

This is the first full week that school has been out, so the kids of the projects, for whom summer camp is something they've seen in the movies, have begun a ten-week stretch during which boredom is the chief enemy. This neighborhood has a serious reputation for basketball—across the street, the Surfside Gardens projects are where the NBA star Stephon Marbury and numerous other playground legends who have graced a local court known as "the Garden" and inspired the movie *He Got Game* came from—so one would expect to see basketballs being bounced left and right. And, as I walk onto this project's playground, I do see a number of kids in various Stephon-related gear, from "Starbury" t-shirts to jerseys with his name and number.

Hoops may be the clothing theme, but the game of choice this afternoon is actually baseball. Twelve black and Latino kids are divided into teams and are playing a real game, with a pitcher, a catcher, a few fielders, and a home run fence. The ball is actually a softball with frayed edges, and there are only three gloves (total!) among the group, but the kids are playing as seriously as if they'd been let onto the field at Yankee Stadium. My approach to the "field" is barely acknowledged, and even when I tell them I'm here to talk about the Brooklyn Cyclones—that baseball team the mayor swears will change their entire neighborhood for the better— the kids barely look up from their debate over how many outs there are.

One kid is essentially running the game, and he shows a passion that anyone who has played a version of sandlot baseball can appreciate. With the little whiskers he's got for a mustache and the fit, 5'5" frame that is holding up his ultrabaggy jean shorts and stylishly loose, short-sleeved, button-down top, Anthony Otero looks like the oldest kid out here. But, beyond the looks, Anthony stands out for his take-charge attitude—this kid is at once the game's umpire, official scorekeeper, and best player. Anthony says that he "has to be in charge of the game, because none of these kids know how to play right." His stern response is belied by the fact that he says everything with a smile and chuckle—Anthony may be the obvious leader of this little crew, but he's no playground dictator. He's a street-smart but cheerful teenager who is both bossy and funny at the same time. Anthony is happy to talk about himself and his friends, but he also makes it clear that he can't understand why anyone would care about what he had to say. A fourteen-year-old resident of Building Two at the Coney Island Houses, Anthony is doing what he says he'll do every single day of the summer: "Hang out with my friends and play sports. Sometimes we play basketball or handball, but usually in the summer we play baseball. That's my favorite sport."

Anthony's friend Josimar Aleman comes over and talks about how the kids play sports "because there ain't nothing else to do around here, and we ain't trying to get in trouble."

In September, Anthony will begin high school at nearby Lincoln High on Ocean Avenue. Even though the Cavallaro middle school that Anthony recently finished up at didn't have a team and Lincoln High has stringent academic requirements to play sports, Anthony has every intention of making the Lincoln junior varsity team—as the starting centerfielder—this upcoming year. "And if I do well enough there, I think I could even make it up to the varsity," says Anthony confidently.

As for his academic pursuits, Anthony isn't as confident. Starting at Lincoln, which is the zoned neighborhood high school for the projects down here, is not even a sure thing for Anthony until he gains some credits in summer school. "Oh, yeah," he adds with a smirk. "That's the other thing I'll be doing every day this summer—going to school. But that's just in the morning, so I'll always be back here playing ball in the afternoon."

Although Anthony and his friends have seen the stadium go up in rapid fashion and confess to having heard about the Cyclones through the local TV news (and/or their parents, who watch said news), they haven't given any thought to attending the team's games. They don't even expect to have their lives altered by the team's presence. Their sphere of knowledge and adventure doesn't seem much bigger than this playground.

Except for Anthony and his crew, the playground is eerily quiet, and one could never guess that a mere fifteen blocks east of these projects, history is being made in loud fashion. Ready to get back to the festivities, I wish Anthony and his friends well and exit the playground on the water side, walking up to the boardwalk that sits between the Coney Island Houses and the Atlantic Ocean. The brilliant ocean makes for a far more pleasant sight than dreary Surf Avenue. The boardwalk leads back to KeySpan, and when I return to the front of the stadium, the crowd has gotten much bigger.

At about 5:10 p.m., the official welcoming parade for the Brooklyn Cyclones comes marching down Surf Avenue from the east, past the subway, past Nathan's, and right to the stadium. It's made up basically of scores of cops, Little League teams, and the mayor and his entourage. The mayor is, of course, the Republican Rudolph "Rudy" Giuliani, the strong-armed city leader who is most responsible for the existence of KeySpan Park. Giuliani, who began his day with an appearance on the *Today* show shot at the stadium, is walking with his mistress, Judy Nathan, and they're both wearing a patented smug grin. There are some boos for Rudy, which highlights the fact that not everyone has enjoyed this controversial mayor's eight-year tenure. Among other headline grabbers, there have been nasty episodes of police brutality and fights picked with the city's cabbies, vendors, street artists, and homeless population, as well as an undercurrent that seemed to pit Rudy against the city's residents of color. Even the genesis of this stadium, beautiful and exciting as it is, has annoyed some critical New Yorkers who wonder why the city should pay for a stadium that the privately owned, ultrarich Mets' organization will profit from. For the most part, however, Rudy is a popular figure at this point in history, particularly in this, his home borough. Rudy was born in Brooklyn and loves to tell stories about how he was a Yankee fan living just blocks from Ebbets Field and how his allegiance to the Bronx team caused many fights in the neighborhood. His family also lived in Long Island for part of his childhood, but Rudy attended Bishop Loughlin High School in the Fort Green section of Brooklyn, just several miles from Coney Island, and he was a student there when the Dodgers announced they were moving to Los Angeles. Yankee fan or no, Rudy has spoken earnestly about the sadness that was felt when the Dodgers moved.

As soon as he gets a microphone in front of him, Rudy announces that this neighborhood, which has gone from rural outpost to vacation spot to tourist capital to immigrant haven to neglected ghetto, is on its way to "once again [being] the center of the universe." Rudy continues with the hyperbole, saying, "this stadium is the first positive thing to happen to Coney Island in sixty years."

It's hard to imagine what Anthony or his friends and family might think of such a bold claim, but those questions will have to wait. For now, in this isolated land of curious day-trippers and sick-day-taking sunbathers, all is good. As the miniparade comes to an end in front of the sparkling new stadium, Coney Island's other amusement attractions continue operations unabated. The Wonder Wheel and the Cyclone whimsically toss their riders through the air, the taps at Ruby's Bar on the boardwalk flow with cold Budweiser, and the shimmering ocean beckons swimmers. Most of the horde didn't come all the way to the dilapidated, smelly Stillwell Avenue subway stop (one of the few stops on the city's massive system that still has a public bathroom, albeit one you can smell from two stops away) for the old-school rides or cheap beer, however. They came here to watch baseball.

As good as everything appears today, one wonders what the city and the organization are doing to ensure that this team, which is essentially being financed by the city and praised by folks who either once lived in Brooklyn or come from better-off parts of the borough, is accessible to and enjoyable for everyone in its immediate neighborhood, as well. The organization says it has done what it could. "We feel that we were pretty involved with the immediate community," says the Cyclones' manager of media relations, Dave Campanaro. "We were working literally out of a trailer in the parking lot while construction was [going on]. We had a big sign out front, so people would come by all the time to find out exactly what was going on. We also made ticket donations to a variety of local boards and groups, so that our immediate community could also become a part of the team."

Regardless of exactly how hard the team tried to appeal to the truly local fan base, the fact is that, as an actual team playing games, the Cyclones already have a huge buzz about them. Not only is tonight's home opener (the Cyclones went 3–3 in their first six road games) sold out, but the team has already sold approximately 80 percent of its available tickets for the whole season. The team's website continues to hum, with fans near and far spilling their nostalgic stories on baseball in Brooklyn. Here are some samples of the fans' passionate writing:

> Baseball, Coney Island, Brighton Beach, The Tokens. I recall taking the Ocean Avenue bus from Shore Road to Ebbets Field and spending all day Sundays going to double headers. Seventy-five cents for bleacher seats, fifteen cents for a hot dog, and a great time. . . . I'll share my second childhood, which starts with the Home Opener, with my kids . . . maybe they'll appreciate what they missed.   —Mark Probert

> I'm a Sheepshead Bay kid (Ocean between X and Y). The '50s in Brooklyn meant Sunday dinners at Lundy's and outings to Ebbets Field. I was there for Carl Furillo Night and Gil Hodges night. I met Campy the summer

before his auto accident. Those were the days. Subway Series? Hell, I
thought that was automatic every fall. Will KeySpan have an outfield sign
that says "Hit this sign, Win a suit" for nostalgia sake?

—Stuart Zuckerman

With the official return of baseball now just about an hour away, Surf
Avenue is overflowing with proud Brooklynites sharing their stories
among themselves and with anyone who has a tape recorder or notebook
in hand. "This feels like old-time Brooklyn," says a Brooklyn resident,
Arthur Kelly, echoing the sentiments of many of the fans on the scene
while eyeing Nathan's hungrily. "You got people buying hot dogs and
going to the beach, plus having baseball back? It's great."

As if the word-of-mouth from the Internet, excited Brooklyn residents,
and a gushing mayor weren't enough to get people fired up about the
Cyclones, the local media have been eating out of the organization's hand.
Well-known older columnists like Dave Anderson and George Vecsey,
from the *New York Times,* and Vic Ziegel, from the *Daily News,* have
written odes to Brooklyn baseball in the days leading up to the inaugural
home game, and today brings out enough TV trucks and crews to cover
the Super Bowl.

Heavy coverage of the Cyclones began in earnest last Monday, when
the team had a light practice and media session to introduce the players
and coaches to one another and to the media. Three players seemed to
cause the biggest buzz among the reporters at the not-at-all-finished
KeySpan. One was Michael Piercy, a twenty-four-year-old from New
Jersey who is not only one of the oldest Cyclones but also a Jersey resident who played in Brooklyn as an amateur. These two facts combine to
make him the Cyclone most aware of what is taking place here. "We've
got big shoes to fill," said Piercy. "This was where Jackie Robinson broke
the color line, there were all the World Series against the Yankees, and I
know that if we don't know all that stuff yet, we will soon." The second
player of note was Tony Coyne, an infielder from Maryland who had just
graduated from Yale. With some funny quotes, Coyne spent the first
week-plus of the season living up to the old sportswriters' adage "Look to

the Ivy League guys when you need a good quote." Finally, reporters seemed to take special note of the Cyclones' pitcher Matthew Gahan, a talkative fellow who is one of two Australians on the Cyclones' diverse roster (the other is Gahan's fellow pitcher Wayne Ough). While the truly "original Cyclones" were getting acquainted with the local press folk and getting at least a little feel for the stadium, Brett Kay was still chilling out in California, working out his contract details.

On June 19, the Cyclones opened play against the Jamestown Jammers in western New York, a good seven hours from Brooklyn (and let's just say that Jamestown, with just 31,000 residents, nearly all of whom are white, is considerably more indicative of the cities in the Cyclones' new league than Brooklyn is). The first Jammers game received little fanfare outside Brooklyn's weekly neighborhood papers, but it remains historic because it was literally the first professional baseball game involving a team from Brooklyn since 1957. The Cyclones won that game 2–1 behind a home run from the infielder Edgar Rodriguez and solid relief pitching from Gahan. These are names that will be memorable on opening night, as well. While Jamestown does not have anything like the atmosphere that KeySpan Park promises, the Jammers organization did try to capitalize on the Cyclones' presence by bringing in the former Brooklyn Dodger Carl Erskine to throw out the ceremonial first pitch. Erskine was a right-handed pitcher with the Dodgers from 1948 until they left Brooklyn, and, as you'd expect from a man with the nickname "Oisk," he was a fan favorite. "This is a great night for the history of Brooklyn," the seventy-four-year-old Erskine told Brooklyn Papers, not exactly going out on a limb. "Bringing baseball back to Brooklyn is fantastic."

Tonight, the hype is far more intense. Besides the requisite firsthand reporting from the likes of CBS 2's Warner Wolf, New York 1's Jay Dow, and representatives of every other big local station, PBS is here as well, capitalizing on the excitement by offering its first-ever live baseball broadcast. "This is an incredible event," says Bill Baker, president of PBS/Channel 13. "Channel 13 is part of this community, and this game is important to this community. A whole bunch of people—including members of my family—had the idea that we should cover it."

In addition to all the electronic media on hand, more than 300 print credentials have been issued for this game, including for writers from Boston, D.C., Florida, and even London. On the field, of course, the Cyclones who are now warming up will be a far cry from the old Dodgers, who were consistently one of the best teams in the majors until they deserted Brooklyn in 1957. In fact, they'll probably need more development than any professional baseball players that these fans have ever seen. Minor League baseball has been enjoying a boom across America for a good ten years now, but the stadium building and attendance jumps have been taking place in small towns or second-tier cities (Newark, New Jersey, home of the Bears, and Central Islip, Long Island, home of the Ducks, are the closest examples, and both of those are independent teams), while New York City proper has remained the domain of the big leagues. The baseball that fans are about to watch tonight is "Low-A" ball, the second-lowest rung on the six-step Minor League ladder to the big leagues. The players will be smaller, less experienced, and less skilled than the players these fans are used to. Those fans who watch the Mets to see Mike Piazza hit a 450-foot home run or the Yankees to watch Derek Jeter gun someone out from deep in the hole at shortstop will be disappointed by their new heroes' physical shortcomings. It's hard to know if this will temper the excitement that the Cyclones have created just by *existing*.

For their part, the players who make up the Cyclones, not one of whom is a New York resident or possessed any real knowledge of Coney Island before they arrived here some time within the past ten days, know next to nothing about what they are getting themselves into. While much of the team had the brief workout and media session last week, the six days on the road (a three-games-to-one series victory over the Jammers was followed by losing two straight at Vermont) mean that tonight represents the players' first substantial time at KeySpan Park.

And, for at least one player, it's literally the first time at the stadium. That player is Brett Davis Kay, the twenty-one-year-old catcher out of Cal State–Fullerton who perhaps best represents the uncertainty facing these baby-faced baseball players. Last night, a Sunday, Brett was home in

California, hanging out with his longtime girlfriend until 4 a.m. Today brought total chaos. Brett was on a plane at 6 a.m. out of L.A., snuck a couple hours of sleep on the flight, and landed at 5 p.m. at La Guardia, where, he says, "some guy, I don't know who he is, came and picked me up after I'd waited, like, forty-five minutes." Brett, his three bags of luggage, and the "$150 my mom slipped me before I left" were brought straight to KeySpan Park. A native of Villa Park, California, in the heart of Orange County, Brett is a legitimate Mets prospect who goes 6'1", 190 pounds, without the normal squattiness one associates with catchers. He's got dirty blonde hair, cropped close to minimize his widow's peak, and even fairer eyebrows, with a boyishly handsome face that serves as the entry point for an engaging, easygoing personality. That personality is not really on display this evening, however, as Brett is nervously beginning the long climb to the "Bigs" in the midst of the most hyped Minor League baseball game ever.

The first words out of Brett's mouth as he takes note of the media hordes and overflow crowd are simple and telling: "Oh, crap. This is mayhem." Brett has heard about the Minor Leagues from close friends, but no one has prepared him for this—the crowd, the media, and, perhaps most uncomfortably for Brett, the teammates who have been hanging out and getting to know one another for the past week or so. To add to Brett's tension, the media and fan chaos is a backdrop not just to his introduction to Minor League baseball; today is the first time that Brett Kay has ever been to New York City.

Though he was retired by the time Brett was born, Brett's father, Rick Kay, was a star linebacker and defensive back for the Colorado University football team and then played professionally for the Los Angeles Rams (1973–77) and Atlanta Falcons (1977). Not surprisingly, Brett had a sportscentric childhood and adolescence, including time spent at Mater Dei High School, in Santa Ana, California. A regional power in baseball, basketball, and football, Mater Dei has arguably one of the best high school sports programs in the country, and Brett tried to take advantage of that fact, at various times playing basketball and football and always playing baseball. After graduating from this veritable athletic factory, Kay was drafted in the thirty-fifth round of the 1998 draft by the Houston Astros. Disappointed at being picked so low in the draft, Kay instead took advantage of the full baseball scholarship that nearby Cal State–Fullerton had offered him.

After two injury-plagued and mediocre seasons at Fullerton, Brett blossomed as a junior. He became the team's everyday catcher and helped lead the Titans to the College World Series earlier this month. This year's interminable Major League baseball draft began on June 5, as Fullerton was preparing for the College World Series, and Brett was one of nine Titans who got drafted. It's unique among professional sports drafts because it takes place when so many of the draftees are still playing competitively (whereas professional basketball, football, and hockey drafts take place in the off-season). It was also a key draft for Brett, because, in baseball, players who want to maintain college eligibility can get drafted only after high school or after their junior or senior years of college. Brett explains his draft experience matter-of-factly: "I was out on the field at Fullerton taking batting practice when I got the call that the Mets drafted me," recalls Brett. "I was still focusing on getting my team to win the College World Series, and when I thought about the draft, at first I wasn't that excited. My reaction was that the eighth round is not good enough. I felt like I've worked harder than that—worked my whole life for this—and that I'm better off coming back to school and going pro next year."

For the time being, Kay didn't worry too much about it. Shortly after the draft, the Titans departed for Omaha, Nebraska, the annual home of the College World Series. At the CWS, Fullerton was eliminated by Stanford on June 13 as Brett made the last out of the season. "I'll always have a bitter taste in my mouth about the end of my career because of that," concedes Brett.

With the low–Minor League seasons about to start, Kay and his adviser—Brett's long-time father figure and local baseball coach, Bob Sporrer—got around to dealing with the Mets. "Bob knew about the Cyclones having a new stadium and all that and figured it would be a good place for me to go, so we told the Mets that as long as they sent me right to Brooklyn rather than Kingsport and would give me a decent amount of money, I'd do it." The Kingsport Brett is referring to is in Tennessee, where the Mets' "Rookie Ball" team is located. With a team made up mostly of guys who turn pro straight out of high school, Kingsport is the only stop lower than Brooklyn on the Mets' chain. Given his college experience and his eighth-round draft status, Brett's resistance to going to Kingsport made perfect sense. And, since Brett, as a junior draftee, had the bargaining chip of returning to school, he wanted to take advantage of leverage he would not have if he went back to school for his senior year. "Besides," adds Brett, "I'm not a real studious guy, not a school guy, and I really didn't want to have to take classes any more. I'd like to finish school someday, but now is not the time."

The $72,000 signing bonus didn't hurt. "We bargained a little for money because obviously this is something I've worked hard for my whole life and I wanted to be rewarded, but unless you're a top pick with that perfect body they're looking for you're not going to get a million-dollar bonus. And I may have a decent arm and am able to hit a little bit, but I'm not a prototypical catcher, so I couldn't say that much. Bob and I just decided not to waste much time. I signed with the Mets and came here," explains Brett. "Besides, I understand that the real money doesn't come 'til you make the big leagues."

With the contract signed, arrangements were made to get Kay to Brooklyn as soon as possible. Besides his expressly stated wish and his college experience, Brett's sheer athletic talents figure to make him a good fit at this level, at least once he adjusts to the fact that he's here.

While Kay and even his most experienced teammates (as in six games played) are nervous, and Anthony and his buddies are ambivalent, the Cyclones' fans are fired up. The parking lot is filling up with SUVs that have trucked in from the Long Island and Jersey suburbs and are paying $10 a pop to park. More than a neighborhood event, this evening is taking on the feel of a classic big New York event, with the location merely adding to the allure.

Approaching the stadium's main, gated entrance off Surf Avenue, fans walk past men with "I need tickets" signs and political hopefuls handing out flyers on the sidewalk. These are fans of all ages who have been drawn by some combination of the media, their memories, and just the attraction of affordable family entertainment to an area many of them had written off years ago. Upon entering the stadium, many sound like first-time visitors to Yellowstone Park. "Woooowww," they gush. "It's beeaauutifulll."

And it, KeySpan Park, most definitely is a sight to behold. KeySpan (named—thanks to a twenty-year sponsorship deal for undisclosed millions and with absolutely no taste at all—for the regional energy conglomerate that bills New Yorkers once a month) is a totally modern structure made of glass, concrete, and metal that rises above Surf Avenue with a futuristic feel. Walking up the cement steps inside the main entrance and turning right to face the field leaves one facing a wonderful sight.

The field itself is perfectly manicured, with reddish-brown dirt that lacks a single spare pebble and grass that looks lush enough to sleep on. From above, one can see that the grass is unadorned with the annoying shapes many stadiums now mow into their lawns, leaving the only decoration a stylized "Cyclones" that has been spray-painted behind home plate. Just beyond the playing surface is the kaleidoscopic outfield wall, lined with billboards reminiscent of old baseball stadiums. Some national chains are represented on the wall, but most signs are for more relevant advertisers, from New York's WFAN sports radio station to the Brooklyn Brewery and Nathan's Famous. Best of all, at least for the nostalgic folks who have been posting their messages on the Cyclones' website, is the presence of the nostalgic "Hit this sign and win a free suit" sign. In its original incarnation at Ebbets Field, the sign was sponsored by a Brooklyn clothier, and later borough president, Abe Stark, who famously never had to actually give out a free suit because no one ever hit his sign. Here at KeySpan, the sign is sponsored by Garage Clothing, a men's store in the nearby neighborhood of Gravesend. And, given the sign's left-center-field location, odds are that Garage will be giving out a suit or two this season. One final billboard of note, which references the old suit sign as well as the current neighborhood attractions, is the one that promises, "Hit this sign and win a free ride on the Wonder Wheel." Located well above ground, the Wonder Wheel billboard is an unlikely target, but it's a cool aspect of the eye-pleasing backdrop nonetheless.

The stadium has a neat, perfectly scaled scoreboard in left center with a mini video screen to show highlights and a little Cyclone coaster above it. Looking around, it's clear that *everything* in the stadium is kept to scale. The dimensions of the park are big league enough, going 315-LF, 412-CF, 325-RF, but everything else, from the scoreboard to the promenade to the press box behind the seats, is slightly smaller than you'd see in the big leagues, appropriately reflecting the fact that this is a 7,500-seat stadium and not Shea. As Brett notes, "this is a little big-league ballpark."

The display of colorful beauty continues beyond the outfield fence. Beyond left field are the famous rides of Coney Island, from the Cyclone to the Wonder Wheel, which look grand during the day and like pure magic when the sun sets. Beyond the fence and the bleachers in right field, the sun is reflected on the calm ocean. Swimmers and boaters enjoy the water while Steeplechase Pier, which seems to jut out on a straight line from home plate through right field to the beach, holds a mass of fishermen, blasting their salsa music and hoping to get lucky. Further around in right is the Parachute Jump, a ride that must have been amazing in its day but that hasn't been active for some time. Thank goodness, however, the city put a fresh coat of red paint on it, and it now makes a beautiful peak for the Coney Island skyline.

Walking away from home plate while inside the compact stadium, one follows a cement concourse that turns into wood, perfectly replicating a boardwalk. A sea breeze is constantly blowing. Filling up the main seating bowl—6,500 seats divided between old-school bleachers down the left- and right-field lines and forest-green folding seats between the bases—are fans of all ages, overjoyed at what is taking place before them. Kids laugh at the sight of the Cyclones' mascot, Sandy the Seagull, while middle-aged adults bask in the realization that baseball is back in Brooklyn. As a thirty-two-year-old Brooklynite named Paul Massoni, sitting along the first-base line tonight, says, "It's great. Brooklyn hasn't had a team to call their own in forty-four years. Hopefully, this team can bring the city and community together. What can you say bad about it?"

While there are loads of kids on hand tonight, a good percentage of the crowd —maybe 10 to 15 percent—looks old enough to have seen the last game played in Brooklyn, and many are happily sharing their "I remember when . . ." tales to anyone who wants to hear about vintage Dodgers such as Jackie Robinson and Pee Wee Reese.

The fans are not just in love with the nostalgic and beautiful setting— they're also in love with the price. Parking, concessions, and souvenirs are at your typical baseball stadium level ($10 for parking, $5 for a beer, and $16 for a Cyclone t-shirt), but the tickets themselves are cheap—$5, $6, $8, or $10. As one woman sitting with her kids along the first-base line gushes, "These seats would cost something like $60 at Shea Stadium. These prices make the whole night much more affordable." To help add space in the wake of the fans' overwhelming response, the Cyclone organization has added semipermanent silver bleachers beyond the right-field fence. The bleachers hold between 1,000 and 1,500 additional fans, giving KeySpan a "capacity" of 7,500, although even that number may increase. The bleachers, which were literally a last-minute addition, look like they belong at a high school football field. As one construction worker at the field says, "I think they just figured, why not? It's at least 1,000 more seats and people want to come, so the team just did it. They'll be working on this stadium all season long, anyway."

Further evidence of the stadium's unfinished nature can be found in the empty storefronts built into the stadium on the Surf Avenue side, which are all clearly unfit to house businesses at this point. All together, there are 9,000 feet of retail space available for three or four businesses, and though the Cyclones say that three are basically rented already and that these will be year-round businesses, all there is tonight is some hanging wires. Further along the stadium façade are the main ticket windows (mobbed with people hoping for a miracle ticket) and the Cyclones' team store, a two-story souvenir store that is in working order and that is similarly jammed with eager buyers. The team says, in fact, that it has already sold more than 9,000 official caps (at $18 to $22 a pop).

There is no sign, however, of where a promised Brooklyn Baseball Museum will go. Some light painting was going on inside the stadium earlier this afternoon, but those workers have disappeared for the night. As another stadium employee tells me, "They'd never let this come out in the news, but this stadium is far from being finished. It was originally going to open in 2002, so they've had to rush like crazy. In the last couple of weeks they've been paying some people *triple* overtime just to get it ready for tonight."

In any event, the bleachers are here, and the Cyclone organization sees the added seats as an opportunity to be more generous with its tickets. "We always had the ability to build these seats; we just didn't know if we'd have the demand. But we've seen the demand go through the roof," Jeff Wilpon, the Cyclones' CEO, told the *Daily News* on Thursday, while explaining that the majority of bleacher seats will be sold only on game days—"For people that didn't have the forethought to buy tickets, we want them to feel they can still see the games and be part of the community."

Despite the last-minute adjustments and their uncomfortable nature—metal bleachers have their limitations—the bleacher seats are still an outstanding vantage point from which to watch a game. Even the last row of seats is only about thirty feet from the field of play, and when crystal-clear twilight descends on the evening, one can see the lights of the Verrazano Bridge a little to the west and the majestic top of the twin towers of the World Trade Center due north. [*By the time the Cyclones' second season began, the twin towers were obviously, and tragically, no longer a part of people's views, from KeySpan Park or anywhere else. The bleachers remain a beautiful vantage point, but with one less landmark in their range.*]

At 7 p.m., Ed Randall, a famous New York baseball announcer and the emcee for the night, gets the festivities under way. "Ladies and gentleman, baseball is back in Brooklyn!"

A lot of backslapping follows Randall's enthusiastic introduction. Fred Wilpon, co-owner of the Mets, speaks, followed by his son, the aforementioned Jeff Wilpon, who says that Rudy the Mayor "is the greatest baseball fan to ever hold office." While the senior Wilpon is a former

Brooklyn resident who is obviously thrilled to be bringing baseball back, he leaves much of the public commentary to his son. Speaking with the media a couple days ago, Jeff Wilpon spoke of how many people had stopped him while he was in the area overseeing construction just to share memories, in a more old-school "chat room," so to speak. Most of the talk was positive, but it was often delivered with regret, as well; it has not been easy for Brooklynites to get over the loss of their beloved Dodgers.

"It's very important that we're bringing baseball back," Jeff Wilpon told reporters. Wilpon brings better baseball knowledge to the table than most of the sport's executives, thanks to his college baseball career at the University of Miami and a brief professional run in 1983 with the Jamestown team (then known as the Expos). "But I don't want people to misunderstand and point their finger at the Cyclones and think it's an attempt to take the Dodgers' place. I don't ever expect to fill the void, the hurt, and the disappointment of the Dodgers' leaving. Hopefully, this will fill a part of it."

Other luminaries on hand for the pregame ceremonies include enough local politicians to fill an entire seating section: U.S. Senator Chuck Schumer ("the first senator from Brooklyn in 150 years"), Congressman Jerrold Nadler, City Council Speaker Peter Vallone, State Senator Marty Markowitz, and Brooklyn Councilman Herbert Berman.

When Randall gets to the player intros, he announces that there will be "no booing" in the stadium. Of course, this being Brooklyn, New York, he gets booed for this announcement. Then Randall introduces the visiting Mahoning Valley Scrappers (based in Niles, Ohio, a suburb of Youngstown that, like Jamestown, New York, could not have less in common with Coney Island), and the boos get even louder. Then the Cyclones are introduced, with particularly warm applause for the coaches, Bobby Ojeda and Howard Johnson, and the manager, Edgar Alfonzo, all with their strong Mets' connections. From a marketing standpoint, the Cyclones are brilliantly conceived, and this coaching staff is a perfect example. There are thousands of Minor League managers and coaches in America, many with about as much name recognition as the average mailman. But, rather than settle for some name with no cachet, the Mets' organization assigned three men with strong Mets' affiliations to the Cyclones' staff, ensuring that even if the players aren't celebrities, big-time fans will not be left wanting. Alfonzo, besides bringing impressive Minor League coaching experience to his job as Cyclone manager, is the older brother of the Mets infielder Edgardo Alfonzo, a very popular player in New York. [*Edgardo Alfonzo has since moved on to the San Francisco Giants, but he remains a very popular player in New York.*] The organization obviously figures that, since fans love Edgardo, they'll love his brother, too. The Cyclones' hitting coach is Johnson, who was a fan favorite with the Mets between 1985 and 1993, when he played multiple positions in the field, hit home runs and stole bases on offense, and generally gave new meaning to "HoJo." Ojeda, who is the Cyclones' pitching coach, is a former teammate of HoJo's and another great name from Mets' history. "Bobby O" was with the Mets from 1986 to 1990, and in his first season in New York he was one of the biggest reasons for the Mets playoff and World Series victories. Though Kay has barely met his new pitching coach on opening night, he's definitely a guy Brett is excited to play for. "I remember Bobby O as a funky lefty that won big games for the '86 Mets. I think it's great he's my coach."

In addition to the Mets' connections, this night also features a couple of heartfelt tie-ins to the old Brooklyn Dodgers. One of the people Randall introduces to the crowd is Joan Hodges, who receives very warm applause. Joan's husband, Gil, was the first-baseman for the Dodgers throughout the '50s, from their 1955 title team to the last team to play in Brooklyn to the L.A. team. After his playing career, he got into coaching and was the manager of the 1969 "Miracle Mets" when they won the World Series. Throughout his career, Hodges and his wife maintained close ties to Brooklyn, which made particular sense since Joan is a Brooklyn native. Earlier this year, Mayor Giuliani signed legislation to rename Bedford Avenue between Avenues L and M, the street on which Gil Hodges and his family lived near Ebbets Field, Gil Hodges Way. "Although he passed away nearly thirty years ago, Gil Hodges remains a beloved figure in New York City," Giuliani said at the time. "He is part of the city's cherished baseball lore. He helped lead the Brooklyn Dodgers to victory over the New York Yankees to win the Brooklyn Dodgers' only World Series, in 1955, and he coached the Miracle Mets in 1969, when they won their first World Series. Gil's achievements represent all that is good in baseball, and it is a pleasure to rename this section of Bedford Avenue Gil Hodges Way in his honor."

Joan Hodges maintained ties to the area after her husband died of a heart attack in 1972, and on this night she admits she never thought baseball would again be a part of the area. "I didn't think I'd live to see baseball come back to Brooklyn, so this is very special for me," she says. "These fans are the best in the world, and I'll always consider this home." For the singing of the national anthem, the Cyclones have brought in the Tokens, the old doo-wop group famous for its recording of "The Lion Sleeps Tonight" (a catchy tune that was played throughout pregame warmups tonight).

After the Tokens sing, there is an extensive "first-pitch" ceremony, which on this night should be called "the first pitch*es*." Besides having the Wilpons and Mayor Giuliani toss pitches, the Cyclones have brought back the infamous old Dodger reliever Ralph Branca to throw out a "first pitch" to Joe Pignatano. Having Branca and Pignatano here is another crafty tie-in to the Brooklyn days. Branca was a great pitcher for the Brooklyn Dodgers when he pitched for them from 1944 to 1953. His finest season came in 1947, when he was the pitching star on Jackie Robinson's first team, a magical Dodger team that won the National League pennant and lost a thrilling, seven-game World Series to the hated Yankees. In '47, the twenty-one-year-old Branca put up numbers that would seem impossible today: he compiled a 21–12 record in thirty-six starts and seven relief appearances (Branca credited his young arm for his durability) and finished in the top five in strikeouts and earned-run average. Overall, Branca went 80–58 as a Dodger, and he's snuck into the hearts of Mets' fans thanks to the fact that his daughter married Mets' manager Bobby Valentine, making Branca a relative of the Mets' organization. But Branca is unfortunately best remembered for being the pitcher who surrendered the "the shot heard 'round the world" home run to

Bobby Thomson in the Dodgers' 1951 playoff loss to the New York Giants. On this night, Branca gets a warm applause, proving that real Brooklyn fans either remember the good times or forgive the bad times. As for Pignatano, he was a rookie catcher in 1957, and though he played in only eight games that season, he is a part of Dodger lore because he caught the final innings at Ebbets Field. Those were special moments for the man known as Piggy, which he shares with the *Daily News's* Ziegel tonight. "I grew up in Brooklyn, made it to the big leagues in Brooklyn, and then I had to leave Brooklyn. Moving 3,000 miles, it killed me." Tonight, Piggy—who lived for much of his life a couple of blocks up on West 15th Street—is part of a rebirth.

Finally, the game begins. The first professional pitch in Brooklyn since 1957 is delivered at 7:19 p.m. by the Cyclones' Matt Peterson, a tall, nineteen-year-old righty from Alexandria, Louisiana. While the inexperienced Cyclones are destined to play a lot of sloppy games this season, tonight's tilt is a taut, well-played pitchers' duel. The Cyclones' first hit is a single by the second baseman, Leonardo Arias, in the third inning, though Arias also gets in the KeySpan record books by fumbling a ground ball in the top of the fifth, allowing an unearned run to score. That run is the only one that Peterson allows, along with just three hits.

In the bottom of the sixth, the Cyclones get a single from their speedy leadoff hitter, Angel Pagan, but he is promptly thrown out stealing.

The Scrappers come back in the top of the seventh against the reliever Gahan with a leadoff single of their own, and then, with two outs, they get a run-scoring bloop single into short left field. It's a play that the Cyclone shortstop, Robert McIntyre, even though he had to go back on the ball, probably should have made. Those fans in attendance who know what to expect of low–Minor League baseball are not surprised at this play, nor are they disappointed, given how dramatic the evening has been already. The top of the seventh ends with the Scrappers up 2–0.

Minus that fielding faux pas, the defense all night is quite solid, with Arias's miscue the only officially scored error of the night. Where the difference between the majors and the minors is more pronounced is with the hitters. Many of the players who are new to the pro game are using wooden bats competitively for the first time (colleges and high schools use aluminum only, though some amateur summer leagues use wooden bats), there's a steady breeze blowing in from the ocean, and the batters are facing better curveballs than they ever have. The defense can respond to this lack of firepower by playing the outfielders extremely shallow (as the Scrappers and Cyclones do all evening) and being a little more aggressive in fielding ground balls (which both teams do as well, turning several double plays with aplomb). Besides these advantages, which are inherent in any low–Minor League ballgame, KeySpan presents an added bonus for the defense and pitchers—the strong ocean breeze.

The fans don't seem too worried about the differences, and why should they? That same ocean breeze feels lovely, and the beer and the hot dogs taste great. And with the Scrappers—who are to the Cleveland Indians what the Cyclones are to the Mets—seemingly unafraid of the historic surroundings, the game reaches the late innings very close.

In the bottom of the seventh, the Cyclones manage two hits but leave both men stranded, and after a scoreless top of the eighth, Brooklyn gets yet another leadoff hit, this one being Arias's second hit of the game. With one out, McIntyre hits a roller to short and sprints to first. The Scrappers' shortstop makes an athletic throw to first, but, to the naked eye (and to the television replay I'll watch later), McIntyre is safe. The umpire, however—one of just two umps on the field, as opposed to the four per game in the Major Leagues—sees it otherwise. McIntyre is called out, and the Brooklyn fans show their world-renowned emotion, booing loudly. The Cyclone manager, Alfonzo, even comes out for some semitheatrical arguing, but obviously the ump does not change his call. The inning ends when the Cyclones' starting catcher, Michael Jacobs, strikes out for the fourth time, an ignoble feat that has earned a place in the baseball lexicon as a "Golden Sombrero."

Of course, one of Jacobs's backups is technically Brett Kay, who was too nervous and discombobulated to put on his uniform or introduce himself to the players, though he does bump into the reliever David Byard, a chummy fellow. "The team gave me a uniform, but I wasn't ready for that. These guys had been together for a good week, and I was just pretty scared. Byard was cool, and the atmosphere was exciting, but I couldn't play that night," says Brett, who is so new to the team that he doesn't even appear in the fancy $5 programs the team is selling briskly. "They also gave me some tickets, so I just walked around the stadium most of the time, amazed at how much excitement there was—and for a Minor League game. It's crazy! When the game got close and I wanted to watch, I went and chilled out with the maintenance crew guys."

The maintenance guys (also known as the "grounds crew" in baseball parlance) do indeed have their own little "box-seat" section down the right-field line, and it affords Brett a perfect view for the late-game heroics of his new teammates.

The Scrappers put a base runner on in the top of the ninth, but Gahan continues his impressive relief work and gets out of the inning.

Down 2–0 in the bottom of the ninth, the Cyclones get a leadoff walk from John Toner, the outfielder. Two outs later, Edgar Rodriguez comes to bat. Rodriguez, whose home run was the key blow in the Cyclones' first game last week, works the count to 2–2. Now, as if this is a movie or something, Rodriguez crushes a home run toward the scoreboard in left field, and the game is tied. The crowd explodes, as fireworks do the same. All night, these fans have been up, cheering whatever on-field moments they could to help illustrate how happy they are to be here. But a truly important, game-tying home run? It sets off group hugs and cries of joy. And it's still a big crowd, too. Because the game has moved so fast and the weather is so heavenly and the history so thick, people have not left this game early. An educated guess would put the crowd in the bottom of the ninth at 95 percent of capacity, including lots of screaming kids.

In the tenth inning, the Cyclones send out Brett's buddy Byard to pitch. Byard, a hefty righty from Cambridge, Ohio (coincidentally just two hours from the Scrappers' home base of Niles), gets an out and then gives up a single and a walk. The crowd, lively and feisty as ever, *boos* Byard! But Byard induces a double play to keep the score tied at two heading into the bottom of the tenth. In the bottom of the tenth, with the crowd screaming the whole time, Arias leads off with a walk. A misplayed bunt and an intentional walk load the bases for Jacobs, who has a chance to make up for his miserable performance thus far. Jacobs is up to the task, hitting a sacrifice fly to deep left field to win the game for the Cyclones. The win goes to Byard.

After the game, Jacobs, in his third season of pro ball, is asked what he made of the crowd. "I'm used to playing in front of 1,000 people—if we're lucky," he says. "There's no way I'd want to pitch in front of all these people."

Brett is not around to talk after the game and is too exhausted to even think about what has happened, but the Cyclones who have been here for a few days know the significance. "It's a big deal," says the Cyclone reliever Blake McGinley, a skilled relief pitcher who looks not a day over fifteen. "I mean, it's been almost fifty years since the Brooklyn Dodgers were here. As you can see by the crowd, that's a big thing for everybody else, but it's a big thing for us, too. So to come back and win on that home run by Edgar? *Awesome.*"

Asked later what he thought of all the opening-night media attention, Brett says, "I didn't understand exactly what was going on. I didn't know why there was such a frenzy, and I hadn't figured out what a big deal it was to win that game."

The fans lucky enough to be in attendance surely share McGinley's sentiments, however, and the 7,500-plus go home happy. A historic moment had rarely been this fun.

Leaving KeySpan on this gorgeous night, most of the fans feel as if they've been given a gift. It's not like there's been, at least in the past several years, a huge public outcry demanding that baseball be brought back to Brooklyn or that much of anything be done in Coney Island. But now that it's happening, with the first game over, people act as if their lives have been waiting for exactly this.

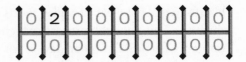

The First Few Brooklyn "Home Stands"

Two days after opening day, while Brett and the Cyclones get ready for another game against the Scrappers, the scene is the same at the Coney Island Houses: Anthony and his friends are playing baseball. The approximately 120' x 120' square of blacktop that the kids have transformed into a baseball field in the aquatically named Nautilus Playground sits between the project buildings, which face out on Surf Avenue, and the seedier end of Riegelmann Boardwalk, which runs along the beach. Being far to the west of the rides, excitement, and crowds, this end of the boardwalk has few businesses and a predictable lack of sanitation or police presence. The area around the boardwalk, on both the beach and the playground sides, not far from the kids' home plate, is littered with fast-food wrappers, wind-blown newspapers, and even the occasional item that was dropped off at high tide, pieces of trash so altered by their time at sea that you can't guess what they used to be. As for the ocean, the dreariness of the projects and the presence of trash lessens some of its majesty at this locale. When residents of the Coney Island Houses go to the beach, they tend to walk a little east before setting up shop. The few pedestrians who follow the boardwalk as far down as these projects are often Russians who have taken a long walk west from their homes in Brighton Beach; occasionally, I'm told by some adults in the Coney Island Houses, the Russians' walks involve fighting off mugging attempts from project kids. None of these young baseball players gives off any criminal vibe, however, and that's probably not a coincidence. In fact, members of this group make it clear they play sports to counter interests in less savory activities. This thought process, which was mentioned by a couple of Anthony's friends the other day, is very mature. One can only imagine how much more of a boost these kids could get toward sports and away from trouble once the Cyclones have the opportunity to improve community outreach.

Geographical notes taken, it's time to address the matter of professional baseball. The conundrum is that there's a pro baseball team playing within walking distance of where these kids who love the sport live, and yet the same kids haven't indicated an interest in seeing the Cyclones play.

Eager to repeat and expand on my questioning from the other day, I engage Anthony, who's sitting on the bench as his "team" takes its turn at bat, in a little Q and A.

You told me the other day that you all love playing baseball, right?

"Yeah, definitely," says Anthony with an eager smile as his friends gather around, momentarily pausing the game.

And are you all baseball *fans* as well?

"What do you mean?" Anthony asks.

You know. The Yankees, the Mets, watching games on TV?

"Of course. I watch, like, every single Yankee game with my mom. Man, I *love* baseball."

So have you ever been to a Yankees or Mets game?

"Nah."

No? Why not?

"I think it's, like, too far. Or it's too hard to get tickets."

This is the answer of someone who was raised without the whimsy that extra money can provide, but also of someone who has been tragically cut off from the world at large. "Too far"?! No one who has ever been to these Houses and to the other projects around them would argue that they aren't secluded from the city in a dismissive fashion. And, a ride from the Stillwell Avenue subway station to Yankee Stadium or Shea Stadium could take a good ninety minutes. But, still, we are talking about stadiums based in the same city that Anthony resides in, and yet he's never been.

Without the chance to really digest what he said, and from my own relatively spoiled perspective of attending fifteen to twenty Major League baseball games a year, I can only give Anthony a silent, quizzical look. To this, he says simply, "*This* is where we hang out. Every day."

Getting back to the original focus of this little interview session, the Brooklyn Cyclones, I tell Anthony and his head-nodding friends—twelve-year-old Anthony De Los Santos and fifteen-year-old Josimar Aleman—that their admission that they love baseball is indirectly getting at the beauty of the Cyclones' birth. After all, what the Cyclones' presence means is that there is a professional baseball team playing just a short walk from these kids' apartments. And, as I was just there two days ago, I explain to them that it really is a cool stadium and a fun environment. So wouldn't it be obvious to these kids that they should go watch the Cyclones play?

"Well, I don't know if we'll go to any games," says Anthony shyly, wiping his sweat away with his Derek Jeter jersey. "I mean, we couldn't get tickets or anything like that. I think I heard that the games are all, like, sold out."

Some may be, sure. But didn't the team put up signs, or maybe send someone over here to talk about the team, or how to buy tickets, anything?

"Nah, nothing like that. I don't think the team cares about us over here either way."

But it's *so* close, and you love baseball. You must be planning on going to at least one game.

"Okay, I think there's one. I mean, like I said, my mom is a big Yankee fan, and she told me she got me tickets for a game against the Staten Island Yankees—it's August 13. I'm a Staten Island Yankee fan too because they're part of the Yankees. If this was a Yankee team in the stadium, then maybe I'd go more. But, other than that game, I don't think we'll go at all."

And you don't think the team will ever reach out to you?

"No. You're the only person to ever come here and talk or ask about the Cyclones. I think they're more worried about over there." Anthony gestures east. Toward the stadium, its well-heeled fans, the world at large?

This is the most disturbing and hard-to-understand aspect for me. Here is a healthy, fun kid, with a pure love for baseball (no small feat in this era of hip-hop and hoops) that he shares with his friends, and even though they live just blocks from the stadium, they feel no connection.

There is another approach running through my head that might get the youths and the older people of the projects more involved. *Even if the city and the team don't care too much about getting these neighbors in the stands as fans, they'll at least want them working for the team, right? Didn't Rudy Giuliani himself talk about all the jobs this team would bring to the neighborhood?* So the question is posed to Anthony and crew: how about working there; they must be hiring kids from around here?

"I don't know if they are. I haven't heard anything like that," Anthony replies. "But I don't really want to work there, anyway. Maybe I'll play there some day."

And that's that. Anthony shows enough interest in his one potential trip to illustrate that he could be excited about this team, but he still seems to view the Cyclones as out of his reach. My interrogation over, I retire to a shaded bench that sits next to the boys' makeshift stadium.

The kids go back to playing. Some of them seem to lose interest by the inning, but the premise of this game is again six on six, and all twelve resist whatever urges they might have to quit midgame.

Facing east in the direction of KeySpan, the basketball and handball courts sit empty behind me. Straight ahead, on the other side of the "field," are a couple of swing sets. Home plate is to my right, with a backstop that backs up nearly to the boardwalk behind it. There are no official bases, though lines or cracks that make do have been assigned in areas close enough to approximate first, second, and third. The outfield is not quite as big as it should be for kids of this size, and only a fifteen- or twenty-foot fence that protects a little pathway in between the field and Building Three keeps down the number of potential home runs.

When Anthony isn't batting, the game tends to get a little sloppy, with the "players" haphazardly running the bases and fielding lazily. But when

Anthony comes up to bat, everyone snaps to attention. With Anthony batting and the bases loaded, one of his teammates yells confidently, "It's all up to Anthony," but Anthony pops out. As Anthony trudges back into the field and takes his position as pitcher, he reminds his playmates that "game is seven," which is said loudly, for the benefit of the weed-smoking twenty-somethings who linger off to the side and want to get into the next game. Throughout the action on the tar field, Anthony issues verbal commands and admonitions to his fellow players. "Get that ball!" "I told you, no bunting allowed."

Besides talking nonstop, Anthony is energetically willing this game toward a suitable ending, by pitching, settling disputed calls, and showing the most polish when it's his turn to hit (this achievement is tempered somewhat by the awkwardness with which some of the other kids hold the bat). He also, no doubt, is a reason the game has made it this far—the other kids don't want to let him down after all he's done to provide a structured and entertaining afternoon activity for them. When Anthony comes up to bat again in the next inning (none of the kids actually utters the word "inning," but I'm trying to track the game in baseball lingo) with a runner on, it's known that his team has five runs. The kid serving as pitcher throws a fat lob, and Anthony crunches it, sending the tattered softball flying over the fence and off the wall of Building Three. Raising his arms triumphantly, Anthony rounds the "bases" with a smile.

With this game over, many of the boys announce that they're returning to their apartments at the behest of their grandmothers. The weed smokers amble over to try to get their "next," but it seems unlikely that Anthony's crew can stay focused for another game, or would even want to, given that these guys won't be as fun to play with.

It's time to return to KeySpan for this evening's game, but not before repeating to everyone the question of the day: are *any* of you going to a Cyclone game soon? "No," they shake their heads and shrug.

With or without the kids from Coney Island Houses, Cyclone attendance in general suffers little dropoff from the first game. The media buzz quiets a bit after the opener, but the team tops 7,000 fans for games two and three, as it did for opening night, and gets a couple of sellouts in the games after that.

Juxtaposing the "everything is wonderful" aura that surrounds the team's higher-ups with the confused looks in the Coney Island kids' eyes regarding the team, it seems that Giuliani and his Cyclone cronies did not have the Anthony Oteros of the world in mind when this project began. The video of the opening home game, which I taped on PBS/Channel 13 and watched when I returned home, is fun viewing, but the interviews with the likes of Rudy and Wilpon are fawning to the point of bordering on propaganda. On the broadcast, Jeff Wilpon puts things most concisely and simply when he says, "The mayor gave us the money, and we brought the project to completion, on time and on budget."

The businessmen behind this project are not planning on being scrutinized for the way the Cyclones came together, but that doesn't take away the fascinating history of the project. In 1997, the Mets' owners began discussing the idea of bringing a Mets' farm team to the New York area. At that point, ownership of the Mets was split primarily between Nelson Doubleday and Fred Wilpon, and they were convinced that the area could support such a team. They thought that Suffolk County, which forms the eastern end of Long Island and where there are lots of Mets fans who are not always up for the lengthy trek to Shea Stadium, would be a perfect locale. The Mets thought Single-A would be the right level, and their plan was to move their New York–Penn League affiliate from Pittsfield, Massachusetts.

Several months later, the Yankees' principal owner, George Steinbrenner, came to Giuliani asking whether the city would help build a Minor League stadium on Staten Island that the Yankees could use. The Yankees were taking over the Watertown [Connecticut] Indians franchise of the New York–Penn League and thought that they could move that team to Staten Island. Since the Mets and Yankees share the New York "baseball market," they have to approve any new Major League–affiliated team that wants to come to the area. The Yankees had initially blocked the Mets' idea for a stadium on Long Island, so it was unlikely that the Mets would be okay with the Yanks building on Staten Island. Not for business purposes, per se, but because guys like Steinbrenner and Fred Wilpon are serious businessmen, if one makes life difficult for the other, the rules of the game dictate that the favor must be returned.

For a lot of reasons, Giuliani wanted the plan for the Staten Island Yankees to come to fruition. For one thing, Giuliani is an avowed Yankee fan, and he and Steinbrenner have had a good relationship. For another, Giuliani is desperate to have baseball stadiums as part of his legacy. While he'd made it apparent over the years that he'd do his best to free up city money to build new stadiums for both the Mets and Yankees, Giuliani also knows the city's voters would never go along with such a deal. This has reportedly been upsetting to Giuliani, since he's so vocal about his support for the local teams and he's openly stated his desire for new Yankee or Met stadiums to be built or at least begun during his tenure. So, Giuliani turned to the Minor Leagues, forcefeeding these new Cyclone and Staten Island Yankee stadiums to his constituents. Finally, the mayor was aware that the northern tip of Staten Island was stagnant, with few businesses opening and little excitement. He thought that putting a stadium there would be a financial impetus for the whole area. But, again, he needed the Mets' approval, and if the Mets built a stadium in Suffolk, Rudy would get nothing out of the deal.

So Giuliani put on his thinking cap and pulled out the city's checkbook. Giuliani knew that Fred Wilpon was assuming an ever larger role with the Mets and that he was the man to cozy up to for future business. Giuliani also knew that before Wilpon went to the University of Michigan (class of '58) and later became a major player in the New York City real estate market as cofounder of Sterling Equities, he had grown up in Brooklyn. And Wilpon considered himself a Brooklyn guy at heart, a Bensonhurst native who had loved the old Dodgers. A deal was concocted. Give Staten Island to the Yankees, Rudy promised the Mets' leaders, and the Yankees will let you have Brooklyn. What's more, the city will build new stadiums for both franchises. It didn't take long for Steinbrenner and Wilpon to agree to such a sweetheart deal, and by 1999 sites were being scouted for a Brooklyn stadium.

For Fred Wilpon, the idea of putting a team in Brooklyn was particularly exciting. Though he's been a part-owner of the Mets since 1980 and has lived on Long Island for years, Wilpon has ties to Brooklyn (and to the Dodgers legacy) that are irrefutable. Wilpon's father ran a funeral parlor on Coney Island Avenue, and Fred attended Lafayette High School along with the Hall of Fame pitcher Sandy Koufax; Wilpon and the famous Dodger lefty have stayed in touch to this day. In fact, the reclusive Koufax still stops by Mets' spring training every year, and many say that is because of his ongoing relationship with Wilpon.

While the Yankees came to Staten Island and spent the 1999 and 2000 seasons playing at the College of Staten Island without a hitch (even winning last year's New York–Penn League title), the Brooklyn baseball team needed a place to play. As far as a permanent home, the Wilpons scouted several locations before, the company line goes, Fred Wilpon fell in love with the picturesque Steeplechase Park locale.

Just as he had "redevelopment" as a major motivation in Staten Island, Giuliani's dual motive in providing a home for the Cyclones was his vision that corporate giants could come into Coney Island and turn it around as they had Times Square. To Giuliani, getting a deal to bring the Cyclones to Coney Island represented the area's start down a road that would one day lead to chain restaurants, chain hotels, and throngs of visitors with their wallets open—just like the old days (well, except for the chain part).

While some confusing deals were being arranged between the Mets and the Blue Jays related to which affiliate would eventually come to Brooklyn, it finally became certain that the Brooklyn Baseball Company would be in charge of a team in 2000 and that a Coney Island stadium probably wouldn't be ready until 2002.

This gave Giuliani another idea. The mayor proposed letting the Brooklyn Parade Grounds, a sprawling Parks Department plot across from Prospect Park, serve as the temporary home for Brooklyn baseball. People in Lefferts Gardens, Park Slope, and Windsor Terrace did not like the idea of massive construction and then crowds in their neighborhood, so they fought Giuliani and the Brooklyn Baseball Company until they killed the Parade Grounds idea. Taking a page from the Yankees, who'd temporarily set up their team at the College of Staten Island, the umbrella Mets' organization instead placed its homeless New York–Penn League team at St. John's University, in Queens. Dubbing them the Queens Kings in a play on the official name of their future home borough, Kings County, the city spent $6 million to upgrade the St. John's stadium.

The season at St. John's was a relative mess, as the team attracted little attention and even fewer fans—a total of 38,662, in fact, the worst total in the entire New York–Penn League. The Queens debacle did create a stronger focus on Coney Island, and by February 2000, the City Council was voting on a Jack Gordon–designed stadium that would be ready for 2002. By August 2000, with the St. John's plan failing and Rudy cajoling needed support from other city politicians, a sped-up construction plan had begun that would have the new stadium ready for the 2001 season.

The next step for Rudy and his Brooklyn Baseball cronies was to name the team. Beginning on the press-friendly groundbreaking day in August 2000, the team held a contest in conjunction with the *Daily News* and the sports radio station WFAN that received more than 7,000 entries by November, when the winning name was announced. There were some amusing entries in the contest, such as "Hot Dogs," "Honeymooners," and, of course, "Da Bums," but none made as much sense as the winner. At a November 29 press conference, Hizzoner explained: "We're proud to announce that the Mets' new minor league team will be known as the 'Brooklyn Cyclones,' in honor of Coney Island's signature roller coaster. The Brooklyn Cyclones will no doubt draw people to the neighborhood, initiate the redevelopment and economic growth of Coney Island, and add to Brooklyn's reputation as a legendary sports borough."

Jeffrey Wilpon, executive vice president of the Brooklyn Baseball Company, added, "The fantastic response to the 'Help Us Name the Team' sweepstakes demonstrates what we've known all along—that New Yorkers are eagerly looking forward to the return of professional baseball to Brooklyn."

"For years, the Brooklyn Cyclone has been the last word in heart-stopping summer thrills for roller coaster riders at Coney Island," said Fred

Wilpon. "Now the Brooklyn Cyclones are going to bring the heart-stopping thrills of professional baseball to Coney Island."

It was not surprising that the main beneficiaries of the city's largesse were excited, but Giuliani also took a little time to try to explain how the common folk would benefit from this project, as well. New York City (with Giuliani behind the proverbial Wizard of Oz curtain on all the press releases) took the opportunity of the name-announcement ceremony to say that the construction work needed to build the stadium and to make improvements to the immediate area would create 700 jobs. And, with thirty-eight home games and the up to thirty-five "nongame events" that the city has a right to hold, KeySpan Park would create "approximately 240 full- and part-time jobs." (The Coney Island Houses apparently never got the memo.)

The stadium sponsorship deal with KeySpan—which Giuliani said would be split between the team and the city—became official in January 2001. Like almost all the financial agreements related to the stadium, officials were tight-lipped about who was making what from the deal. For reference, Richmond County Bank had agreed the previous summer to be the naming sponsor of the Yankees stadium in Staten Island, and, according to the *News*, the bank "revealed it would pony up $400,000 annually for at least nine years." It's safe to say that the KeySpan-Cyclone deal is much larger. Giuliani made sure that financing the project never turned into a huge issue, despite the protestations of Brooklyn borough president Howard Golden. Giuliani had authorized the use of city money, and there was no stopping him, even as the costs soared past his initial estimate of $20 million for building the Cyclones' stadium; Rudy's city would finance the building of the stadium.

On opening night, Giuliani told TV viewers that "the $37 million it cost to build this stadium was worth it. We'll get that back in economic development within a year." Jeff Wilpon sang a similar tune, telling reporters that "this is an economic development project and we think it will bring 200,000 to 300,000 new people to Coney Island."

There was no in-depth explanation of the numbers (and Wilpon's remark sounds particularly suspect because the Cyclones' healthy season ticket sales indicate that there won't be nearly that many "new" visitors; most will come over and over again). Even for enterprising reporters, measuring the costs and benefits is difficult because most of the figures relating to the lease and to sponsorships, including the massive amount that KeySpan had to come in for to acquire stadium naming rights, are not being released to the public or the press.

Throughout the Cyclones' stadium process, there was one extremely loud public voice of dissent—that of the aforementioned Brooklyn borough president, Howard Golden. Golden, a Democrat, had been borough president since 1976, and term limits would finally force him to leave office at the end of 2001. And, while Giuliani faced the prospect of leaving office without getting a Major League stadium built, it looked like Golden would exit public office without getting a much more personal project built—the Brooklyn SportsPlex—directly because of Giuliani and the birth of the Cyclones/KeySpan Park.

For the past fifteen or so years, there had been talk in Brooklyn of a SportsPlex. Fought for aggressively since 1995 by an organization called the Brooklyn Sports Foundation, the SportsPlex sounded like a wonderful idea with two admirable goals. It has been explained as an indoor arena with approximately 12,000 seats. Given that the city has a huge gap in arena sizes, with nothing falling in between Madison Square Garden's 19,000 and St. John's Alumni Hall's 6,000, the Sports Foundation figured it could attract lots of events to the SportsPlex. Besides having the potential for for-profit events, including the Ice Capades, the circus, pro track and boxing events, pro basketball exhibition games, and major college basketball games, the SportsPlex could host countless high school events. This would be a huge help for nearby high schools, such as Lincoln and Grady, whose facilities are dated and getting older fast, not to mention being way too small for the attention their stellar basketball programs attract. Ironically, the SportsPlex always planned to use Steeplechase Park, the same locale that now has KeySpan Park sitting on it. And, to hear SportsPlex supporters tell it, a building that would draw visitors to Coney Island in the winter is even more appealing and logical than one that would attract folks in the summer, given that even rundown Coney

Island has maintained the ability to draw close to 500,000 visitors on a hot summer weekend. As Anthony says, there ain't too many kids that get excited about heading down to the ancient and bleak Abe Stark Recreation Center, adjacent to the stadium, for an afternoon of ice skating. Although the arena's advocates had no problem explaining how the SportsPlex would be used, the long-time problem facing the SportsPlex was money, or lack thereof. But in 1995 the idea got a boost when Governor George Pataki and his state government committed some $30 million to the project, which was at least temporarily matched by Giuliani. The total was then raised again when Golden promised $7 million of Brooklyn money, theoretically giving the project $67 million.

Once the determined Giuliani entered the Minor League stadium–building business, however, all bets on the future of the SportsPlex were off. In January 1999, as the Met and Yankee organizations were getting excited about city-funded stadiums, Giuliani said that to worry about the SportsPlex before taking care of the stadiums would be "putting the cart before the horse." He went on to say that "you need the major investment of something that will draw enormous numbers of people to Coney Island to turn it around. [The Mets' farm team will mean] 5,000 people to Coney Island forty times a year, and there's nothing else to guarantee that." Giuliani also reiterated that he was not canceling the SportsPlex altogether: "The ballpark idea is going to happen, and then the SportsPlex will also happen."

By late February 1999, Rudy's plans were coming into focus. With little fanfare, the city signed contracts with the Met and Yankee organizations to build the stadiums. As the *Daily News* explained the contracts, the *maximum* rent the teams would owe the city (if they sold out every game of their 6,500-seat stadiums) was only $510,000, a low number given the cost of building the stadium. Hizzoner had this memorable comment when the details were made public: "There are people who are constructive visionaries and then there are people who never accomplish anything in life. The borough president and I are constructive visionaries."

The borough president Giuliani was referring to was Guy Molinari, a Republican, of Staten Island. For his part, the Brooklyn borough president, Golden, was appalled with the deal and could not have found Giuliani's arguments any less convincing. In fact, Golden announced a plan to sue the city in the wake of February's announcement. Besides maintaining that the SportsPlex was a better fit for the community, Golden had a major answer to the "5,000 people forty times a year" claim. To paraphrase Golden, his response was, How about 5,000 (or more) people *seventy* times a year?

In June 1999, with the Staten Island Yankees already playing on Staten Island, the Coney Island/Mets' plan was discussed in a public hearing for the first time. While there were complaints from Coney Island business and community leaders who still believed in the SportsPlex idea and wanted to make sure that any stadium deal included major neighborhood improvements, the loudest objections came from Golden. On the day of the hearing, Golden released a report through his borough office that explained how, if the city wanted a baseball team in Coney Island, it could do much better than a Single-A team. Golden knew that the Mets and Yankees wanted to use their veto power over Major League–affiliated teams to keep the level of play in the city at a low level, thereby lessening the potential impact on attendance at Met and Yankee games. That alone bothered Golden, because his study showed that Minor League teams could draw quite well without affecting Major League teams, and he also knew that Major League teams have no say over independent teams, the like of which had started in Newark (the Bears), Long Island (the Ducks), and Montclair, New Jersey (the Jersey Jackals).

The biggest problem Golden had with Single-A ball was the smallness of it. This is a borough president who said in 1998 that he was speaking with the O'Malley family (which had moved the Dodgers to Los Angeles and was putting the team up for sale) about moving them *back* to Brooklyn and giving the city three Major League teams again. After all, when standing alone from the rest of New York City, Brooklyn has a population of more than 2.4 million people, according to the 2000 census, making it by far the biggest U.S. city not to have a baseball team. The Class-A season is only seventy-six games long, which means that even if a team were to reach the unlikely maximum of four home playoff games, it would host only forty-two games a year. And, logically, a Single-A stadium can be built only so big. Double- or Triple-A Minor League teams' seasons are nearly as long as those for the majors, generating close to eighty home games a year, and there wouldn't be anything weird about a 12,000- or 14,000-seat stadium for that level. Independent teams might not draw quite as well as Double- or Triple-A–affiliated teams, but they could easily hold their own in a 10,000-seat stadium, and again, their season home games number closer to eighty than forty. What Golden's thirty-plus-page report, titled "Out at First! The Giuliani Administration's Missed Opportunity," details over and over again, with examples from metro areas around the country that are all smaller than New York, is that Brooklyn could easily support a high-level Minor League team.

Golden's report, combined with their own apprehension about the lack of a SportsPlex promise, was more than enough for the members of Coney Island's Community Board 13 to vote against the stadium initially, though Giuliani threw enough money at the project that even most of the local politicians came around, except for Golden. By April 2000, against the loud wishes of Golden, construction of the stadium was under way. And there was no longer a promise that the SportsPlex would ever get built. The entire episode was considered a victory for the overbearing Giuliani and a depressing loss for Golden, who had been a relatively popular borough president over his lengthy tenure. The two's divergent roles in the project played out on opening night. While Giuliani shook hands, preened for the cameras, and was as press-friendly throughout the historic evening as he'd ever been, Golden attended the game quietly and avoided the cameras altogether.

Ironically, the game program that the Cyclones sold on opening night and sell through the first couple of weeks includes a quarter-page advertisement for an auction to benefit the SportsPlex. The ad copy reads, "The Brooklyn Sports Foundation, developers of the new SportsPlex, congratulates the New York Mets and welcomes the Brooklyn Cyclones (our future neighbor) to Coney Island. Please join the Brooklyn Sports Foundation for the August 16th game at KeySpan Park. We will be conducting a Sports and Entertainment Fantasy Auction during the game, with hundreds of exciting and unique items available for bid. For more information about BSF or to reserve your tickets, please call 718–875–7000." With or without some little print ad, however, few people close to the situation—particularly those who work for the Cyclones—have any expectation that this excellent idea will ever come to life.

Through the Cyclones' first eight home games, at least, Golden's views seem extremely prophetic. The Cyclones are averaging more than 7,300 fans a night, which is almost a complete sellout. It's not hard to imagine selling at least 10,000 or 12,000 seats a night on at least sixty evenings per year and bringing that many more people to Coney Island. As far as Dave Campanaro, manager of media relations for the Cyclones, knows, however, nothing like that will ever happen.

There is at least one constituent of Golden's who was also heavily against the building of KeySpan, although this gentleman's thinking is far to the left of even that of the Democrat Golden. The dissident is Robert Lederman, a political activist and Coney Island resident who has been arrested throughout the city over the years for displaying anti-Rudy art (some catch phrases, which are written above nasty caricatures of Hizzoner, include "Adolph Giuliani," "Fooliani," and "Jailiani") at rallies and on street corners. Lederman has a website devoted to his commentary on many New York City issues (www.baltech.org/lederman/), including essays that lambaste the mayor for agreeing to spend the city's money to finance a stadium for the Mets. Basically, the entire process that landed the Cyclones here has galled Lederman. The lanky, middle-aged protester attracted some attention at the parade before the first Cyclones game, when his boos were the loudest of the day. Standing on the Surf Avenue sidewalk just east of KeySpan property with a "Fooliani—Corporate Welfare" poster, Lederman shouted, among other things, that "my kids can't get new pencils in their schools, and yet this city is building stadiums for billionaires." In Lederman's mind, the use of city money to build a stadium for the Mets' franchise amounts to "welfare for billionaires."

Lederman is not the only one who thinks this. Kevin Baker, who wrote the historical novel *Dreamland* (which was set largely in turn-of-the-century Coney Island), has referred to the building of KeySpan as a form of "corporate welfare." One more sour note came from the renowned sports and stadium economist Andrew Zimbalist, an economics professor at Smith College, who said, about KeySpan Park specifically, as well as about countless other projects across America, that "the economic impact of a stadium does not justify having taxpayers build it." The antistadium rants of Zimbalist, the *Village Voice* writer Neil deMause, and others even have their own home on the Internet (www.fieldofschemes.com).

All the gripes that can be uncovered by digging for them are by no means a regular subject of public discourse in Brooklyn these days, however. For the most part, the subject has been debated behind closed doors by a small group of people, while it seems that whenever the general public thinks about the Cyclones, it's in a positive way. In a story that ran on June 23, the *New York Times* perfectly captured the common attitude toward those who dared question the Cyclones' birth. Andy Newman wrote, "Let the economists grumble that $39 million—the amount Rudolph W. Giuliani, in the soft twilight of his mayoralty, lavished on a minor-league stadium in Coney Island—would have been better spent on an industrial park. Let Brooklyn's own borough president fume that the city would have been far better served by playing fields for high school and college teams. All of that, for the moment, is beside the point. People are talking baseball in Brooklyn again."

For many years, baseball was probably the *most* talked-about topic in Brooklyn. The most linear connection to the famed Brooklyn Dodgers of the 1940s and '50s began in 1890, with the Brooklyn Bridegrooms, the borough's first National League team. In 1899, the team became known as the Brooklyn Superbas, around the same time that a former clerk named Charles Ebbets was coming into power within the organization. By 1900, Ebbets was the sole owner of the Superbas, and he had visions of a stadium that could bring in big crowds and replace the team's Washington Park, a grandstand located at Third Avenue and First Street that had opened just a few years before. In 1911, the team adopted the name Dodgers, as in Trolley Dodgers, in light of Brooklyn's busy electric trolley system that sent residents scurrying to "dodge" the conveyances all over the borough. In 1913, Ebbets moved the team into his self-named stadium, Ebbets Field. From 1914 to 1931, the team was known as the Brooklyn Robins, in deference to its well-liked manager, Wilbert Robinson. Robinson led the team to the World Series in 1916 (when they lost to the Babe Ruth–led Boston Red Sox) and 1920 (a loss at the hands of the Cleveland Indians), but he couldn't get them over the championship hump. A frustrating trend had been established. From 1932 to 1938, the Dodgers—as they were again known—were among the bottom feeders in the National League, but when Leo "the Lip" Durocher was brought in to manage the team in 1939, things changed for the better. Throughout Durocher's eight-year stint as manager, the Dodgers were one of the best teams in the National League, winning the 1941 pennant and having only one losing season.

While modern-day New York City and the Cyclone organization clearly have some challenges ahead of them as far as making sure that fan interest remains high and that no one gets too concerned about how the stadium got paid for, there are specific, on-field baseball challenges inherent to every Minor League baseball team. As a subsidiary of the Mets—who define success by wins and losses—the Cyclones must ultimately rise above the hoopla to present solid baseball and stick to the main purpose of developing players for the Major Leagues. This could be a difficult goal in Coney Island, because the players are being placed in a more intense situation than they had expected from Minor League baseball. Normally, guys at this level are just worrying about adjusting to wooden bats, tighter strike zones, and tougher curveballs; here in Brooklyn, they need to worry about how they play in front of screaming fans.

"Maybe it's hard for some guys, but I think for most of us, the fans and attention are our adrenaline," says Brett Kay. "I mean, even if I didn't expect there to be this much attention here in Brooklyn, I like having fans, and I'm sure I play better when more people are watching."

A little more than a week into his stint with the Cyclones, Brett is speaking with more confidence, and with good reason. Just as the team has been challenged to develop the players, the players too have been challenged to improve. And, in the world of Minor League baseball, when a player meets the challenge of a certain level, he moves up the ladder, freeing a spot for the next guy. And that is exactly what has happened with the Cyclones' catching situation. It's possible that Mike Jacobs, the Cyclones' opening-day catcher and hero (he's the one who drove in the winning run in the tenth inning after striking out four times earlier in the game), will be called up by the Capital City Bombers soon. Moving Jacobs to the more advanced Class-A team of the Mets that plays in Columbia, South Carolina, will open up playing time for Brett. So, after a week of barely playing and barely talking, Brett Kay makes his first start on July 1 in a home game against the New Jersey Cardinals.

For now, Kay is right behind Jacobs on the organization's rung of catching prospects, and he's eager and able to show why he should be seen as at least Jacobs's equal. In his second start, July 2 at KeySpan against the Lowell Spinners, Kay goes 4-for-5 with a home run, a double, three runs scored, and three RBIs in a 14–4 win. "I'm so happy," Kay says after the 4-for-5 performance. "Yesterday I was only 1-for-3 with two strikeouts, which I hate. So to come out and hit a home run in my first at-bat and then get four hits was pretty sweet. . . . I'm getting comfortable, and I finally feel all situated with the team and the level of play. We're all getting to be buddies, and I think I'm going to be all right."

One of the things Brett has going for himself as he tries to claw up the Minor League ladder is that he's a catcher, a position for which the Major Leagues often find themselves bereft of prospects. After an initial aversion to donning the "Tools of Ignorance" as a kid ("Why would I want to play catcher if it meant always being in the dirt blocking balls?" he says with a laugh), Brett eventually realized it was a better ticket to adulthood than any other pursuit.

"I was an athletic kid, and I started having visions of playing professional baseball when I was seven or eight years old. I always pictured myself playing in Shea Stadium, against the Mets, and hitting a home run to right center field off of Dwight Gooden. All the time I'd have that picture in my head," recalls Brett with amazing clarity. "So, from then on, I was watching these guys on TV with the hope that one day I'd get to play with them. I played football and basketball, too. I was a raw football player—my dad was obviously a player, and I think that rubbed off, but I quit football so I wouldn't get hurt. And basketball, well, I was good at that, too, but me and the basketball coach—who was also the school's athletic director—we hated each other, and things didn't work out. I got kicked off the basketball team."

The coach/AD that Brett clashed with was Gary McKnight, a hugely successful basketball coach and near-legendary figure in California prep sports. Talking to Coach McKnight today, he chuckles at the mention of Brett's name. "Brett was some athlete. Obviously he was a great baseball player, but he was some basketball player too," McKnight says. "But let's just say he was a high-maintenance kid. He's done a lot of growing up since then."

To hear Brett talk now, run-ins with authority were nothing out of the ordinary for him. "I was a good athlete, but I was a rough kid. I was the kid other kids were told to stay away from. I've toned down so much from those days, and I'm still maturing."

Part of the roughness came from home. Brett's father, the former football player Rick, had what Brett calls "the worst temper in America." Brett's parents got divorced when Brett was ten, leaving him, his older brother, Eric, and his older sister, Kelly, with their mother, Sandy. Brett's father was basically out of Brett's life. "After they got divorced, my dad wasn't around too much. He moved all the way around the country. First he was in northern California, but he'd still come to see me play maybe once every two months. Whenever he came, I'd play real well. Then he was in Chicago, Arizona, I don't really know. He might've coached some youth leagues in Chicago or something, but he never coached me."

Rather than get into any serious trouble, however, Brett used baseball and some new mentors to create a new focus. "When I got out of Little League, I got a call about a team I should play for. The team was coached by Bob Sporrer and Mike Robinson, who were big baseball guys in Orange County," Brett relates. "My parents had gotten divorced, and I had no father figure in my life, and I had very little discipline. And these guys instilled discipline and looked after me. Bob was the head coach, and I played for him from age thirteen to eighteen, and he's been just as big a part of my life since I finished playing for him."

As a high school sophomore, Brett played mostly center field and hit .390 with seven home runs, twenty-six RBIs, and seven stolen bases. Brett then switched to playing primarily catcher, but his offense did not suffer in the slightest. He hit .458 with eight home runs, twenty-nine RBIs, and six steals as a high school junior and .389 with seven homers, twenty-seven RBIs, and seven steals as a senior. In both of his final two seasons, Brett was named Most Valuable Player of Mater Dei's South Coast League, as well as picked for the All-CIF (California Interscholastic Federation) First Team. The honors, athleticism, and catching ability (remember, he became a catcher largely because of its pro potential) were the reasons that Kay believed he'd be a pretty high draft pick right out of high school. Getting taken in the thirty-fifth round by the Astros was not nearly good enough for Kay, however, so he headed about fifteen miles from home to one of the best college programs in the country.

"When I was playing in high school and thinking about college, Fullerton was not my first choice at all," recalls Brett. "I wanted to go to the South—Florida State, Mississippi State—or maybe even Arizona State. Then some other big schools recruited me, like Miami, Stanford, and Texas, but nothing really came through. Then Fullerton came up big for me with a full scholarship at the same time that I was realizing that even though it's close to home, it is a great program."

Kay is right about that last part. He might not have paid the local college much mind as a kid, preferring, if he was going to watch baseball at all, to head to nearby Anaheim Stadium for Angel games, but Fullerton had won national championships in 1979, 1984, and 1995, and the Titans almost always qualify for the College World Series. It's also the school that has produced relatively famous Major Leaguers Jeremy Giambi, Mike Harkey, Mark Kotsay, Brent Mayne, Phil Nevin, and Tim Wallach. And, while it doesn't have quite the national baseball name of a Texas or Miami, Fullerton draws about a thousand people per game, and Fullerton's baseball sports information director, Ryan Ermeling, says that it's "one of the extremely rare Division 1 colleges that has higher attendance for baseball than men's basketball."

But Brett wasn't worried about the big picture of Cal State–Fullerton baseball when, on September 3, 1998, just weeks into his freshman year, he received an unexpected jolt when his father died in a car accident. It didn't make for a great start to college, but with the help of his family and his father figure, Brett made it through his freshman season and continued to follow his dream. "I had a lot of struggles that first year," Brett concedes. "From what happened at the beginning of the year to not really playing much during the season [Brett played in only twelve games and hit just .133 with two RBIs], it was tough. But I think I learned from everything I went through that year, and it's helped me later in life."

As a sophomore at Fullerton, Brett became a bigger part of the team, playing about half the time and hitting four home runs as the Titans got to the NCAA Regionals. Brett also exhibited his fearlessness and athleticism by getting hit by eight pitches and bunting for hits regularly. As Fullerton's Ermeling says, "Brett is the king of drag bunting." This is not a phrase baseball people usually use to describe a catcher. Brett's attitude seemed to rub off on his team as well, which went 17–4 in games that Brett started at catcher.

Brett rose to his junior-year challenge by putting together his first solid season at Fullerton. Brett started at catcher in forty-eight of the Titans' sixty-six games—a solid percentage of playing time for a catcher who suffered a broken thumb in midseason. In those forty-eight starts (and in one appearance off the bench), Brett finally showed the offensive versatility he had exhibited in high school. Brett batted .323 with seven home runs and forty-three RBIs. Overcoming the broken thumb and getting hit by seven pitches showed his toughness, while Brett's eleven stolen bases in fifteen attempts were a really impressive showing by a catcher. Brett was equally impressive behind the plate, throwing out eleven base runners in thirty-one attempts and making only four errors all season. He did all this while catching one of the best pitching staffs in the country, which included the All-American Kirk Saarloos, who threw a no-hitter (with Brett catching) on April 8. [*In 2002, Saarloos became Brett's first contemporary to reach the Bigs, starting seventeen games for the Houston Astros.*]

Brett also exhibited an ability to perform best when the games mattered most. He hit a disproportionate .352 in Big West Conference games and earned First Team All-Conference accolades after the season, as well as All-Regional honors for his play in the NCAA Regionals.

The New York Mets, among other teams, noticed Kay's exploits during his crucial junior season. And, while the major ink and big bucks go to the guys who get taken in the first round or two, the Mets didn't spend an eighth-round pick and give out a $72,000 signing bonus to a guy to be nice. No, they brought him to Coney Island and appear to have handed him the starting catching job because they, as an organization, want production and growth out of Kay. "I think it's clear that Brett has the physical tools to make the big leagues," says the Cyclone manager, Edgar Alfonzo, after one of Brett's first games in the lineup. "What this year will tell is if he has the mind and personality to make it."

With several games under his belt, Brett's feeling good, physically and mentally. "The jump from college to here doesn't seem that big to me," says Brett. "You can tell guys have nastier stuff and a better idea of how to pitch than the guys did in college, but I feel like I can handle it. I'm having a little harder time with the catching because Bobby O is letting me call the pitches and I don't know these guys yet, but that will come."

While Brett is feeling better and better about his on-the-field role with the Cyclones, the first couple of weeks of the season have been totally hectic off the field, at least as it relates to the essential need of shelter.

"The whole thing with where I'm staying has been a cluster, to be honest," explains Brett on July 8. "When I got here, they weren't sure where

I was going to live; some people were in hotels. I stayed in a hotel and then out in the dorms at St. John's College [he means the University, thirty minutes away in Jamaica, Queens, where last year's Queens Kings were housed]. When we got to St. John's, we had to wait outside because they hadn't cleared it. Staying in the dorms is brutal. *Brutal.* We have one van, and we have to leave as a group. It's, like, a big deal for guys to get shotgun and all that stuff. It just isn't any fun. I can't say it's a good experience, but I guess it's a way to get close to a bunch of the guys. I'd like to get a bit more settled and not stay there all summer."

In the rush to usher the Cyclones into Coney Island, the city and the team didn't spend a whole lot of time thinking about where these young men would sleep. That may seem like a concern that would exist throughout the Minor Leagues, but the fact is that in most of the small towns that fill up the New York–Penn League, there's an old-fashioned tradition that works well—host families. The Cyclones' urban location, however, creates a challenge for the organization. The host families with which low-level Minor Leaguers in small towns typically stay, including Kingsport and Columbia, the teams above and below the Cyclones in the Mets' organization, cook and do laundry for the players while allowing them to feel as at home as possible. And, at the higher levels of the Minor Leagues, players can afford to rent apartments, and teams can help facilitate those deals. As has been noted already, the housing stock in Coney Island is not exactly where a baseball organization wants its future to be residing. And, with the first-year players making only $850 a month (including Brett, obviously, who says that the most any Cyclone makes is $1,100 a month) and lacking assurances that they'll be in Brooklyn for very long, guys are not going to go out and rent a place in Bay Ridge, Park Slope, or any other cozy Brooklyn neighborhood. Instead, the Cyclones are spread out in a hodge-podge of housing situations. One or two players live with the manager in a house, some others are actually being hosted by a man with a home (and a borrowable car) in Staten Island, and the rest are staying either in St. John's dormitories or in some converted classrooms at Xaverian High School, in nearby Bay Ridge. There is one player, the pitcher Harold Eckert, who hails from suburban New Jersey and who stays at home with his parents, but the rest are in an unsettled situation when they're not on the field.

"I think coming up with housing was the least of their concerns," says Brett, stating the obvious about his team's owners. "I know that it's a much easier situation for guys I know on other teams, but it makes sense here—New York is a tough place for anyone to find a good place to live."

The housing crunch is no less a problem for the Cyclones' visitors. New York–Penn League teams coming in from out of town stay at the out-of-the-way Radisson Hotel at Kennedy Airport.

There is an unfortunate irony in the lack of housing for the players, given the identity of the man most responsible for bringing the team here. In his time as mayor, Rudy Giuliani has undermined and battled the homeless, trying to kick them off the streets without providing safe shelter as an alternative. At the same time, Giuliani has shown little compassion for the city's project residents, such as the Oteros, who are forced to live in buildings with broken elevators, poor heat, and smelly, rat-infested stairwells. There are literally thousands of apartments within walking distance of KeySpan Park, and it's unlikely the team or the city would feel safe letting a single player stay in one, with or without a host family.

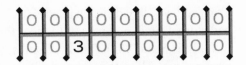

Kay and the Cyclones Become Celebrities

It's Tuesday, July 10, and the Brooklyn Cyclones have their first off day of the summer. Obviously, the potential for things to do in and around New York City is practically limitless, especially on clear, hot days like this one. There's beaches, zoos, parks . . . and that's just in Brooklyn! But if the guys want to be chaperoned around—and since many of these men are young, naive, and totally unaware of how to get around the city, it's probably a good idea—the choices have been whittled down. Brett explains after the fact, "We had our first day off, and if you wanted to go to the city with the team, some of the guys were given a choice—to go to MTV for *TRL* or to go to that famous sandwich place, Carnegie Deli. I went to MTV."

TRL, short for *Total Request Live*, is MTV's weekday-afternoon countdown show, where the videos that the viewers want are played in countdown fashion. Before and after the videos, guests chat with the host about whatever they've been up to, and people always give the impression that they're having a grand old time. It's hard to think of a show that has a broader appeal to America's teens than this show, since it so clearly makes them a part of it, from the fact that they can vote to the live studio audience. So it's not a total surprise that the Cyclones whom Campanaro, the media relations director, brought to the show name the experience as the highlight of their young season, without too many ideas of what could top it. "It was me, Ross [pitcher Peeples], Forrest [outfielder Lawson], [pitcher Matt] Peterson, [infielder Danny] Garcia, and Mike [pitcher

Cox], and we all had such a good time," says Brett with a wide smile. "We had a great time, and we got to meet Puffy."

Puffy is Sean "Puff Daddy" Combs, the hip-hop producer and entrepreneur who, like the show itself, is about at the peak of popularity among America's teens. And if the Cyclones keep on receiving this type of exposure, they won't be too far behind. "Besides Puffy, the other guests were Jon Favreau and Vincent Vaughn," says Brett, speaking of the actors of *Swingers* fame. But it's not like the Cyclones were just bystanders on the show. The program's host, the teen hero Carson Daly, interviewed the Cyclones as if they were stars in their own right, joking with them about their chances of making the Mets and telling Lawson that he should've said he hit a home run last night because "there's chicks here."

As Brett himself says, "The girls loved us. Carson was talking, like, 'These are the Cyclones,' and the girls started screaming. At one point Puffy took my hat, and kept it. Then he hugged me."

Brett even got a shot in the spotlight that his teammates didn't. "They did a contest with one of Puffy's videos—'We Don't Stop'—where you had to name all the cameo appearances in it. I won, so I got a CD, an autographed shirt, and hugged Puffy. It was definitely a lot of fun, and it's something I told my friends about."

Not that the players would care or take note of this, but there is irony in the Cyclones' spending time in Times Square. Remember that, as the home of a washed-over amusement zone that has been transformed into a cheesy tourist destination very different from its not-so-long-ago status as a seedy locale, Times Square has been mentioned by the Wilpons, Giuliani, and other politicians as the model for what Coney Island can become. Through economic incentives and draconian law enforcement, Giuliani turned the Times Square area from a grimy city center where peep shows far outnumbered legit theaters and drunks had the run of the place to a family-friendly (*tourist*-friendly, most of all) spot where you can eat off the sidewalk. The fact that the home of teen Americana, MTV, placed its signature show in Times Square speaks volumes about the image rehabilitation that has taken place in Times Square over the past decade. Now Rudy wants to do the same thing to Coney Island. If the city can pull off such a transformation in Coney Island, many Cyclone players, who seem drawn to the lights and excitement of Times Square in ways that New Yorkers never seem to understand, would probably be happy. And none would be happier than Ross Peeples. A native of small-town Cordele, in Crisp County, Georgia, who had never been to New York before he became the pitching ace of the Brooklyn Cyclones, Peeples is falling in love with Times Square.

Peeples and his mates are beginning to understand and revel in what less than one month as New York athletes has done for their lives. Some Cyclone players have already enjoyed free drinks at Brooklyn bars and choice tables at Manhattan's swank China Club restaurant, and the guys are surreptitiously starting to employ the "Met bomb" or "Cyclone bomb" on unsuspecting females. This amusing tactic of "dropping the Met/Cyclone bomb" involves guys using the fact that they are pro baseball players to pick up girls, enjoying increased success when they tell the white lie that they are playing "for the Mets."

On the MTV day, while most of his teammates stayed in the city into the evening to eat, drink, and sightsee while also using their newfound fame to hit on girls, Brett headed back to Brooklyn. With a serious, long-time girlfriend back home, Brett can appreciate the squeals of approval from young women that he got on the show and has gotten at the stadium, but he's not interested in taking it further. So he and Campanaro got on the train, leading Campanaro to a great story. "Brett and I left, and the rest of the guys stayed around in the city," tells Campanaro, a resident of Cobble Hill, Brooklyn. "When we were taking the train home, I had to kind of tell Brett where to go. I'll never forget the look on his face while riding the F train. He was as pale as can be, and when we took one of those sharp turns, he looked up and asked, 'Are these things supposed to shake so much?' He was terrified. That was his first time being on the subway."

To have spent any time with Brett Kay is to be particularly amused at the story Campanaro tells. Brett has an absolutely goofy demeanor, and he tends to take things to the extreme, good and bad. When Brett laughs, which he does often, he laughs loudly. And when he's annoyed, after a bad at-bat or a loss, for example, he's likely to snap at the first person to speak to him. So it stands to reason that when Brett's scared, he's really scared.

Brett also has an amusing tendency to sprinkle his quotes with curse words, only to apologize for cussing when he remembers that someone is writing down or tape-recording his words before resuming his cursing shortly thereafter.

Even if Brett tries at first to give writers and reporters the impression that he's just your average Minor League baseball player, spending minimal time on the Internet or simply getting beyond mundane baseball questions with him is enough to tell you that he's a unique cat. And it's not just finding out that Brett's birthday is October 31, or that he says the rushed flight he took from L.A. to New York for opening day is the "last plane I'm taking until I'm on a chartered flight with a baseball team." (From now on, Brett says, his trips east for spring training are going to be done by car or train.) While at Cal State–Fullerton, Kay bragged to the Sports Information Department that he once played Sony PlayStation for *three straight days,* a fact recapped on the Titans' webpage. Perhaps even weirder than his propensity for video games is the guy Kay named as his favorite player—Pokey Reese, of the Cincinnati Reds, a so-so infielder known more for his funky hairstyles and cool nickname than for his play. With the Cyclones, Kay's increased role on the team soon earns him a spot on the "Player Profile" section of Brooklyncyclones.com. There, it's disclosed that Kay's favorite athlete is Darryl Strawberry (Brett told me that Strawberry has always been his favorite player, meaning that Pokey was apparently a short-term, and bizarre, fave). As his favorite musician, Kay's Cyclone entry names the hideous shock rocker Marilyn Manson. Finally, it's disclosed that Brett's nickname is "Walt Flanagan." Kay reluctantly addresses the last fact when asked about it in person: "How do you know that's my nickname?" he asks me with mock anger. Told that it's right there on the website for the entire Internet-surfing world to see, Brett laughs. "Oh, yeah. Well, you know those Kevin Smith movies—*Clerks, Mallrats, Chasing Amy,* and *Dogma*—plus that new one about Jay and Silent Bob that I have to see? Anyway, Kevin Smith likes to do things that link his movies together, and one of them is that he has this character, 'Walt Flanagan,' appear in every movie. I just think it's the funniest name, and one day my brother started calling me that."

It isn't hard for Brett's good humor to show through to the Cyclone fans. Although a specific "fan favorite" may vary a bit from day to day depending on what happened in the previous game, it's quite possible that Brett Kay is the team's most liked player. His choices for favorite athlete and musician notwithstanding (Darryl Strawberry and Marilyn Manson are not exactly role models most parents encourage), Kay is very charming with the fans.

By July 12, with the Jamestown Jammers in the midst of a three-game series at KeySpan, Kay and his teammates on the Cyclones are heating up even more than the vintage New York summer weather. The Cyclones' record is 15–7, which is good enough for first place in the McNamara Division, and they're riding a winning streak that will stretch to twelve straight games. Along the way, the Cyclone players are generating from fans even more squeals of delight during their games (and even their pregame batting practice sessions) than they did at the *TRL* taping. The KeySpan Park screams are different in that they don't come exclusively from cute girls, but to most Cyclones, it's a flattering experience just the same. "I love the fans, and I love helping them out, giving kids stuff, all of that," says Brett, looking out of the dugout while a throng of boys and girls, median age about twelve, look in from all angles screaming the players' names and begging for autographs.

"Playing here, like, our home games, is just *awesome*," continues Brett in his California accent and lingo. "We've got 8,000 fans a night, and all the guys on the team are totally awesome also. This type of atmosphere is like playing in the big leagues everyday."

As the pitching coach Bobby Ojeda, who played all over the minors before he reached the majors, says, "This situation is the best experience you could ever have at this level."

Brett's appreciation for what he's experiencing translates into the way he treats the fans. "It seems like we're heroes to the young fans we have," he says. "And that's really cool. We get to interact with the fans a lot, and I know I do it whenever I can as far as giving stuff out. I'm sure I've given away the most stuff on the team."

Kay doesn't seem slick enough to make this stuff up in order to put on a show, so it's pretty appropriate that, as soon he finishes rhapsodizing on the joys of being a Cyclone, Kay digs into his equipment bag and pulls out a bat he recently cracked. "Want this bat?" he asks one of the reporters in the dugout. Before the reporter can finish his awkward review of the idea in his head—*well, I'm supposed to be a neutral observer, but that bat is pretty cool and Brett might make the majors*—Brett checks in again. "Yeah, right," he says with a laugh. "I'm going to give it to that kid over there." And with that Kay dashes the length of the dugout and hands the bat to a kid who can't believe his good fortune. The fast-moving Kay is gone before the lucky kid (or the kid's beaming father) can even offer a thank-you; he's left the dugout area to sign autographs for a different group of kids down the right-field line.

Kay is merely the most eager of an entire group of guys who, for the most part, see player-fan relations as not only a responsibility but a joy. "The kids are great here," says the reliever Blake McGinley, a skinny kid with bookish looks. "I like to sign autographs and talk to them. They look up to us; I mean, some of them have told me that one day they might want to play for the Brooklyn Cyclones, so I want to make them feel comfortable when they're here."

Besides the catcher Kay, the majority of the team's most eager autograph signers tend to be the pitchers, like McGinley. This makes sense, since, on nights that they know they won't pitch, pitchers have heaps of downtime before, during, and after the game. It's not necessarily a good excuse, but position players theoretically have to always be mentally ready for a game, and for some of them that process may not include spending quality time with young fans.

Another pitcher who can't get enough of the attention is Harold Eckert. "It's awesome here, and I don't think signing autographs for these kids will get old at all," says Eckert, the Edison, New Jersey, native who attended Florida International University. "Me, I love kids. I went to school and studied teaching and stuff like that, so to see them around is great. It gives them something to look forward to. I play baseball, and a lot of them do, too. You never know who's gonna make it. I just tell them to keep working hard." Eckert, with a big, jovial face, actually looks the part of substitute gym teacher, so it's not difficult to see why the kids seem to enjoy laughing with him so much.

The fans even have a fan in the Cyclone starting pitcher Luz Portobanco, the one player on the team that you could actually call surly on occasion. A cocky, 6'3", 205-pound right-hander with great stuff, "Porto" gives off the feeling that he thinks he should be in the majors sooner rather than later. Still, get him at the right time and the Nicaraguan (by way of Miami) will smile at the situation he's in. "Sometimes, all the attention is tiring, having people ask for your auto-graph before and after *every single game.* But it also is a good feeling—I know that we are heroes to these kids."

That Portobanco, a Nicaraguan with handsome features and caramel skin, can be a hero to the largely white crowd of youngsters speaks to the diversity of this sport, this team, and this borough, and anyone who knows his Brooklyn Dodger history would consider it appropriate that the Cyclones are so diverse. With the influx of players from Latin American countries such as Cuba, the Dominican Republic, Mexico, Nicaragua, Venezuela, and the U.S. commonwealth of Puerto Rico, Spanish has become baseball's second language, and this team is a perfect example. Sitting in the Cyclone dugout, one hears almost as much chitchatting in Spanish as in English. Besides Portobanco, the team's Latin players thus far this season include the infielders David Abreu (Dominican Republic), Leonardo Arias (DR), Edgar Rodriguez (DR), and Joel Zaragosa (Puerto Rico); the outfielders Noel Devarez (DR) and Angel Pagan (PR); and the pitcher Yunior Cabrera (DR). And the Cyclones' manager, the Venezuelan Alfonzo, is the first Latino baseball manager in New York. The Cyclones' roster also includes black and white Americans from all over the country, as well as the two Australians, creating a diverse, inter-national mix.

It's an appropriate mix in Brooklyn, because few teams in the history of pro sports are as linked to race as the Brooklyn Dodgers, thanks to the organization's landmark decision, in 1947, to put Jackie Robinson on the field. Until that time, baseball was as strictly segregated as anything else in America, and black players were expected to play in the Negro Leagues if they insisted on playing the sport at all. But, by 1947, the Dodgers' GM, Branch Rickey, felt that the time had come to bring a black player up to the big leagues, and with the strong-willed Robinson playing for the Dodgers' farm team in Montreal, Rickey felt that the Dodgers had the man for the job. Without going into all the details, it's fair to say that Robinson did not have an easy task in front of him. First, he had to overcome his teammates, who ostracized him and many of whom tried to circulate a petition to keep him from playing for the Dodgers. And once Robinson won over his teammates (well, all but the most bigoted) with his blazing speed and win-at-all-costs determination, he still had to deal with abject racism from opponents, coaches, and fans whenever the Dodgers were on the road.

One place the California-raised Robinson was a relative hero, however, was in his new hometown of Brooklyn. As Peter Golenbock wrote in his 1984 book, *Bums,* about the Brooklyn Dodgers:

[By 1945] there were three million people in Brooklyn, and hardly a Mayflower descendant among them. The populace had landed in boats all right, but they had streamed past the Statue of Liberty and docked at Ellis Island. Brooklyn was different from the rest of the country. Everyone came as a minority, and they discovered that when they arrived in Brooklyn, everyone was the same: Everyone was poor. Everyone was struggling. No one felt persecuted, unless they rooted for the Giants or the Yankees instead of the Dodgers. Although different areas had different ethnic characters, there was little serious prejudice.

And even if there wasn't a lot of mixing between blacks and whites, many fans swore they didn't have a problem with Robinson. One fan Golenbock quotes in *Bums* said, "When Robinson came up, all of a sudden we saw Negroes not only as human beings, but we lionized them. You'd say, 'Oh my God, there are wonderful people in there.'"

While there were certainly some working-class adults who were appalled at Robinson's presence, young Dodger fans didn't seem to care what he looked like, as long as he helped their beloved team. "I don't remember a lot of ethnic or religious segregation in my neighborhood," recalls Steve Asch, a gregarious New York City businessman who was a seven-year-old Flatbush resident and Dodger devotee when Robinson debuted. "I lived on Martense Street, between Flatbush and Bedford near the old Garfield Cafeteria, and very close to Ebbets Field. What I do remember is that my friends and I all loved Jackie Robinson. *Loved him!*"

By the end of the 1947 season, Robinson was the National League's Rookie of the Year and the Dodgers were the National League champs. More important, at least from a societal aspect, fans of all colors were flocking to Ebbets Field as well as to the road stadiums the Dodgers visited, and baseball was on its way to becoming a fully integrated sport.

In Brooklyn baseball's new incarnation, the crowds at KeySpan Park are disproportionately white (like they are in professional ballparks across America), but the support does seem to unite across many neighborhood and class divisions. The white players such as Brett have little to say about the subject beyond this: "What matters to me is that guys have a team-first attitude, and I can't say enough about these teammates," Kay says. "I don't care about the other stuff."

Meanwhile, to Latin players such as Portobanco who have heard horror stories about Latin Minor Leaguers being stuck in the middle of some midwestern town without any Spanish speakers around other than some teammates, Brooklyn is close to heaven. The ocean breeze feels familiar, and many people—inside, and, even more frequently, outside the stadium—have made the players comfortable. "I've got an uncle up here in Brooklyn, but I'd never been able to visit him. I always wanted to come here because when I was living in Miami and going to college there, the people always told me I would blend in here because I'm Latin and because of how I dress," says Portobanco, who has been living in the same house as the team's manager, Edgar Alfonzo. "Miami was a great place to be, and when I joined the team it became my first time here. If anything, everything I had heard made me think things would be crazier. But it's been a lot of fun. There are a lot of people in the neighborhood that I can speak Spanish with, and I've gotten some real good Latin food."

To reflect the borough in the ultimate sense, the team should probably have a local player or two, in the way that the local Puerto Rican Anthony Otero dreams of being a Cyclone. But the fact is that Brooklyn is no baseball hotbed, notwithstanding Nautilus Playground in the afternoon, and teams simply can't assign roster spots to appeal to fans. Even so, in the event there is a Brooklyn sandlot player with the skills to make it, the Mets' organization has scheduled an open tryout for August 3 at KeySpan for anyone who thinks he's got what it takes.

Despite the fact that none of the Cyclone players are from Brooklyn, and regardless of their racial background, the players have quickly become a big deal in the New York sports scene, and most of them are enjoying the new status immensely. While any fan could cite the pre- and postgame autograph chaos—and the corresponding smiles—as proof of the players' celebrity status, there are also some subtle experiences inherent in being a Cyclone that the players love.

One thing that Brett has quickly learned to love is the media attention, particularly after games. "Man, we grew up watching ESPN, guys getting interviewed in the clubhouse," Brett says. "So to have that—the lights, the cameras, the interviews—here, at this point in our careers, it's awesome."

Brett is right. While not quite as intense as the postgame scene at Shea Stadium, where scores of reporters trip over giant food spreads in their rush to players' mammoth lockers in order to get an awful cliché out of some overpriced relief pitcher, the postgame locker room at KeySpan is about as "big league" as you can get without actually being there. Well, the "lockers" are pretty spartan, with wooden dividers separating them, but there is carpeting, a table with paper plates and leftover concession food for the guys to snarf down, and plenty of room to get around. There's also the occasional sand particle, which has blown from the beach to the boardwalk and into the stadium and somehow clung to a player's uniform. Have the beach and baseball ever been so intertwined? It's not likely.

But, as Brett says, it isn't even the better-than-normal physical amenities of the locker room that thrill the players—it's the energy and the attention they get. Besides the weekly Brooklyn papers with their own beat writers, the dailies are sending writers out occasionally, and there's even some cable networks coming to talk to guys. Some want material for general features on the city's new team, and others are beginning to hype the upcoming "Ferry Series," which will start on July 14 and pit the Cyclones against their obvious geographic rival, the Staten Island Yankees. It's enough to make the guys feel like they're in the "Show," as the Major Leagues are often referred to.

And even if every Cyclone player does not love the spotlight, most at least greet reporters with a smile and maybe even an anecdote or two. This is a pleasant change of pace from big leaguers, who often treat reporters as if they're carrying a disease and rarely utter more than the blandest of quotes.

The visible joy that Brooklyn Cyclone players feel before, during, and after the games is inevitably rubbing off on the fans, many of whom are following this team with the passion like that with which their parents and grandparents followed the Dodgers and all of whom are guaranteed the minimum of a fun evening when they go to see them play. As much as the Cyclones have going for them, with the physical beauty by the stadium and the historical aspect of the season, the beautiful Minor League fan-player relations on display at KeySpan Park are by no means exclusive to Brooklyn. The Minor League baseball formula—take young prospects and have them play their hearts out in front of appreciative fans who sit close to the action and haven't been gouged for parking and tickets—has been working with remarkable success throughout America for generations, and there's been a boom for some twenty years now. As far back as the summer of 1990, *Sports Illustrated* dedicated an issue to the "Minor Miracle" (that was the cover line) that was taking place across the land as small cities built Minor League stadiums and watched the people file in.

The premise of the issue, which featured eight different stories and fifty editorial pages devoted to the sport, was captured in the following passage:

> The Minors are offering good, clean, relatively inexpensive fun and food for the whole family. They are giving towns a sense of civic pride and providing them with their own piece of Americana. They are giving fans an opportunity to spend some time with their neighbors, to talk about the great season so-and-so had here on his way to the big leagues. For those and other reasons, the "bush leagues" have never seemed lusher. Last year the National Association of Professional Baseball Leagues—the minors—drew 23,103,593 fans, the highest minor league total since 1952, when attendance was 23,103,373. But back then there were 324 clubs in 43 leagues and only 16 major league teams. In 1989 there were 190 minor league franchises in 19 leagues, and there were 26 big league teams. [In 1989] eight different leagues set attendance records, and the Buffalo Bisons of the Triple A American Association counted 1,116,441 fans, becoming the first minor league team to draw more than a million two years in a row. In 1989 the Bisons outdrew the Chicago White Sox and the Atlanta Braves. . . . Says Jerry Leidler, a Hollywood producer with interests in three clubs (Reno, South Bend and Welland, Ont.), "The minor leagues are thriving in part because of a tremendous renaissance all across America—people trying to find their roots, to get a little closer to home. As major league baseball becomes more and more packaged, and more and more players make $3 million a year, it gets harder for the average fan to relate to the majors. And it gets easier to relate to the minors. They're cheaper, more fun for the family, and people are enjoying themselves."

Remember, that excerpt is from *1990*.

In 1997, Fodor's put out a book called *Ballpark Vacations*. While the book's authors, Bruce Adams (contributor) and Margaret Engel, cover Major League stadiums thoroughly, the book is much more intensely devoted to the best road trips people can take to see Minor League baseball, giving full travel information for eighty-five different ballparks. If the duo were working on a second version now, KeySpan Park would probably warrant an entire chapter all by itself. Here, in the year 2001, Minor League baseball is celebrating the one hundredth anniversary of the aforementioned National Association of Professional Baseball Leagues, the sport's governing corporate body—and it's doing so with the sport even healthier that it was at the start of the '90s. The 2001 season features more than 200 teams, and attendance is projected to be higher than 33 million, a figure reached for the past seven seasons. Much of *Sports Illustrated's* 1990 issue featured the small-town and even small-city charm of Minor League baseball, examining closely teams in places that feel lucky to have any pro sports (Bend, Oregon; Peoria, Illinois; Medicine Hat, Alberta; Salinas, California), as well as legitimate cities that remain too small ever to get a big-league team (Buffalo, Toledo, and Raleigh/Durham). Raleigh/Durham is home to the team that the Cyclones are chasing for the title of most famous Minor League team—the Durham Bulls, who achieved their fame thanks to the classic baseball flick *Bull Durham,* which stars Kevin Costner as an aging Minor League great. In fact, *SI's* special issue credits that film greatly for the Minor League boom. A huge coincidence that is somehow fitting within the quirkiness that is Brett Kay's life is uncovered when he is asked—in light of the Daly/Puffy/Vaughn/Favreau interaction at MTV—who the biggest celebrity he's ever met is. "I'd have to say Kevin Costner," says Brett. "He went to Fullerton and he'd come down to our games and practices a lot. That was always pretty cool."

On the last page of the *Sports Illustrated* Minor League issue, in the magazine's then-signature "Point After" column, the well-known baseball writer (and inventor of Rotisserie Baseball) Daniel Okrent waxes poetic about the joys of Minor League baseball, specifically as it's played in Pittsfield, Massachusetts's Wahconah Park. "Imagine this," writes Okrent.

> You're in an old wooden ballpark where the action is so near at hand you can sometimes hear the batter talking to the umpire. . . . The players exert themselves ceaselessly, sprinting towards first on every routine pop-up, chasing every impossible foul fly. After the game, the players linger behind

the dugout and greet the kids in the park with autographs and pats on the head. If this is your idea of heaven, you ought to visit Wahconah Park.

The incredible irony in rereading this column is that Wahconah Park—a unique stadium built in 1919, before night games and sunset were ideas to consider and hence the home of the occasional "sun delay" because home plate faces the sun—is where the Mets' Single-A franchise played before the Wilpon/Giuliani team decided to bring Minor League baseball to Brooklyn. Wahconah Park (now the home of the Houston Astro–affiliated Pittsfield Astros) is not nearly the cash cow that KeySpan is, nor does it hold hopes of rejuvenating a neighborhood, but its ancient beauty reflects the more traditional way that Minor League baseball has been seen as a glorious summer pastime.

To illustrate the difference between the Cyclones' experiences and the more typical Class-A experience, the *Journal News* Mets' beat writer Kit Stier recently asked some Mets' players to recap their memories of professional baseball at the low level. Jay Payton, a Mets' outfielder, was a college star at Georgia Tech and then went straight to Pittsfield, where apparently players don't hold the stadium in the same regard as sappy baseball writers. "I remember when I left college and went to Pittsfield, I was wondering if I had made the right decision after walking into that clubhouse," Payton said. "It was not quite as clean as Georgia Tech was, the field wasn't as nice as ours was at Georgia Tech, the clubhouse wasn't quite as nice. . . . You're like, 'Man!' But on the same note, it motivates you to get out of there."

In any event, what the Cyclones (as well as the Newark Bears, Long Island Ducks, and dozens of other Minor League teams) are a part of is the most recent boom in Minor League baseball—the sprouting up, and subsequent success, of teams in "Major League areas." These teams, with names like the San Jose Giants (in the San Francisco Giants' and the Oakland A's market), the Tacoma Rainiers (in the Seattle Mariners' market), and the St. Paul Saints (in the Minnesota Twins' market) are proving that even fans who *could* watch big leaguers often prefer the affordable, small-time scene. In fact, they are the fans—fans who have cars and disposable income but who may not like all the trappings of the Major League game—that the minors are reaching out to more and more. This is a major point of Howard Golden's study. As Golden's "Out at First" says, "There is no doubt that a market area of this demographic . . . will make a minor league team successful in Brooklyn, and there is ample evidence to suggest that the presence of a team will not adversely affect the Yankees or Mets . . . even if it was a high level team playing as many as 69 home games per season."

So far this summer, the first-place New York Yankees are averaging more than 35,000 fans a game and have a good shot at setting the franchise's *all-time* attendance mark, while the middling Mets are averaging about 32,000 per game, a still-impressive figure about in line with how the organization has done since its glory days in the late '80s. The point is that Minor League baseball is booming, to some degree, in "Minor" and "Major League" cities throughout America and Canada, and the Cyclones are simply taking that boom to another level. As Brett says, "I do know we've played in front of some good crowds on the road, and my buddies on other teams and in other leagues have told me about some of their crowds being pretty good. But there is *definitely* no place like Brooklyn! You know how the St. Louis Rams are called the Greatest Show on Earth," Brett continues, referencing the NFL's high-powered offense. (It's "Turf," rather than "Earth," but I don't want to disrupt his flow.) "Well, they're wrong. The Brooklyn Cyclones are the Greatest Show on Earth."

A big part of the show is the approachability of the players as I have described it. Minor League players are, as a rule, considerably more pleasant to fans than big leaguers are. Sometimes Major League players have reason to be cynical—there are stalkers of both sexes out there, and players know that anything they sign could be up on eBay within a day, which tends to knock some of the charm out of autograph chasers. Plus, in bigger stadiums with abrasive ushers, even the earnest fans have a tough time getting close to the players. Incidentally, in my experience at some fifteen different Major League stadiums, I have to say that no ushers are as rude and domineering as the ones at Shea Stadium. Fans who try to sneak into the lower section at Shea Stadium—even when it's less than half full—are treated as if they were trying to trash the field. The old, crotchety ushers at Shea are probably just doing what they've been told, but they sure are harsh about it. Thank goodness, the Mets' organization hasn't let such an attitude trickle down to this level. At KeySpan Park, the ushers wear cheery tropical shirts and cheerier smiles, while interaction between fans and players is encouraged and enjoyed by all parties. The Cyclones' media relations manager, Campanaro, sees the connection at close range, and he's been very impressed. "Players throughout the Minor Leagues are strongly encouraged to interact with the fans and sign autographs—that's part of what makes the experience so great," begins Campanaro when asked whether the players are "taught" to be so good with the fans. "Though it has to come from within the player, too. You can't just make someone be good with the fans. Some guys are great at it and can sign stuff all day long. Others don't feel the same way and can get overwhelmed by the whole thing, especially if they're struggling on the field. We've been really lucky in that almost every player so far has warmed to the experience, especially guys like Brett, Ross Peeples, Jay Caliguiri, and Robert McIntyre. . . . I think part of it is that they can see how passionate our fans are, and they feed off of it."

It is also easier for fans to identify with players at this level, and this makes fans' dreams of baseball success seem not so impossible. For one thing, every player is not a physical specimen. While the Major Leagues are filled with giants such as the California Angels teammates Mo Vaughn (6'1", at least 275 pounds, first baseman) and Troy Glaus (6'5", 245 pounds, third baseman), the Cyclones have guys—who start, no less—like the outfielder Frank Corr, who checks in at 5'9", 200 pounds. Where steroids are considered a significant problem in the big leagues, at this level they're thought of more as a fear that hasn't quite been realized yet. Among the catchers, Brett's size (6'1", 190 pounds) is just about in line with big-league catchers, but he certainly doesn't come off like a monster. Brett is definitely physically fit, but there's nothing intimidating about his build, and his personality is so warm that few fans would be fazed by him no matter what he looked like.

Another factor in the positive player-fan relationship is that the players at this level do not make millions of dollars, and few ever will. For the first time ever, the average Major League salary this season is more than $2 million. Even the minimum salary is $200,000. The point here is not to debate the merits of such high numbers—these are highly skilled entertainers who produce millions of dollars in ticket and TV revenues, and we'll leave it at that—but they do explain another reason why Joe Fan might not feel he has a lot in common with these millionaire stars. While a couple of Cyclones got six-figure signing bonuses, Brett's $72,000 is more indicative of what most decent prospects get. And that bonus money is a one-shot deal. Single-A players' monthly salaries, remember, are a meager $850 a month. Plus there's the factor of guaranteed contracts. Major League contracts in this era are guaranteed, which means exactly that—a shortstop who has earned a Major League deal can subsequently hit .192 with one home run and make thirty-eight errors in the field and still be cashing biweekly checks that are worth more than most fans make in a year. Imagine how many "working stiffs" would welcome a guaranteed contract, as opposed to walking around worrying whether the next budget cut will be their last. Here in Brooklyn, at the Single-A level, if a Cyclone hits .192 for long, there's a good chance he's going to be looking for a new job. As the Cyclones' manager, Alfonzo, a veteran of the Minor Leagues, says, "The whole point of Minor League baseball is to move up. If you're doing well, you get promoted, and you have to be happy about that. And if you're not doing well, you can get demoted and someone doing well can replace you. And from this team [meaning low Class-A], if you're not doing well, you can get cut." A lot of working fans can relate to that type of employer pressure.

The cost of the "Brooklyn show" remains a huge factor in the Cyclones' appeal, as well. As one of the happy mothers in the opening-night crowd noted, a ticket that would've cost her $60 at Shea cost $10 here. For a family of four, you're talking about $240 instead of $40, just for tickets. The way Minor League baseball's cost structure is set up, going to a Cyclone game with your family is not unlike going to the movies (yeah, movie tickets are too expensive these days, but that's another story). And for fans for whom cost is no object and for whom the desire to live it up trumps all else, KeySpan does have twelve luxury suites in the deck behind home plate and a party deck down the left-field line that can hold groups of up to fifty guests and provides personal waiter service for $3,000 a game.

Of course, KeySpan Park has crowd-drawing advantages over probably every other Minor League park in the nation. There's some great stadiums out there, for sure, from the retro flavor of Durham Bulls Ballpark to the Mississippi River scene that plays in front of you at Davenport, Iowa's John O'Donnell Stadium to the breath-taking mountain views from Lindborg-Cregg Field in Missoula, Montana, but it's hard to top the eye candy a fan enjoys while sitting in the stands at KeySpan Park. The autographs and giveaways are nice, and the baseball is usually entertaining, but, while perusing the scenery this evening, it hits me that it would be tough not to enjoy oneself here even if the team stunk and its attitude was worse.

Inside the twenty-plus rows of the main seating area, you sit on green seats adorned with nifty cup holders, a nice nod to the past. On the side of the seats is the image of an old-time player holding a bat, flanked by two little circles, each with a logo. One is the trademark B of the Brooklyn Dodgers, the other the interlocking NY that signified the old New York Giants and then the early New York Mets, which are the teams that the National League–affiliated Cyclones most closely represent. It's a nice touch.

At the top of the seating area is a concourse, one that's so wide you could drive a truck through it. The width is welcome because it allows for major foot traffic without overcrowding. And, because there are no barriers between the concourse and the seating area, you can always see the field while you walk around, be it to the barbeque pit down the third-base line, the conventional refreshment stand on the first-base side, or the souvenir shop right in the middle. Because the concourse is one story above street level and the team wanted to have the store open even when the stadium wasn't in use, it created a two-level store, with the levels connected by stairs; fans inside can enter from the concourse, while fans outside can enter from Surf Avenue. In addition to the interior entrance to the ultrapopular souvenir store, which is called Cyclone City, the concourse behind home plate also holds the elevators and stairways up to the luxury boxes and the press area. One final touch on the concourse is a dry-erase board, which always displays the day's updated New York–Penn League standings. Such a board was commonplace in old stadiums (they used chalk back then), and it's a cool addition here, too, not least because the Cyclones are at the top of the list.

Where the palette of most concrete stadiums is various shades of depressing gray, KeySpan counters that with well-placed blues, greens, yellows, and oranges. One of the unique elements of the stadium is the colorful neon rings around the lights at the top of the stadium's pinwheel-style light towers. The rings are different colors, blue or pink or green, and they add to the festive feeling at the stadium. Bright yellow and blue canopies hang over the concourse down the first- and third-base lines. These colorful canopies conjure images of an amusement park while also seemingly acknowledging Los Angeles's Dodger Stadium, which has similarly shaped overhangs. Lighting KeySpan's main concourse are Mets'-themed blue, orange, and white lights that seem to further acknowledge Coney Island's carnival history. Unlike some fluorescent lights, these are not all that ostentatious, and they work well in the overall KeySpan tableau.

On the field, this July 12 game against the Jammers is a crisp and well-played contest, with the Cyclones' starter Ross Peeples finally giving up his first run of the season but still maintaining control of things on the mound. The Cyclones' first hit of the game comes on Jay Caligiuri's third-inning, two-run homer, his first of the year. With the red-hot Cyclones ahead in the late innings, I decide to take a break from watching the game and follow the concourse out to the bleachers again. As the cement concourse turns into boardwalk-style wood, the effect is completed by the constant sea breeze blowing sand particles onto the pathway. To the right of the elevated concourse is the 1,100-car parking lot. There's nothing pretty about a parking lot, but the convenience of this one is impressive. For all but the latest-arriving fans, this is a clean, safe lot that is just feet from the stadium's entrance. Following the boardwalk around, I reach another well-conceived concession stand. Besides the peanuts and cracker jacks people have been getting at stadiums since at least 1908 (when Jack Norworth wrote the sport's signature song), this concession stand has some homegrown treats for sale, namely Brooklyn Italian ices, Brooklyn Brewery beer (brewed in Williamsburg), and Nathan's dogs (obviously a national chain now, but their genesis was just a home run away). The elevated concourse-turned-boardwalk then passes the Cyclones' bullpen, below to the fans' left. There the Cyclones' relief pitchers can be seen warming up, spitting sunflower seeds, watching the game, or just messing around. There's usually a coach and other staff and security in or near the bullpen to help maintain a certain level of professionalism, because otherwise the number of requests for balls, gloves, phone numbers—and the willingness of the players to oblige—could really get out of hand. Beyond the bullpen are more bathrooms and then a left turn that leads to the bleachers, which sit behind right field. The comfort of the bleacher seats remains an issue, but the views are still outstanding. Surveying the scene from the stadium again, I am again amazed at just how much one can see from KeySpan Park, even with its location out on the edge of New York City. The lights on the massive Verrazano Bridge, which spans Brooklyn to Staten Island, are visible to the west, while the tips of the World Trade Center, in downtown Manhattan, are in sight to the north.

It's nights like these that have generated all the poetry and meaning attached to baseball and that other sports—regardless of their TV ratings or fan demographics—have never been able to match. As the former Kansas City Royals' pitcher Steve Busby once said, "Baseball to me is still the national pastime because it is a summer game. I feel that almost all Americans are summer people. That summer is what they think of when they think of their childhood. I think it stirs up an incredible emotion within people."

In Coney Island, inside KeySpan Park, those emotions are readily visible.

Ask Brett about KeySpan and he gets so excited. "It's not one of the nicest places I've ever played in, it's *the* nicest," he says with a wide smile. "The ocean, that cool parachute jump in right, then you've got the nice, big scoreboard in left. And with 8,000 people watching? Wow! What else can you say? It's the most fun place you could ever play."

If the players go on to forget individual games in this season, and *when* the fans do, they will still remember this ballpark. To some degree, every baseball stadium is memorable—for a certain ad on a fence, or the contour of the seats, or the mountain or skyscraper you can see if you look in a certain direction. But few, if any, stadiums, have as much going for them as KeySpan Park. The bleachers end about 200 feet from the boardwalk, which is right on the beach. To link the stadium with the boardwalk, the team built a skinny, boardwalk passageway from the right-field corner out to the boardwalk. There is a little ticket booth that sells bleacher seats out there, and an entrance directly to the stadium. In the space between the boardwalk and the field next to the walkway is an ugly vacant lot, strewn with weeds. Showing that they have a plan for that, too, Campanaro tells me that a Little League field will be built there in time for the 2002 season. Not a bad idea. [*Indeed, it opened in June 2002.*]

The salty sea breeze that the folks in the bleacher seats feel on their necks is a welcome sensation and feels wonderfully out of the ordinary at a professional baseball game. As one coat-and-tied Long Island–raised stockbroker, sitting in the bleachers on his first-ever trip to Coney Island (not just the stadium, the neighborhood), says, "The subway ride out here is a bitch, but that ocean breeze sure feels good after a day at the office." A few fans have joked that KeySpan is like "Candlestick East," a reference to the old San Francisco Giants stadium that sat by the water and was notorious for its cold winds. The difference in Coney Island, as the businessman said, is that the breeze feels good here. These are eighty- and ninety-degree days with wicked humidity that we're in right now; people may joke about the wind on particularly breezy nights, but nobody's going to complain about it.

The crowd is filled with this type of satisfied response—not necessarily about the breeze, but just the overall joy these outsiders feel upon making their first trip to Coney Island and the stadium. There's another type of fan here, as well, the type that was out in full force on opening night. These are the ones with Brooklyn or even Coney Island ties, who used to live nearby or had a grandfather or cousin who was "always talking about the glory days," as one fan said. It's not surprising that these groups of fans are here, nor should they be denied their pleasure even if they and their families left the area twenty, thirty, or forty years ago. Build a stadium this beautiful in a place with as many peripheral attractions as Coney Island still has, and people will come. This doesn't quite explain why city residents had to finance the project, but it certainly explains why the project itself was a good idea.

One thought prevents my bleacher-bound self from completely slipping into reverie as the Jammer game winds down to an eventual 5–4 Cyclone win—what about the local kids? I haven't seen Anthony in over a week, at which point he was reiterating that the August 13 Yankee game would be the only time he'd come here and that he wasn't even that sad about it. I never should have worried.

I didn't see Anthony that night, but the next afternoon, several hours before the Cyclones' series with the Jamestown Jammers winds down, I return to the Coney Island Houses. Sure enough, Anthony and his boys are playing baseball. Anthony comes over and says rather matter-of-factly that he has already been to a "couple" of games and that I must have missed him and his friends in the stands. Such a quick turn of events! "Yeah, man, Josi [his friend Josimar] got us a bunch of bleacher tickets for one of the games last weekend. I think they played the Expos or something [indeed, the Vermont Expos were just in town for a two-game series I had missed], and all of us went down there," says Anthony, taking a break from his latest playground baseball game and gesturing at a group of six or seven kids. One of the quieter kids in the crew, I've learned, is Anthony's younger brother, twelve-year-old James Otero, who has attended the games with Anthony. Anthony continues, "I guess Josi just thought it would be something different to do. It was so fun. We had these bleacher seats [Cyclone CEO Jeff Wilpon did presciently say that the bleacher seats were meant to create more opportunities for people to see the team], but we just moved down to the front row. Nobody said nothing to us, so we just stayed there. And we got autographs afterward. Look at my glove—I got it signed by a lot of the guys."

Anthony is even understanding the player-fan dynamic. "I think that the guys mostly care about making it to the majors," he says. "They have to care about that. But it's like they care about the fans also. I think they like us."

Now his buddy Anthony De Los Santos ambles over. "One of the guys on the team gave me his pack of seeds the other day," he says with a broad smile. "I've got them upstairs if you want to see them."

There is, suddenly, enthusiasm over the Cyclones in this overlooked little corner of Coney Island. This talk of sunflower seeds and autographs is so different from last week's lament that the team wasn't for them.

The August 13 game that was supposed to be Anthony's only visit to KeySpan Park is now being presented as just another game for Anthony. None of the kids can give me any real perspective on the matter, however. It seems to be as simple as any other teenage adventure. One day the Cyclones were a distant concept out of these boys' reach. The next, it was an obvious thing they could be doing, walking the length of several football fields to buy some cheap tickets, sneaking into the good seats, making a lot of noise, and watching the sport they all love. "It's not like anyone from the team came here and told us to come out to support the Brooklyn team or anything, but it's pretty easy for us to go," Anthony says. "Now I want to go to a lot of games, and I'll try to get these kids to come with me."

In fact, speaking of games with the Staten Island Yankees, Brooklyn's big rivals host the Cyclones tomorrow and then make their first appearance of the season at KeySpan the next day, July 15. Anthony Otero, in the midst of discovering all the joys of Minor League baseball, will be there.

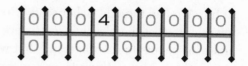

Coney Island's Team Begins
Its Own Rivalry—The "Ferry Series"

The sun-drenched late afternoon of Sunday, July 15, presents a Cyclone home game that has captured the city's imagination more than any game since opening night. It's the Staten Island Yankees' first visit to KeySpan Park. Since the game is a 5 p.m. twilight start, the crowd near the stadium starts to morph from a beach crowd to a baseball crowd by 3:30, and it has the biggest buzz around it since the throng on opening night. Given New Yorkers' predilection for a good rivalry, it's no surprise that this game, and the other Yankee games on the schedule, was the first to sell out after the opener. Looking at this bustling, well-heeled crowd, theoretically the crowd that Rudy and other stadium boosters envisioned bringing to Coney Island, it's worth asking what it would really mean if Coney Island, a place that's been dubbed "the working-man's Riviera," were to be redone.

Beginning in 1829, Coney Island began developing into a playground of the rich. That was when some local residents of Gravesend—named for an English town from which some of their ancestors had come—laid a path over Coney Island creek and built an inn on the sandy strip of land that is today called Coney Island. Previously, the island had mostly been cut off from the mainland by a giant marsh, and few people were attracted to the strip (today the marsh has almost been totally filled in, and "Island" seems more a figure of speech or a metaphor for the neighborhood's isolation than a geological definition). To get all the way out to the area, visitors needed to travel by carriage, which was not for anyone but the upper class. So the rich folks of the time, including Washington Irving and Herman Melville, discovered the glory of sitting by the beach and frolicking in the water, and, shortly after, other inns were built. The original inn's name? The Coney Island House.

Today's Coney Island Houses couldn't have less in common with their ancient, unknown (to most of the residents), singular namesake, aside from being a place of youthful exuberance. These are not children of the elite, however, running around the blacktop of Nautilus playground. It's Anthony and his boys, and while it's no surprise that they're playing a sport (handball) today, it is hard to believe that they seem as excited about the Cyclone-Yankee game (they have bleacher seats, as has become their custom) as they are about their own game of handball. By all the indications he gave three weeks ago, Anthony wouldn't even be making his first trip to KeySpan until the August 13 game against the Yankees, and here he is ready to go to his third game of the season. Like his mother, Anthony is a devout Yankee fan, and even his exciting discovery of the Cyclones' stadium isn't going to change his rooting interests. Anthony may be picking out individual Cyclone players that he's fond of, and he welcomes the autographs of any Cyclone, but whether the Cyclone team wins or loses is still insignificant to him. "The only team I really want to win is the Yankees. My mother pretty much got me into liking them. In this game I'm going to root for Staten Island Yankees, since they're part of the real Yankees, but I don't really care who wins."

Since it's a Sunday, Anthony's father, Anthony Sr., is free of any major obligations, and he's outside playing handball with the group of kids. I've met Mr. Otero, a stocky guy who goes about 5'8", before, but only when he's tired and just off of his job as an auto mechanic in the Red Hook neighborhood of Brooklyn. Today, Mr. Otero is refreshed and whipping these kids around the court in handball. According to Anthony Jr., his pops "taught all of us—every single kid out here—how to play handball." This is no small thing to learn, since, in many ways, Coney Island is the handball capital of the United States, and it hosts the national tournament. Mr. Otero is not lecturing the kids with this type of information, but he has made sure they'll always be able to partake of this neighborhood pastime.

Unlike mother and son, Mr. Otero has no interest in the Yankees, or in any other aspect of baseball. "I don't know why, but I'm just not into it," he says simply, in the same calm tone he uses to answer any query. "I am happy the team is here, though, because Anthony loves baseball so much. I mean, he loves all sports, but baseball is his favorite."

Anthony's mother, Janet, is also hanging out on the playground, but that's not unusual. Most afternoons, while Anthony, his brother James, and their friends run around in the playground heat playing sports, Anthony's mom is sitting on a shaded bench, just keeping an eye on things. Janet Otero is a pretty, petite woman with slightly graying hair and an awkward way of answering my questions; no one else with a pen and a pad has ever asked for her opinion on the future of her neighborhood. As part of a nuclear family in which her husband is the primary wage earner, Mrs. Otero sees it as her de facto job to spend most of her days within the project property, keeping her eyes on "all" of her children. Every couple of minutes, one of them will come up to her, calling her *Mami* and asking for a soda or something. "I'm always watching them," she confirms with a smile.

"My Mom really looks out for us," says Anthony. "She's basically around here, watching us play. If a fight starts, she'll break it up and talk to the kids alone. And my dad is out here whenever he can be, too. People like when my parents are around because they kind of look out for everybody. My parents are cool like that."

Luckily for Mrs. Otero, or perhaps *because* of her, this youthful group that Anthony runs with seems too sweet to get into much trouble. But the fact that they've avoided any major incidents doesn't mean that problems are not lurking around them. "We play sports to get away from all this violence around us," says Josimar. "A lot of kids be messin' with drugs and that bullshit, but we're not those types of kids. We got this," Josimar finishes, with a head nod to the baseball "field" and handball court.

Says Anthony, "Well, you do have a lot of people around here that are always arguing and talking about other people. But I stay away from that. I don't have time for that stuff. I'd rather be playing or going to a game."

Besides her lingering worries about local drug dealers and petty thugs and the abject lack of concern about her complex among the invisible New York police force, Mrs. Otero actually doesn't have many gripes with her neck of the urban woods. "We've been here for thirteen and a half years, since right after Anthony was born. Then we had James, and it's been the four of us ever since," she recalls in her Brooklyn accent. "I think my husband would like to move us out if he could, but the thing is, we've never had any problems. I think it's nice here."

Mrs. Otero is a little quirky, as evidenced by her refusal to take her building's elevator up to the family's third-floor apartment, even if her sons or husband are taking it. "I'm scared of it," she says. More relevant to the Cyclones and her son is that she has no plans to set foot in KeySpan Park, at least not until something else happens that Otero family history indicates will not be taking place any time soon. "I love baseball, but I'm a *Yankee* fan most of all. I watch every single Yankee game on TV. When I first heard about this stadium project on the news, I was hoping we'd get a Yankee team here. I can't go to any stadium of the Mets. I bought Anthony tickets for that one game against the Yankees, but I still won't go," she says.

I ask her if that means she's going to make the trek over to Staten Island to check out the "Baby Yankees." "No, I can't go there, either," Mrs. Otero says with a chuckle that seems to acknowledge my raised eyebrows. "I have to go to Yankee Stadium first. Even my kids tell me I'm crazy. They say, 'Ma, you're going to die before you get to Yankee Stadium, just come to the game,' or whatever. But I can't do it. It's like, my father was a Giant fan, my sister is a Mets' fan, and I love the Yankees. So when I go to a game for the first time, it's got to be Yankee Stadium. That's it!"

Regardless of her rooting interests, Mrs. Otero will be the first person to say that she is happy about the stadium's presence in the neighborhood, especially now that her kids and their friends are spending some quality time there. "I think that the stadium is a nice place for kids to go," she says. "This neighborhood could use a lot of things, and I think the stadium is a great start."

I ask Mrs. Otero about the SportsPlex that almost came to the site instead of KeySpan and that still has an outside shot at getting built in addition to the stadium. "I've never heard of that. You're the first person to ever tell me about it," she says. I fill her in with further details about what might have been, and her response is honest and emphatic. "You know, this place is never that bad in the summer anyway. I think what you're talking about would be a great idea because in the fall and winter this place is a ghost town. That's when the kids get so hyper, but they have nowhere to go. Anthony just has the four walls around him, and he'll be saying, 'Mom, can I play outside?' But it's too cold. So, yeah, we need a place for football or basketball or whatever, a place where the kids could play in the winter," she says.

Darcy Frey's *The Last Shot,* which chronicles a season with the Lincoln High School basketball team and as such was largely set in the Coney Island winter, captures what this place was like then. He writes:

> The Cyclone and Wonder Wheel have been shuttered . . . the boardwalk is littered with broken glass and crack vials. Certain of the neighborhood's urban beach activities continue—guys combing the sand for loose change with their metal detectors and car owners attending to their batteries with solar-powered rechargers. Just behind the boardwalk and the amusement park, where the projects rise up, the cold weather has swept the streets clean. . . . Garbage drifts down empty alleyways like tumbleweed.

Mrs. Otero adds one final clarification. "You know, I still can't say I'd have wanted [the SportsPlex] more than the stadium. In the summer the kids have so much free time, and the stadium gives them something to do. Ideally, they would have built both."

Anthony, a newly formed live-baseball fan, says he thinks he heard people talking about SportsPlex in school a long time ago and has similar thoughts. "I don't think I'd want that more than a baseball stadium, but I would be happy to have a place to go in the winter."

In any event, Mrs. Otero is positive that the stadium is much better than an alternative that her neighborhood had buzzed about in recent years. "What they used to talk about was putting a casino into this neighborhood," she says. "At first, that sounded fun, but I don't need to be going to a casino. And what would that have done for the kids? A casino is no place for kids. If there was anything I worried about because of the stadium it was traffic and stuff, but it seems like the police have done a good job because we haven't had any problems with traffic."

In listening to the Oteros and other people in Coney Island, and even more from looking through the archives of the *Daily News,* I realize that changing Coney Island has been talked about forever. If the idea wasn't a casino, it was the SportsPlex. If it wasn't the SportsPlex, it was a huge movie theater and shopping mall. If it wasn't that, it was a renovated amusement park, or a whole new one designed by the people at Walt Disney. To Coney Island visitors who do little more than get off the subway at Stillwell, eat a dog at Nathan's, and try not to throw it up on the Cyclone, laughing the whole afternoon, talk of "fixing" Coney Island seems silly.

After all, Coney Island contains seemingly endless entertainment in the form of the beach, amusement rides, and even the New York Aquarium, a heretofore unmentioned attraction that sits on Surf Avenue about a mile from the Coney Island Houses, just east of the Cyclone roller coaster. Started in 1896 in Battery Park—making it the oldest continuously operating aquarium in the United States—the New York Aquarium was moved to Coney Island in 1957 as part of Robert Moses's plans for the area. Still, even with its estimated 750,000 visitors a year, the Aquarium seems like nothing to a thrill-seeking visitor when compared to rides such as the Cyclone and the Wonder Wheel and to carnival games that focus on basketball, gun shooting, and horse racing. Turns out that none of it really appeals to life-long resident Anthony, however. "We'll go over to Astroland sometimes," Anthony says without enthusiasm. "We'll walk through there, play the dollar games, go for the balloons, and win prizes and stuff."

I ask Anthony whether he realizes how unique it is to live within walking distance of all this stuff. "Yeah, I guess, but it's not like a big part of my life. When I was little, we never went there."

Anthony's lack of interest notwithstanding, there's no getting around the fact that the overall idea of Coney Island remains remarkable. Especially its urbanness. This is a city-based theme park that is still up and running years after early-twentieth-century attempts to create similar parks failed. Coney Island once had more-or-less peers in Pacific Ocean Park (Los Angeles), Euclid Beach Park (Cleveland), Forest Park Highlands (St. Louis), Riverview (Chicago), and Wonderland Park (part of Revere Beach, Boston). Now these parks are gone. None of these parks were located right in a city center, but they were inarguably urban amusement centers, which Coney Island remains.

Unless you're the rare New York City resident with a car, the Coney Island amusement area is reached from other parts of the city only when you've traversed the entire borough of Brooklyn and come to the absolute end of the subway line. The N, D, Q, and W trains all make their last stop at Stillwell Avenue, the still-smelly station that, in conjunction with the arrival of KeySpan Park, is due for a massive renovation that will commence shortly. [*By 2003, the reconstruction of the Stillwell Avenue stop is in full swing, with all lines but the W terminating elsewhere until the work ends, hopefully by mid-2004*]. There isn't a whole lot going on during the seemingly endless subway ride through Brooklyn, which takes a good fifty minutes from northern Brooklyn nneighborhoods like Park Slope or Boerum Hill. Much of the last part of the ride is above ground, exposing old tenement buildings, tree-friendly backyards, and finally the little Coney Island Creek—which used to be a big marsh—that makes this area an island. The United Nations–style population inside the subway is as interesting as what goes on outside the windows, with numerous riders of African, Asian, Caribbean, European, and Middle Eastern descent, all chattering in their own accents or languages. At no point on the ride, until you're about 100 yards from the Stillwell Avenue stop, is there any sign that you're about to reach a world-class amusement park.

Arriving at the elevated Stillwell station, you can look down on some old-fashioned ocean and beach supply stores selling suntan lotion, beach chairs, and cheap sunglasses. On days filled with brilliant sunshine, with people pouring out of the subway clutching the latest copy of *TimeOut New York*—which put Coney Island on the cover—the place almost feels like Rehoboth Beach or the Jersey Shore. Of course, the urine smell, the towering projects in the distance, and the people begging for money usually snap one back to the realization that this is, as the t-shirts say, New York Freakin' City, but it's a fun illusion.

If the Dodgers are Brooklyn's most famous defectors, Coney Island, as an institution, is Brooklyn's most famous longtime resident. While the Dodgers left Flatbush and moved to Los Angeles, Coney Island the area stayed put, ever more deserted as thousands of people left the area over the years and vowed never to return, turned off by its gritty, crime-laden streets, jeopardizing the future of Coney Island the idea.

Going away from the amusement park area and KeySpan, even on a sunny day with the ocean a block away, you find that somber gray is the dominant color when you walk west on Surf Avenue. Some of the non-project buildings along this stretch of Surf include the Jewish Geriatric Center and Surf Manor, a group home of some sort with numerous dazed individuals resting outside. It seems that every building along this stretch is devoted to the poor or the old or to invalids. There are also many deserted lots, waiting for some type of salvation.

The amusement park history of Coney Island is worthy of entire books, and, indeed, they already exist. A brief account begins around the end of the nineteenth century, by which time Coney Island was an easy place for the moneyed masses to reach, readily accessible by the railroads, roadways, and steamships that hauled people in from Manhattan. Coney prospered after its annexation, in 1894, by Brooklyn, which put an end to its era of lawlessness as a part of Gravesend town, for years under the corrupt rule of John McKane. With McKane out and visitors able to come in, Coney Island amusements became the domain of family-oriented businessmen such as Peter and George Tilyou, a father-son combination that ran one of the first bathing pavilions on the island. Besides the pavilions—where you could rent a bathing suit and a place to change into it—other amusements of the early 1890s included game booths, countless saloons, three racetracks that made the area the horse racing capital of the world, and the Switchback Railway. Perhaps the most important harbinger of the glory days that would soon follow, the Switchback Railway was the world's first roller coaster, a gravity-powered ride that got up to a whopping six miles per hour and had to be pulled, manually, to the top of the track. Still, it was a start, and the Switchback's creator, LaMarcus A. Thompson, made enough money from the project to see its potential; according to Robert Cartmell's *The Incredible Scream Machine: A History of the Roller Coaster,* he went on to build twenty-four more roller coasters.

In 1895, a former navy officer named Paul Boyton, who'd acquire worldwide celebrity of sorts thanks to his penchant for sea-bound swimming feats, opened the aquatic-themed Sea Lion Park. Sea Lion Park was not extravagant, but, with a broad lagoon, trained sea lions, an old-mill water ride, a toboggan slide, and the Flip Flap Railroad—which flung its riders through an upside-down loop—the park was the original enclosed amusement park in Coney Island.

In 1897, the younger Tilyou took Coney Island to another level by opening Steeplechase Park, which sat on the same land that KeySpan Park graces today. Tilyou had opened a ferris wheel in Coney Island in 1894, and several other rides shortly thereafter, but Sea Lion Park gave him the idea to wall in his rides and make an amusement park of his own. Steeplechase's signature ride was a mechanical horse race course, which played off the popularity of thoroughbred racing in the area at that time. Other wild amusements at Steeplechase included the Pavilion of Fun, the Human Zoo, and the Blowhole Theater, where unknowing women were led to stand above an opening that blasted air up their skirts while the crowd looked on approvingly.

In 1902, Tilyou convinced Frederic Thompson and Elmer "Skip" Dundy to move a renowned illusion ride of theirs, called "Trip to the Moon," to Steeplechase after its successful run at the Buffalo Pan-American Exposition. After a year of partnership with Tilyou—and after some 850,000 customers rode the "Trip to the Moon"—Thompson and Dundy decided to use their interactive ride as the anchor for their own park. They bought up the land from Boyton's struggling Sea Lion Park, built around the lagoon, and named their place Luna Park. Thanks to more than 700 workers who put in time day and night— much like the folks who would later whip KeySpan Park together— Luna Park opened the next spring, across the street from Steeplechase. Designed with a mind-bending collection of towers and lights, Luna Park and Steeplechase together presented an unprecedented array of rides and attractions, including the exotic "War of the Worlds" and "The Kansas Cyclone." Luna Park's opening night, in May 1903, attracted more than 60,000 visitors, and the park remained successful for many years.

Seeing Steeplechase Park and Luna Park as models for lucrative amusement parks, former state senator William Reynolds and some other shady politicians raced to get on the bandwagon. Using a whopping 2,000 workers, and buying up loads of property through questionable auctions, they put their park, called Dreamland, together in five months and opened it to tremendous crowds one year after Luna's opening. Dreamland, which was located on the eastern part of Surf Avenue where the Aquarium sits today, jutted out into the ocean and afforded visitors the opportunity to take a steamship from Manhattan right to the entrance—a forebear, of sorts, of the ferry service to Steeplechase Pier that Giuliani concocted in the summer of 2001 for the Cyclone-Yankee "Ferry Series." Many of Dreamland's attractions were blatant ripoffs of attractions at Luna Park, but it did have some original ideas, including Lilliputia, a miniature village with miniature people. In any event, visitors flocked to all three massive parks. Reading the stories and looking at old paintings and photos of the amusement parks, especially when sitting inside the relatively minor attractions that exist today, such as the

Aquarium or the Coney Island Museum, is intriguing. "How," you're bound to ask yourself, "did all of this exist?"

By 1907, while the racetracks—which had become cesspools of corruption—were going out of business, the three parks were attracting families from around the world. Even if amusement parks had become a staple of that era in America, nowhere else were they as spectacular and huge as in Coney Island. As Giuliani said on the Cyclones' opening night, "It's great to have this beautiful ballpark in what was once the greatest amusement park in the world—Coney Island."

The three-headed glory days would not last forever, however, and fire was the main culprit. First came a fire in Tilyou's Steeplechase Park in 1907. Ever the businessman, however, an undaunted Tilyou charged people admission to come watch the park burn, then rebuilt it, with an extension so that he, too, could welcome visitors directly from the ocean to his park.

In 1911, fire destroyed Dreamland. Whereas Tilyou was a Coney Island native committed to Steeplechase and its neighborhood, the greedy Dreamland owners lacked that same commitment and let Dreamland fall, not to be rebuilt. Many of Dreamland's workers landed on their feet at one of the two remaining parks, but the magic was subsiding. Tilyou's passing away in 1914 and the outbreak of World War I further dimmed the brightness at Coney Island.

Steeplechase and Luna Park chugged through the '20s and '30s, efficiently drawing visitors, if not anywhere near the number they had when they were new. Movies and radio had come along to entertain people in their homes, and inevitably some of the magic of Coney Island wore off. The extension of the subway in 1920 ensured that people from the city could reach the area easily and cheaply; while the subway further eroded some of the mystique of Coney Island, it did ensure that lots of people would keep coming. The rich wanted little to do with these newcomers from lower Manhattan, many of whom were recent immigrants, but the parks were happy to have the new visitors. It was during this era that Coney Island became unquestionably a place for the masses as opposed to the elite, a vibe that has lasted until today. The city's building of

Riegelmann boardwalk, in 1923, made Coney Island even more open and accessible. Whereas hundreds of thousands of visitors used to come mainly for the amusement parks, they were now free to walk along the water and hang out at the beach. Besides easing overcrowding in the area, the boardwalk brought people to a new culinary attraction, Childs Restaurant, a branch of the successful early-twentieth-century chain that sat about a block west of the Steeplechase/KeySpan site. The restaurant has long since gone out of business, but the terra cotta building is noteworthy because it still stands on the boardwalk, its marine-themed designs providing a nice change from the largely dreary boardwalk area that surrounds it. If developers have their way, this is the type of building that will be refurbished and reopened with the help of Cyclones-related visitors.

Around the time that the boardwalk opened, independent rides started popping up outside the boundaries of Steeplechase and Luna parks. In 1925, the Thunderbolt roller coaster was built just off the boardwalk to the west of Steeplechase Park. The Thunderbolt operated until 1983 and stayed standing until 2000, when it was torn down, despite the protests of many sentimental locals, to make room for the KeySpan Park parking lot. In 1929, the brothers Jack and Irving Rosenthal commissioned Vernan Keenan to design, and Harry C. Baker to construct, the wooden-tracked roller coaster known as the Cyclone, giving the area its lasting drawing card that was independent of an amusement park. The Cyclone remains to this day one of the most fearsome roller coasters in the world.

As the amusements became more rundown and less, well, amusing, the old parks continued their decline, a descent aided by the Great Depression and eventually by World War II. Millions of people were still coming to Coney Island in the 1940s, but often it was just to go to the beach.

In 1944, fire burned Luna Park to the ground, and the once groundbreaking amusement park was now just part of the land. Its site, on the north side of Surf Avenue, would never again be used for amusements.

Steeplechase, which suffered its second major fire in 1939, hung on for two more decades, luring a new generation of customers to ride the old horses or check out the sideshows. One new addition to Steeplechase was the purchase and installation, in 1940, of the Parachute Jump, which had been used for the 1939 World's Fair, held in Flushing Meadows, Queens. Steeplechase stuck around throughout the '50s, but it was on shaky ground; there were fewer and fewer new rides that outsiders would travel to go on, and the neighborhood had been blighted by the razing of houses and their replacement with housing projects. This led to a fear of crime—which the city never really took measures to counter by increasing the police presence in the area—which further undercut Steeplechase's success. The year 1964 proved to be the final season for Steeplechase Park, and in 1965 one of the Tilyou descendants sold the land to a real estate developer, Fred Trump (yes, as in Donald's father). Trump sold the land to the city without building the housing he'd planned on, but not before overseeing the demolition of nearly all the rides (save for a few that would live on in Coney Island's new park). The Parachute Jump—as a structure, not an active ride—was one of the few things that survived Steeplechase Park's transformation into a vacant lot, and it was given landmark status in 1988.

Even if its wildest era was over, Coney Island is a resilient place, and it would never stop being, in one form or another, the place to go if you wanted to scream your lungs out. As Steeplechase rotted away and the neighborhood began to feel more desolate and less safe, the new park, Astroland, was under construction. Astroland provided little of the wonder that its famous predecessors did, but it was an amusement park, sitting between Surf Avenue and the ocean in Coney Island, and to some people that was enough. In 1975, the owners of Astroland took control of the Cyclone. They gave the coaster its first (and last) major renovation, and they have stayed in business and capitalized on the stomach-turning coaster with the eighty-five-foot drop as it gained unprecedented status as a New York City Landmark (in 1988) and a National Historic Landmark (in 1991).

The Cyclone is so thrilling that, according to one oft-repeated story, Charles Lindbergh found a ride on the Cyclone to be more exciting than his trans-Atlantic flight. The thrills come from the Cyclone's wooden structure, which is surely safe but feels as terrifyingly rickety as an old wooden shack in the midst of a tornado. Except for the work done in 1975, the coaster is basically the same today as when it was built; it is definitely still 110 seconds of pure terror.

Despite the Cyclone's continued allure and Astroland's survival, Coney Island suffered through some miserable years. "It was like all that was left in the '70s and '80s were remnants of what once was," recalls the old Brooklyn resident and fan Steve Asch. "We lived in Park Slope then, and I'd take my kids on bike rides to show them the area, but besides getting some hot dogs at Nathan's it's like the place was a shell of itself."

Remnants, however, of the former dynamism of the old neighborhood remain. A contemporary of the Cyclone roller coaster that has lasted to this day is the Wonder Wheel, a 150-foot-tall ride that takes a ferris wheel to new levels, given its ability to slide its sixteen swinging passenger cars to different heights while rotating around in a tremendous circle. At its highest point, the Wonder Wheel offers views of the ocean to the south, the Manhattan skyline to the north, the Jersey Shore to the west, and Long Island to the east. The Wonder Wheel towers over even the Cyclone, and it's much wider than the Parachute Jump, so from most angles, it serves as the dominant sight of the amusement park area. And, when its colorful lights are lit up at night, out beyond the left-field fence at KeySpan, it's a beautiful sight. The Wonder Wheel was built in 1920 and was owned by Herman Garms Sr., whose son inherited the ride and ran it until 1983. At that point the Garms family put the Wonder Wheel up for sale and sold it to a guy who'd been working at Coney Island for years, Denos D. Vouderis. Vouderis is a Greek immigrant who came to the States as a teen in the 1940s.

In the '60s, Vouderis started working at a restaurant on the boardwalk and managing Coney Island's kiddie park, Ward's. When the Garms family offered Vouderis the Wonder Wheel, he jumped at it, and since that time he has been as big a force as any behind Coney Island's survival. Vouderis did well with the Wonder Wheel, keeping it in top shape and getting landmark status for it in 1989. He eventually was able to expand his operation and opened Deno's Wonder Wheel Amusement Park, which is right on the boardwalk at Denos Vouderis Place (Giuliani and the city having renamed West 12th Street one week before the Cyclones began playing). The park bumps up against Astroland, and they work well together, but Wonder Wheel Park is its own operation, with twenty-five rides, two arcades, live entertainment, and a Sweet Shoppe. There are no crazy gates or other wondrous entry points to the two parks, but it's neat to see that Coney Island is once again home to two amusement parks, plus an amusing *Park* (as in KeySpan).

The Brooklyn Cyclones' presence may or may not lead to further wholesale changes. To Giuliani, the Cyclones represent Coney Island's start on the path to an economic revival. As Mrs. Otero says, "I've heard about them making more restaurants, more rides, a hotel, and I really hope it happens." On one hand, Janet Otero's enthusiasm is understandable— who wouldn't want her neighborhood to be livened up? But, as she and her husband would say later, there is a potential cost to any improvements.

This is the point that the columnist Robert Lederman, the community activist who marched against Giuliani on opening night, made in a column the day after the inaugural game. "Despite being in a crowd of thousands of Mets' fans I was surprised to find so many people in enthusiastic agreement with my sign. As I walked the length of Surf Avenue storeowners who glimpsed the Giuliani painting came out and yelled their encouragement," wrote Lederman, whose thought-provoking protests on behalf of street artists and free speech have been covered over the years by every relevant media outlet in the city. He continued:

> Many applauded. These are the businesses the stadium is supposedly going to bring so much "economic benefit" to. Those who were critical of my painting turned out without exception to be from other neighborhoods. The reality is that this corporate welfare will mean the destruction of most local businesses, including many of the current rides, attractions and restaurants. Numerous former street vendors along the avenue who had rented what were once abandoned storefronts have already been given

eviction notices by the City. When the local landlords start raising rents on apartments, thousands of low-income tenants, many of them elderly long-time Coney Island residents, will be forced to leave the area as well. Of course, this will make lots of room for Starbucks, a GAP, a few more McDonald's, Wendy's, Kentucky Fried Chicken and Burger Kings. Just what Coney Island needed to spruce up its image. As the Mayor said in his press conference, he wants to do for Coney Island what he did for Times Square. That's about as an accurate statement as you'll ever hear from Rudy Giuliani. He wants to take billions in tax dollars and use them as corporate welfare, giving this money not to minority, low-income or immigrant business people who need a boost but to billionaires and the city's wealthiest real estate developers. He wants to sterilize a world-famous part of New York, putting his uniquely bland trademark of decency and deceit on it. Say goodbye to what was left of the old Coney Island. It just went the way of Times Square, the Chinatown New Year's celebration and public access to City Hall. It's been Giulianied.

Lederman's column is perhaps overly dramatic in its extremity, but the fact is that some local businessmen, particularly in the flea market to the east of the subway stop on Surf Avenue, are already feeling railroaded out of town. And Lederman's general point—that Coney Island is ripe for gentrification and that lots of powerful, rich people are watching the area closely—is valid to many locals.

A twenty-something African American, lifelong resident of Coney Island, had gotten at this key concern while speaking to me about his neighborhood last week. "What if the Cyclones do really well?" he asked. "Then you know what's going to happen. They're going to make the stadium bigger, make the amusements bigger, and kick all those people out of the projects and make it expensive there again. Then, I'm telling you, the Mets will be in that stadium before long."

No one has put the possibility of the Mets in print anywhere, but the point is that there are worried Coney Island residents. And, Golden did say that he had had at least preliminary discussions about bringing the L.A. Dodgers back to Brooklyn, so there are clearly people in power who have at least *considered* the idea of putting a Major League team in Coney Island. There is a sad irony in these residents being forced to worry about their future. For the oldest residents, as well as for many second- or third-generation residents, Coney Island was not a neighborhood that they or their forefathers chose to move to. They were placed here, at the whim of a city—specifically, its didactic, Giuliani-esque city planner, Robert Moses—that wanted these poor, typically nonwhite folks tucked into the deepest corner of New York City. And now, after some residents tried to escape quickly and others tried to make a neighborhood out of an underserved wasteland, this generation of western Coney Island residents might end up getting *kicked out*?

The Oteros are not gravely concerned about this issue, but they are aware of it. My bringing it up to the two parents prompted the following exchange. "I guess it [serious gentrification] could happen here," Janet says. "I still remember hearing about it back when we first moved in here all those years ago. A lot of people told me, 'Watch out. They're going to get rid of all you people and build co-ops down here.' And since then, all through the years, I've been hearing stuff like that. But it hasn't happened yet. I think it would be hard to move all these people out."

Anthony Sr.: "Yeah, it would be hard, but it has been talked about more since the stadium came. The talk has been that someone like the Walt Disney company is going to come in and buy everything up. At least all the buildings on the water side of Surf—like the Coney Island Houses."

Janet: "And then they'd turn 'em all into co-ops. They'd want rich people in here, I guess, with the baseball stadium and all that."

Anthony Sr.: "What would happen is that they'd come in, make co-ops, and the current owners would have the first chance to buy them. I would like to do that if I got the opportunity, but it would be hard. So far, rent has always had a cap of about $500 a month, or a little less. If Disney or someone like that took over, costs would go high. Real high."

Janet: "And if you can't pay, they'd just move you, like to the Bronx or upstate, and put us in different projects. But I don't want to move—we live in Brooklyn."

Most Coney Island residents have responded to the haziness about their neighborhood's future with apathy, dulled as they are by their isolation from the city, their relatively low-class status and, according to one expert I spoke with, pure American inertia. Mike Fabricant is a policy and social research expert who heads the Ph.D. program in social welfare at New York's Hunter College School of Social Work. He's also a third-generation Coney Islander who lived on 29th Street, just blocks from where the Oteros live, between 1952 and 1957.

"Part of what's going on in Coney Island is that the city is investing a lot of money to make that a place for working- and middle-class people of color," says Fabricant.

What the city has been trying to do is create some individual housing, apart from the project-style housing that has been dominant. When my family left in 1957, it was because my father was chasing rainbows and wanted to relocate to Florida, but by the '60s there was a massive exodus from the neighborhood, spurred by racial and economic factors. The housing stock that was left behind—attached housing, in our case—was all eliminated. For a while, the area looked like Berlin after World War II.

Now that there is a team in there, the city has spent a lot of money and is trying to attract corporations. These things are magnets for new residents, and there is a good chance that they will want the surrounding area to fit more into their image—that may mean attracting even a different type of person to the neighborhood. It's likely that some of the people who live there do not fit that image.

Still, Fabricant is not certain that the Disney/co-op plan will come to fruition any time soon. "In places where there has been enormous gentrification, such as Harlem [in Upper Manhattan] and Park Slope [in Brooklyn], the housing stock is much different than what is available in Coney Island. Those [gentrified neighborhoods] have old brownstones that people with money want to live in. This doesn't mean that someday middle-class people who want to own a home but feel pushed out of other areas won't turn to Coney Island, but the situation is different."

Given what Fabricant says, Janet Otero's lack of fear regarding the future of her residence seems reasonable. Given the utter dearth of shops, green space, good schools, and, most important, desirable housing, wealthy white folks don't figure to be calling Surf Avenue home anytime soon.

Still, it's in the seemingly hopeless response of the Oteros that Fabricant sees the country's mindset as a whole. "The sense of paralysis that people feel is far larger than an issue amongst the poor," he says. "You can see it in the amount of people in this country who do not step forward to demand better health care or education, *even for their own children.* There's a sense people have of a looming city hall, of a state bureaucracy—in this case, one that feels like it has moneyed interests behind it—that seems impossible to stop."

While rumors swirl about what is or is not coming to the neighborhood around KeySpan Park, the self-contained neighborhood that is KeySpan Park is off to a slow start. The stadium itself has five storefronts carved into it. The one closest to the ticketholder's entrance is occupied by Cyclone City, the souvenir shop. The carpeted, bilevel store (remember, there is an entrance from the street and one upstairs off the concourse) does a brisk business even on nongame days, and it's packed in the hours leading up to a home game.

To the east of the Cyclone City team store is the ticket office, and then the four vacant storefronts. One has a sign touting a restaurant called Oriental Palace that is "coming soon," but that's it. [*By 2003, two of the four vacant storefronts had been rented out, neither to anything called Oriental Palace. While the two spots closest to the ticket office remain vacant, the third one to the east now houses Slices N Ices, a pizza/Italian ice joint that does a decent game-day business—even if the Oteros still go to their old favorite on Stillwell Avenue. The biggest and most successful edition is the eastern-most storefront, which is where Peggy O'Neill's opened in 2002. A sports bar/restaurant with a successful location in Bay Ridge, Peggy O'Neill's uses its outdoor patio on Surf Ave, drink specials, karaoke contests, and a bunch of TVs to draw big crowds before games and even lures people there after games and on off nights. The area adjacent to Peggy O'Neill's has also become home to a Farmer's Market, held every Sunday throughout the summer].*

The fact remains, though, that viability is an issue, given that this is a stadium with only thirty-eight official days of business per year, give or take a boxing match, concert, or playoff game here and there. And, since, as the Oteros put it, this neighborhood is a "ghost town" in the fall and winter, the only independent businesses attached to the stadium that will survive are ones that can draw massive crowds when the stadium is open and then see whether they can draw anyone at all in the off-season.

To try to learn what type of employment opportunities these in-stadium businesses might offer for the likes of Anthony Otero in a year or two, I try to strike up some conversations with the young folks who work in the team store. I don't get very far, however, because when I try to ask the employees how they like working there, how old they are, or even just what part of the city they came from, I'm met with nervous stares. Shortly thereafter, a manager surfaces out of nowhere to tell me that no Aramark employees (Aramark is the concessions giant that the organization has hired to run the souvenir and food stands in KeySpan) may talk to the media, under any circumstances. Anthony himself still says he hasn't heard of anyone from his area getting a job at KeySpan.

And when these businesses do open up, they will be as good a study as any as to just how much the "economic development" that Giuliani promises is reality.

Whether he has his own sources of information, is blindly optimistic, or was flat-out lying to make this project seem like a better idea, Giuliani has promised that a "hotel and lots of new restaurants" are coming to the neighborhood. A New York City real estate expert I spoke to takes issue with Giuliani's claims, if not his vision. "Rudy's idea for Coney Island is well intended and visionary. Brooklyn is a huge borough with millions of people, and Coney Island is a place with land and water that you can develop. Wanting to use the team to lead that development is an idea with merit," the executive says.

But I think [the stadium] is going to be more of an accoutrement, if you will. As far as creating new development, it's a blip. I know that major developers have snooped around and talked about a lot of plans, but I'm not certain anything is going to come of it, because of the politics, the cost, the housing, I don't know what. If you brought the Dodgers back and put them in a stadium with 50,000 people every night, then you'd be talking. As it is, I think it's not much more than a very cool amenity for the neighborhood.

The one new chain that has opened in Coney Island is a Popeye's Chicken on Surf Avenue, while Nathan's, the national chain with the famous local roots, has made plans to expand its operation by adding a large picnic table area next to its famous stand/restaurant, which is across from the Stillwell Avenue subway and the old Shore Theater. Nathan's may be big and corporate now, but no observers of Coney Island's changing tides could begrudge its expansion or its desire to take advantage of the Cyclones' presence.

As legend has it, the hot dog was invented around 1870 by a man named Charles Feltman, who would eventually make the tasty treat almost synonymous with Coney Island. Feltman's Restaurant, on Surf Avenue, was a massive restaurant that became a first choice among Coney Island's hundreds of thousands of visitors, who craved Feltman's surf-and-turf grub, the hot dog most of all.

One employee of Feltman's, a European by the name of Nathan Handwerker, saw more potential for the hot dog than even Feltman. The story goes that Nathan saved enough money working for Feltman's that in 1916 he was able to rent his own space on the same plot of land that Nathan's rests on today. From there, Nathan Handwerker spiced his dogs in his own unique way and tried to steal Feltman's business by selling Nathan's dogs for only five cents each, half the price that Feltman charged. When the Stillwell Avenue subway station opened across from Nathan's, the restaurant was an obvious beneficiary, and while the Great Depression began pushing the more expensive Feltman's out of business, Nathan's cheap hot dogs continued to thrive. By the 1960s, Nathan's was a growing chain, but Nathan's never forgot its roots, adding a small board-walk location behind Astroland Park and holding its annual hot-dog-eating contest every year on the Fourth of July. To this day, the Nathan's by KeySpan Park is open twenty-four hours a day every day, selling under-rated seafood, delicious corn on the cob, and, of course, the most famous hot dogs in the world. No matter what was going on around Nathan's, the restaurant survived, but even if there were years when the future looked iffy for Nathan's, the Cyclones' presence has put an end to that concern.

One person watching this entire state of affairs closely is Dick Zigun, the head of the nonprofit group Coney Island USA, who has been taking a wait-and-see approach to the stadium from the beginning. Zigun, whose official title is artistic director, is one of the founders of Coney Island USA, a proud man who saw the beauty in Coney Island even when almost everyone else saw the area only as an ugly relic of the past. Zigun came to Coney Island in 1979 and started USA the following year. In the Coney Island USA newsletter, available at the headquarters Coney Island Museum a couple of blocks east of the stadium on Surf Avenue, Zigun frankly explains what the organization is. "Coney Island USA is an official, tax-deductible charity with I.R.S. 501 (C)(3) status," he writes.

With admission to the dingy but entertaining second-floor museum a mere ninety-nine cents, Zigun solicits money to support some of USA's many activities. Foremost among those activities is the Mermaid Parade, which began in 1983 and was meant to pay homage to the Mardi Gras parades that were held in the area in the first half of the century. Held every summer on the boardwalk, the parade most resembles Greenwich Village's famed Halloween party in that it attracts thousands of visitors, including many members of the city's arts community, who turn out in outrageous outfits. This year's parade took place on June 30, and, with the Cyclones out of town, the organization made a nice offer to Zigun and his cronies, allowing them to bring the parade into the stadium. It was a gesture that spoke to the ability of the neighborhood's freak-show history to blend in with its potentially antiseptic future.

In the mid-1980s, when Coney Island USA was run out of an office on the boardwalk, Zigun started Sideshows by the Seashore, a modern-day freak show that appealed to the area's freak-show-friendly past and prides itself on allowing performers to do wild things, such as swallow swords and walk on glass. To provide a fun experience for those with a curious mind, Zigun took care to show off interested, talented(?!) performers without exploiting genetic defects (no midget colonies or premature-baby incubators such as used to be shown off during Coney Island's early-twentieth-century freak-show heyday). Today, the sideshow is held just down 12th Street from the museum, and Zigun says it draws close to 70,000 visitors each year.

Zigun also works tirelessly to protect area landmarks, and, for those who want some more conventional learning for their donation buck, he and his organization offer an "Ask the Experts" series on Sunday nights in the summer. One panel scheduled for later this summer is titled "The Future of Coney Island," a subject that could not be more apropos given all that is going on in the famous area. In his midsummer 2001 newsletter, the goateed and top-hat-wearing Zigun—who was a 2000 inductee to citylore.org's "People's Hall of Fame"—offers his blanket assessment of what's going on while also repeating his pitch for money to help keep his organization alive.

> New York City's beach is the place where American popular culture invented itself. Coney Island in the 21st Century is a neighborhood with landmark rides and a new baseball stadium. . . . Gentrification has reached Coney Island with Keyspan Stadium [sic] completed and [construction on] the new Stillwell Avenue Subway Station underway [sic]. New businesses are opening up all over Surf Avenue and our lease is up in four years. We once had to move out of an earlier building on the boardwalk and we want to stay put for a long time in our new home. We are not afraid of growth and change in Coney Island as long as the progress does not pass us by.

Zigun's words are echoed by many local businessmen, though few have the influence or wherewithal to voice their position as loudly as Zigun can. Right across from KeySpan Park is Gargiulo's Restaurant, a massive Italian restaurant that's been around since 1907. Though people with the

team have told me that Gargiulo's will be one of the main local businesses to benefit from the Cyclones, if the people there are excited about the
team you wouldn't know it right now; the restaurant currently has a sign
up: "Closed for vacation, July 2–July 20."

A couple of blocks from the stadium and Gargiulo's, the manager at
the only sports store I've seen in the neighborhood, Sneakertown, has
said that the presence of the new team has been good for business. Very
good in one regard, in fact—the store has sold out all its Cyclone hats.

Following the boardwalk back from the Coney Island Houses as the July
15 sun drips slowly toward the ocean, I walk right past the stadium and
head for a pregame beer at Ruby's, which sits between Stillwell and 12th
on the boardwalk and is the closest boardwalk bar to KeySpan Park. The
beautiful day obviously has brought masses to Coney Island looking for
tickets to tonight's game, but many more people came for the beach and
its immediate surroundings, such as Ruby's Bar.

Boasting a sign adorned with the bar's name next to Budweiser's name
and a logo that announces that Ruby's is a "Proud Supporter of Cyclones
Baseball," and, judging from the "free soda" coupons the business handed out on opening day, this seems like a business that is pretty invested in
the team. Not necessarily so, says Sam Rodriguez, the seventy-ish bartender and manager of Ruby's who came to Coney Island from his native
Puerto Rico fifty years ago. "When the sun is out, people come to the bar.
When it's not, they don't," the leather-faced Rodriguez says simply about
the place that the Coney Island devotee Rubin Jacobs once proudly
owned. Jacobs died in the spring of 2000, but Rodriguez is trying to maintain the place's old-fashioned vibe, which includes old beer memorabilia
and photos of Coney Island that effectively tell much of the area's history tacked up all over the open-aired business's sea-and-smoke-stained
walls. The place's aura is enough to have earned it *New York Press*'s award
for "Best South Brooklyn Tavern," according to the plaque that hangs
among the memorabilia.

Joshua Gossman, a sixteen-year-old serving food from Ruby's snack
bar, tells me that "things have picked up" over the season's first couple of

weeks, but Rodriguez is hesitant to credit the Cyclones with any boost in business. "There might have been a few more people here than we normally have on the night of the first game, but not really since then," he says with a what-can-you-do chuckle. "The new generation of people coming to the area for the games seem to like just going into the stadium and drinking inside. I've seen more people walking by on the boardwalk after games, but they're not coming here. I say business was still better forty years ago."

Even on a tourist-, yuppie-, and baseball-friendly Sunday afternoon, there are some definite regulars at Ruby's, including some pretty "freaky" folks (who needs to pay for Dick Zigun's freak show when you can drink beers in the company of middle-aged guys with multiple body pierces and wearing nothing but tattoos and Speedos?). Most of Ruby's customers look like they'd be entirely out of place inside KeySpan—the whole freak-show-friendly attitude hasn't really permeated the wholesome ballpark, notwithstanding its support of the Mermaid Parade—but some of this evening's patrons are indeed talking about the nearby stadium. Most of the commentary centers around the costs of the stadium's food and drink and how they're not only higher than on-the-street prices (what stadium doesn't gouge like that?) but are higher than those at the Staten Island stadium. Two casually dressed men sitting in Ruby's outdoor area on the boardwalk, a good seven or eight beers into their day, to judge from the word slurring, show me their tickets to prove that they'll be at this evening's games. "But we'rre doing our, um, drinking, and, uhhhh, eating out here," says one, stumbling over his words as if they were a raised plank in the way of his aural stroll. "It's waaaaay too, uhhh, expensive, in there."

As New Jersey residents in the midst of their second Cyclone-centered trip to Coney Island, they are an example of the potential new visitors to the area—baseball fans from northern Brooklyn or Manhattan, or even the suburbs, who are curious enough to come to the neighborhood well before gametime and check things out a little. And, while "checking things out," to spend some money.

The well-known stadium economist Andrew Zimbalist has said that one of the problems with publicly subsidized stadiums is that in *most* cases they just recycle entertainment money within one community. For example, Zimbalist has said, people would spend just as much if you built a multiplex, which wouldn't cost the municipality nearly as much as a stadium (and, because multiplexes lack the political power of baseball stadiums, a municipality wouldn't even do that). Speaking before Congress on stadium financing in July 1999, Zimbalist stated:

> Although teams and leagues often hire consulting firms to publicize purported positive economic impact from sports stadiums, all independent academic studies have found that there is no statistically significant positive effect from having a new team or stadium on an area's economy. This fact alone does not mean that there should be no public subsidization of new stadium construction. If the voting public in an area believes that having a new facility or team would enhance the local culture and create a positive consumption value for its citizens, then the public may very well decide to expend tax dollars in support of sports teams—much the same way they may decide to use public funds for park construction (albeit in the case of sports teams the subsidies are eventually appropriated by the private owners of the franchises). The voters, however, need to understand that they are voting for cultural, not economic, value. The voters are also entitled to make this election without the threat of extortion by the monopoly sports leagues.

Obviously, the people of Brooklyn did not get to vote on whether or not they wanted KeySpan Park. This was a Rudy Giuliani project all the way, and Rudy has said on several occasions that he doesn't think Zimbalist has a clue. What stadium defenders point out is that money is actually coming into Coney Island from all over that wouldn't normally be spent here. And, even with all the wild amusement park rides, when it comes to standard family entertainment this neighborhood is in many ways lacking. As the Oteros said, even with the stadium, the SportsPlex would be a good idea. And the privately funded multiplex that has been proposed might not be awful, either, given that there's no movie theater in Coney Island or in adjacent Brighton Beach.

Still, as the bartender at Ruby's lamented, it takes a curious fan to come to Coney Island and put his money anywhere but into the Cyclone organization's pockets. Given its all-in-one appeal, with concession stands and ample sources of amusements, KeySpan Park—home to the Brooklyn beers, the Nathan's dogs, the Dippin' Dots ice cream, not to mention mascots, music, and games—will not necessarily be a massive impetus for people to spend money with local vendors. And what happens if and when the stadium-based storefronts get finished and a few more restaurants or bars come in? Those will be independently run, but they will not be "Coney Island businesses" in the true sense. In other words, thirty-eight nights a summer, 7,000 people, many of whom can get what they need inside the stadium, are not necessarily going to change the course of the future for Coney Island businesses.

If you walk from Ruby's back to the Surf Avenue entrance to KeySpan via Stillwell Avenue, you pass the only baseball-themed amusement in the area. Sporting its own "Welcome the Cyclones to Brooklyn" banner, this outdoor batting cage offers everything from slow softball (like slow toss) to medium baseball/softball (70–75 mph) to "super-fast" (supposedly 95+ mph). When you stand in one of the batting boxes—helmet on, beat-up bat in your hands—the ocean is one block south, and KeySpan's center-field fence is just a vacant lot away behind you. It's got to be the world's best setting for a batting cage. There's a healthy crowd today, and while the cashier says she hasn't noticed a whole lot more customers in the wake of the Cyclones' arrival, the cage always seems to be doing fine. As Anthony would tell me later, "It's always crowded when I've been there. I've been there probably three times in my life, and there's always a long line for the slow or medium cages. So I would always go in the fastball cage, and it's coming like 100 miles an hour. You can't hit that!" From the batting cage, it is just a two-minute walk to the stadium.

Not too many of the Cyclone players have an opinion on the matter of the neighborhood. Given their age, where they're from, and the fact that

With the famous Coney Island amusement park rides looming in the background, final preparations are made for opening day. Held on June 25, 2001, this Cyclones game against the Mahoning Valley Scrappers represents Brooklyn's first professional baseball game since 1957. *(Photo by George Napolitano. Courtesy of the Brooklyn Cyclones)*

Cyclone players line the first-base line before opening day. Beyond the right-field fence is the spectacular Parachute Jump, a once-active ride that has been standing in Coney Island since 1941 and is now a National Landmark. *(Photo by George Napolitano. Courtesy of the Brooklyn Cyclones)*

With arms and legs aggressively poised, Brett Kay prepares to make solid contact with the pitch. For the season, Brett hit .311 with five home runs and eighteen RBIs in 180 at-bats, striking out just twenty-eight times. *(Photo by George Napolitano. Courtesy of the Brooklyn Cyclones)*

Anthony Otero practices his batting stance in the confines of his parents' modest apartment in the Coney Island Houses complex. (*Courtesy of the Otero family*)

The entrance to the far end of the Coney Island Houses, located just off of West 32nd Street. The complex includes five fourteen-story buildings, all an identical reddish brick. (*Photo by Justin Borucki*)

This nondescript playground is where Anthony spends nearly all his free time. The classic New York City Parks Department sign "greets" visitors, while the sprawling pavement doubles as a baseball diamond, at least when Anthony is around to organize the transformation. The Oteros' Building 2 stands in the center of the image. *(Photos by Justin Borucki)*

At the opposite end of Nautilus Playground from the baseball area is the basketball court used in Spike Lee's 1998 movie *He Got Game.* Here, Anthony's younger brother, James, shoots around. *(Photo by Justin Borucki)*

Despite his good-natured charm away from the field, Brett remains a fierce competitor with a serious game face when it comes time to play. *(Photo by George Napolitano. Courtesy of the Brooklyn Cyclones)*

Few Cyclone players are as good with the press as Brett. Not only does he answer all questions, but he does so thoughtfully, often without the clichéd jock-speak most sports reporters are used to hearing. (*Photo by George Napolitano. Courtesy of the Brooklyn Cyclones*)

Brett Kay and Ross Peeples share a smile while the KeySpan Park scoreboard shines behind them. Despite never having been to New York before their season with the Cyclones, Brett (from Villa Park, California) and Ross (from Cordele, Georgia) both fall in love with their new city. (*Photo by George Napolitano. Courtesy of the Brooklyn Cyclones*)

Fans walking into the Cyclones' sparkling stadium. For the 2001 season, the team averaged more than 7,800 fans per game, by far the best in the New York–Penn League. (*Photo by George Napolitano. Courtesy of the Brooklyn Cyclones*)

most are scared to focus on much more than advancing up the baseball ladder, expecting them to be sociologists would probably be unreasonable. The most thoughtful Cyclone on the subject of Coney Island is the pitcher Harold Eckert, the player who hails from just forty-five minutes away in Edison, New Jersey, and who is living with his parents during the season. "It's a little weird that they haven't had a team here before," says Eckert. "Maybe people were scared because they heard Brooklyn was a bad area. I remember hearing that when I was growing up and people spoke about old Coney Island. But it's actually a great area. There's people walking around, everything's cool, you can say hi to everybody."

Eckert also feels that Brooklyn's baseball history trumps any neighborhood concerns. "I think they needed to just take advantage of the fact that this is a baseball town—they used to have the Dodgers here! That's what makes it the best thing," he continues. "You've got these little kids, ten-, eleven-, and twelve-year-olds coming out to see the game and cheer, and they're loving it, and at the same time you've got these fifty-year-olds and we're bringing back memories from when they were young and everything was good. It's awesome!"

Brett Kay has still barely adjusted to being on this team and working his way into the lineup, let alone taking in the surroundings. He does say, however, that he's trying to explore a bit. "I've been walking around a little bit. Haven't been to Nathan's, but I've gotten food at a couple places. I love it. The boardwalk and all that? How could you not think it's a cool neighborhood?

"And with baseball, it sounds like people felt maybe they should leave Brooklyn for the Dodgers," Kay continues thoughtfully. "But I think we're proving that it was a good idea to put a new team here."

The players have no problem talking about this Yankee series, however. As tonight's starting pitcher Portobanco said the other day, "We want to whip their ass."

The Staten Island Yankees' first visit to KeySpan comes after the Cyclones have made their own first visit to the Yankees' gleaming ballpark in St. George (no, not Steinbrenner), Staten Island, last night, July 14.

The game in Staten Island was played before a sellout crowd of 6,809 (with an average attendance in 2001 of about 5,000, sellouts are not nearly as common on Staten Island as they are for Cyclone games) that included a Yankee-hat-wearing Giuliani ("You know I'm a Yankee fan," Rudy told reporters at the game. "Don't give me a hard time.").

Rudy went home unhappy because his old pet team, the Cyclones, won the game by the score of 3–1. The win pushed the Cyclones ahead of the Yankees and into sole possession of first place in the New York–Penn League. They were already in first place in the city's heart, however. Not one month into the Cyclones' first season, their classy caps with the old Brooklyn "B" of Dodgers fame interlocking with a new-age "C" are ubiquitous on people around the five boroughs (with reports trickling in of "BC" sightings around the country). Even with the fact that they're the defending champs and are a Class-A affiliate of the *real* defending champs, the Staten Island Yankees, in contrast, have not captured the imagination of people outside Staten Island.

The "Ferry Series" provided the perfect opportunity to check out Richmond County Ballpark (the Yankees' field in Staten Island). It doesn't have the variety in colors that KeySpan has, but Richmond County (another sellout name, this one is for a local bank that's sponsoring the team) has some nice features just the same. Foremost are its own stunning vistas. With home plate backing into the island, almost all vantage points look out toward New York Harbor, affording views of the Statue of Liberty and the Manhattan skyline. Most spectacular is the view of the Manhattan skyline that one can see clearly over right field. That's where the massive Twin Towers loom, looking so big that famed lefty home-run hitter Barry Bonds would probably try to reach them with one of his monster homers. With the water almost directly behind the outfield fence, there is no logical place to put bleacher seats, and, anyway, demand for tickets is not quite as high as it is at KeySpan. The Yankees' stadium is incredibly convenient; it has its own stop on the Staten Island commuter rail line and sits just to the west of the Staten Island Ferry terminal. Given this ferry's pre-eminence as the way to get from the island to Manhattan, the ballpark is easier to reach from lower Manhattan than

KeySpan is. Ask Brett about the Yankees' home and he says, "It's a nice park and all, but we have everything in Brooklyn. We walk around the neighborhood and people know who we are."

Richmond County Ballpark opened one day before KeySpan did, and Giuliani took a similarly huge role in those proceedings, saying proudly, "This has to be one of the most beautiful ballparks in America . . . Major League or Minor League. This is ten times more beautiful than Guy [Staten Island borough president Guy Molinari] and I ever dreamed it would be."

After taking a short break from Minor League baseball to get back to actually running the city, Hizzoner is once again focusing on baseball, thanks to the inaugural "Ferry Series" (through which he reaps the benefits of being associated with America's pastime). Days before the series began, Giuliani took great pride in announcing special ferry service to shuttle people to and from the Ferry Series while seeming to take credit for its existence. "You've heard of the Subway Series between the Yankees and the Mets. Today I'm pleased to announce the *Ferry Series* between the City's newest baseball teams—the Staten Island Yankees and the Brooklyn Cyclones," the mayor said in a press release. "This unique, round-trip ferry service will go between St. George and Coney Island on the eight different dates when these two teams play each other. It will give fans an easy way to catch their teams playing at rival venues—not to mention a beautiful way to see our City, which, after all, comprises three islands and a peninsula."

Iris Weinshall, commissioner of the city's Department of Transportation, added, "DOT is delighted to offer this ferry service. It will give fans of both teams the easiest way to get to games—avoiding the roadways and instead sailing the City's beautiful waterways and harbors. We hope taking this ferry will become a City tradition—along with taking in baseball games at these beautiful new ballparks."

On one hand, all the hype sounds like so much government propaganda, but it's legitimate in that the baseball fans of New York *are* excited about this rivalry. New York's media, particularly its tabloid newspapers, like nothing more than a rivalry to spice up the sports pages. Large numbers of writers are covering the Cyclones and the Staten Island Yankees for the first time since their opening games. Plus, as if this were a fictional season that Giuliani himself had drawn up, the teams come into their first meeting tied for first in the New York–Penn League's seven-team McNamara Division. And, even though most people have never heard of the players on the teams and "Coney Island versus Staten Island" doesn't have quite the ring to it that "Flatbush versus the Bronx" once did, you can't get much more intense than a game pitting a National League club from Brooklyn against an American League club that's linked to the Yankees.

The World Series—matching teams from baseball's American and National Leagues and representing the only time teams from the rival leagues could play—was begun in 1903. The first New York team to make a dent in the Series was actually the National League Giants, who played at the Polo Grounds. The Giants got to the Series four times (winning in 1905 and losing three straight from 1911 to 1913) before either the National League Brooklyn squad (alternately known as the Superbas, Dodgers, Robins, and finally Dodgers again) or American League Yankees (originally Highlanders) could make one. Brooklyn made the Series in 1916 and 1920, losing both times, while the Yankees made their Series debut in 1921, when they lost to the Giants. That outcome was repeated in 1922 before the Yanks won their first title in 1923. The Yankees won the Series again in 1927 (with the famed Murderer's Row batting lineup that featured Babe Ruth and Lou Gehrig), '28, and '32. After the Giants won one in 1933, the Yankees won four straight between 1936 and 1939, the first two by beating the Giants. While the Giants were a good team in the '30s, they always seemed to play second fiddle to the Yankees. The Dodgers, meanwhile, had a pretty miserable decade, six times finishing below .500 and never even reaching second place in the National League. Either way, a trend was established that would last well beyond the 1930s: the Yankees were the baseball kings of New York.

In the 1940s, the Brooklyn Dodgers became arguably the premiere franchise in the National League, suffering only one losing season and reaching the World Series in 1941, '47, and '49. The problem, all three seasons, was that the team they played for the World Championship each time was the Yankees. And, each time, the Yankees won. Whereas the old fans of the Dodgers had to cope with the fact that their team stank in general, the new problem for Dodger fans was that they were good, but they couldn't quite get past those damn Yankees. If anything, this sense of frustration increased fans' devotion, in much the same way Chicago Cub fans stay devoted to a team that hasn't won a title since 1908. "Nineteen forty-nine was when I really got hooked in," says the Brooklynite Asch, who was nine years old at the time. "That team won the pennant, and I was hooked, as were lots of other people in Brooklyn. We went into every year thinking they could beat the Yankees."

Indeed, with the help of a *Brooklyn Eagle* headline, the unofficial slogan of Brooklyn fans had become "Wait 'til next year."

The Yankees defeated Philadelphia to win the 1950 Series, and then, in '51, the Dodgers battled their other archrival, the Giants, for the National League pennant. The playoff series came down to one game at the Polo Grounds, a game that has been immortalized in places as diverse as the *Wall Street Journal* and Don DeLillo's novel *Underworld.* That game, like so many crucial Yankee games, ended in crushing fashion for the Dodgers, as the Cyclones' opening-night guest Ralph Branca surrendered a series-ending home run to Bobby Thomson, the so-called shot heard 'round the world. "That's a game that got my ass kicked," remembers Asch. "I stayed home from school that day so I could watch the game on TV, and when the home run was hit, I threw my shoe into the TV. My old man, who actually didn't have the fervor for the Dodgers that a lot of my friends' parents did, was not at all happy when I did that."

Still, like their fans, the Dodger teams of that era were nothing if not resilient—which they needed to be. After the hated Yankees beat the hated Giants in the '51 World Series, the Dodgers got back there in '52 and '53, only to lose to the Yankees twice more. By now things were getting desperate. "The frustration was overwhelming," Bill Reddy said in Golenbock's *Bums.* "[The Series losses] gave you a feeling that God and everybody was against you. What the hell. What could you do? Wait for the next year? But next year never seemed to come."

Finally, after neither the Dodgers nor the Yankees made the Series in 1954, the Dodgers beat the Yankees in 1955. The borough of Brooklyn rejoiced. What's relevant to this season of Minor League baseball, however, is that the years of frustration and disappointment had imbedded anti-Yankee sentiment in many Brooklyn residents. And if most of the original Yankee haters themselves are no longer around, the hatred has certainly been passed down to younger generations.

A few years after the Dodgers left New York (for good measure, the Yanks beat the Dodgers again in the penultimate Brooklyn season, 1956), the New York Mets, a Queens-based National League team that would play the Yankees only if they somehow made the World Series, were founded. Despite being an expansion team, the Mets were a respectable outfit before long, winning titles in 1969, 1973, and 1986 and earning respect for their never-say-die attitude. Many Mets' fans were people who had been Dodger fans, and before long they too were hating the more famous and more successful Yankees. As the current Cyclone pitching coach and former Mets' pitcher Bobby Ojeda told the *Times,* "[Mets' fans] would tell me about how much the Dodgers meant to them." The converse of that was how much they hated the Yankees, even if the teams didn't play each other for the first thirty-five years of Mets' history.

The year 1997 brought the fan-friendly baseball traditionalist hell of interleague play. This invention, courtesy of baseball commissioner Bud Selig, provided a forum for Major League teams to play between fifteen and eighteen games a year against teams outside their league. While this has led to some ugly match-ups—Royals–Pirates, Marlins–Blue Jays— baseball fans have tended to embrace the "natural" rivalries that interleague play has brought from the barroom to the field, such as between the Cubs and the White Sox (Chicago), the Dodgers and the Angels (the "freeway series"), the Giants and the Athletics (the "Battle of the Bay"), the Indians and the Reds (Ohio), the Cardinals and the Royals (the "I-70 series"), the Marlins and the Devil Rays (Florida), and the Expos and the Blue Jays (Canada). Of course, none of the interleague series garner as much attention as the Yankees–Mets "Subway Series." Six times every summer, the teams play, three times in each park, and every game of the rivalry has been a sellout. Before each three-game series between New York's teams, the city's tabloids devote special sections to the match-ups, and you'd be hard pressed to find a more topical water cooler topic in city offices while the series is going on. The Met–Yankee rivalry reached its apex in the fall of 2000, when the teams met in the World Series—a legitimate, old-fashioned Subway Series, like the old Dodgers-Yankees battles. Appropriately, given their historical role as the city's baseball bully, the Yankees won the series. And, in case anyone had been living under a rock and forgotten the Yankees' all-time organizational dominance, that Series victory was their third straight and their twenty-sixth overall.

To capitalize on people's interest in Brooklyn Dodger history—including the team's rivalry with the Yankees—there are concrete plans in place to build a Brooklyn Baseball Museum into the KeySpan Park structure. Like the storefronts, the museum opening fell victim to the rushed nature of KeySpan's opening, but it is a good idea [*one that was realized by the 2002 season*].

In any event, it's not at all surprising that this new Cyclone-Yankee rivalry has people fired up. The *Daily News* even lent the series its own level of importance to the weekend by inserting a Subway Series–style supplement on the Ferry Series.

Brett did not have any big hits in last night's game on Staten Island, but that's okay with him because he was due to have a quiet game. In the last week, the affable catcher has been red-hot at the plate. On Friday, July 13, in the last pre-Yankee game, Kay hit two two-run home runs in a 7–4 win over Jamestown. The second broke a tie and led to the victory, which was played before a season-high 7,925 people. After the game, Brett, whose batting average stood at a team-high .415, said humbly, "Things are going pretty well right now." Not coincidentally, the game on the thirteenth represented Brett's first game as the Cyclones' exclusive top catcher, since Mike Jacobs finally got promoted on the twelfth. Clearly, Brett is up to the challenge.

As Brett adjusts to the New York–Penn League, some of his former college teammates are doing the same, including one he'll be seeing in the Ferry Series. Not only did Staten Island's third baseman, Aaron

Rifkin, play at Fullerton, but his career has been very similar to Brett's. Both Brett and Aaron grew up close to the Fullerton campus, and both had sports ingrained in them when they were young. While Brett's love of sports came from his football-playing father, Aaron's came from his baseball-loving father—Yankee-loving, to be exact. They each developed in high school to the point that they thought they'd be high picks without needing to go to college, but, while Kay went in the thirty-fifth round out of Mater Dei, Rifkin was a fifty-fourth-round choice from Etiwanda High School; being chosen so low was not nearly good enough for them to turn pro. While Kay went right to Fullerton, Rifkin put in a year at Division III Chapman University before transferring to Fullerton. While playing for the Titans, Rifkin, who usually batted directly in front of or behind Kay in the batting order, bloomed even more than his buddy, at least in the eyes of scouts, as he was a fourth-round pick of the Yankees, four rounds sooner than Brett got taken by the Mets. "It'll be great to play against Aaron, because we really became friends on and off the field. Then, all of a sudden the college season ends and you don't see these guys anymore," says Brett. "I can't wait for him to see what it's like here."

Brett won't mind beating him, either. As he says, "We already know we want to beat the Yankees more than any other team."

The Cyclone-Yankee crowd at KeySpan is huge (7,935); the fans are much more enthusiastic than their Staten Island counterparts (many of whom were not born and bred on the Island and lack the intense borough pride that so many Brooklyn residents possess), and louder than they've been all season. While the opening-night crowd was politely excited, watching history being made in an evening that brought them back to their childhoods, tonight's is actually rowdy, proof that the ghosts of Yankee-Brooklyn pasts have somehow lived on in some of today's fans. The fan taunting is increased because of the tendency many Brooklynites have traditionally shown for making fun of their southwestern neighbor, yelling the old "you live on a dump" jokes (in reference to the presence of the massive Fresh Kills landfill that sits in the heart of Staten Island). The Brooklyn fans also feel confident mocking Staten Island's baseball heritage, which, except for an American Association team in 1886 and

1887, is basically nonexistent. "Our fans are incredible," Brett would say a couple days later. "I mean, the stadium where they play the College World Series doesn't compare. And Staten Island? Ha! That place is nothing compared to here. These are loud, amazing fans."

The game is as tensely played as any since opening night. The biggest key for the Cyclones is the pitching of Portobanco, who throws seven innings of two-hit, two-walk ball while striking out five. Clearly, Porto's admitted enthusiasm about facing the Yanks is manifesting itself in a stellar performance.

Offensively, the only real attack comes in the sixth inning. Highly touted Danny Garcia beats out an infield single. Then the rehabbing Mets' outfielder Tsuyoshi Shinjo (more on him in a moment) walks, putting Cyclones at first and second. Jay Caliguiri follows with a bloop single, and the Cyclones have a 1–0 lead, which is all they need, thanks to Portobanco's strong starting pitching and Blake McGinley's two perfect innings of relief. The win is the first-place Cyclones' tenth in a row.

As if the game needs any more excitement, Shinjo's presence in KeySpan Park adds just that. It is common practice for Major League players who have been injured to do rehab stints in the minors. What level the players go to is usually a matter of convenience, and with that being the case, the Cyclones are obviously a convenient location for any injured Mets who need to get back in playing shape. This is a fact that has been touted about the Cyclones since they were born—not only do you get to see Mets of the future, the logic went, but you'll get to see currently injured Mets, as well. Shinjo, a Japanese import, is starting as a Cyclone for the second straight game while he rehabs a strained left quad. Last night in Staten Island, Shinjo had one hit and one RBI, and fans in KeySpan tonight are excited to see the big leaguer in action. Even the players are happy about their temporary teammate, who will probably rejoin the Mets after this game. "This is just another highlight, getting to play with a guy who's at the level that we want to make it to," says Brett.

Tonight's game has been televised on local cable—quite a feat for Single-A baseball, and a nice treat for home-bound Cyclone fans, since non-TV games can be followed only via radio on the Internet or at 90.9

FM, the frequency for the Kingsborough Community College radio station, with reception that's good for about six blocks. Afterward, the Cyclone players watch the postgame coverage from the locker room, which includes an interview with the pitching coach, Ojeda, who's asked about Portobanco's seven shutout innings. "If Porto's mind and arm are attached to his body at the same time," says the New York–Penn League's most famous pitching coach, "he's gonna be tough to beat. He certainly was today."

While Anthony Otero and his friends have a good time at the Yankee game, taking an inning or two to watch closely then an inning or two to wander the concourse and enjoy the scenery they never thought they'd be a part of, Anthony isn't changing his opinion on what the game meant. "They nothing compared to the Mets and Yankees," Anthony says later. "But I do like to watch [these teams]. I still root for Staten Island Yankees to win. They're my favorite team in the Minor Leagues because they part of the Yankee organization. Every game Staten Island plays here, I'll be here."

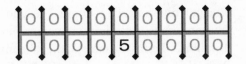

Kay and the Cyclones Take the New York–Penn League by Storm

With the two Yankee wins that kick off the Ferry Series, and with seven more victories in the next eleven games, the Cyclones have established themselves as the team to beat in the McNamara Division of the New York–Penn League. Sitting in second place, of course, are the Yankees, who recently got their first win in four meetings with the 'Clones in a game in which the Yankee Shelly Duncan ran over Brett, who was not pleased.

This league, which was formed in 1939 and is one of Minor League baseball's best known, is made up of fourteen teams in two divisions, the McNamara and the Pinckney-Stedler. The Cyclones' McNamara Division includes not only them and the Yankees, but the New Jersey Cardinals (from Augusta, New Jersey), the Hudson Valley Renegades (Fishkill, New York), the Pittsfield Astros (Pittsfield, Massachusetts), the Lowell Spinners (Massachusetts), and the Vermont Expos (Burlington, Vermont). The Pinckney-Stedler Division is made up of the Auburn Doubledays (New York), the Mahoning Valley Scrappers (Niles, Ohio), the Batavia Muckdogs (New York), the Oneonta Tigers (New York), the Jamestown Jammers (New York), the Utica Blue Sox (New York), and the Williamsport Crosscutters (Pennsylvania).

The New York–Penn League's streak of sixty-two straight years in operation (with no end in sight) is the longest of any Class-A Minor

League division. The original league had six teams—Olean, Batavia, Niagara Falls, and Jamestown in New York; Hamilton, Ontario; and Bradford, Pennsylvania. With ballclubs in Pennsylvania, Ontario, and New York, it was named the PONY League. The combined attendance for the first season in '39 was 267,212, with each team playing a full schedule (as opposed to the short season that is played now). The PONY League set an attendance record in 1946, with 500,599 for eight teams, and in '56 the league changed its name to the New York–Penn League. Television and shifting populations brought a slump for Minor League baseball throughout the '60s, and the New York–Penn League was not immune to these problems. By 1965, the league was down to six teams, all in New York. The worst attendance was in April and May (not surprising since these teams were playing in northern and western New York cities, which are also known as "really cold!"), so commissioner Vincent McNamara suggested a "short-season" league. The eighty-game season McNamara devised was a hit not only with fans but also with the Major League teams, which liked the idea of having a place to send their June draft picks for a fresh introduction to professional baseball alongside fellow greenhorns.

Since 1968, the New York–Penn League has been healthy, and the short-season format it uses became a model for other leagues around the country. In the 1990s, with costs rising, the New York–Penn League followed the nationwide trend of moving to bigger, more affluent markets. In place of little towns like Elmira, New York, came bigger markets like Lowell, Massachusetts; Staten Island; and, of course, Brooklyn, which is taking the New York–Penn League to heights, in terms of attendance, media coverage, and brand recognition, that it has never reached before.

With Ruby's Bar shut down on this Friday evening because of a problem with its water supply, I decide to head into the stadium early to check in with the red-hot Cyclones. So far in this 2001 season, the Cyclones have been the cream of the New York–Penn League crop, leading the league offensively (team batting average), in pitching (team ERA), and, most important, in wins. The team's success is a result in large part of its absurdly good home record. Going into the July 27 home game against

Hudson Valley, the Cyclones sport a 25–12 record overall, with eighteen of those wins and just two of the losses coming here at KeySpan Park.

The Cyclones have not lost a home game since the last two games of their season-opening series with the Scrappers, and as they prepare to entertain the Renegades of Hudson Valley (affiliated with the Tampa Bay Devil Rays), it's fair to say that the Cyclones' players have a healthy swagger about them. The success the team has had and the confidence you can see in the players' eyes raises an obvious question: Does all the hoopla surrounding the team and all the history being represented make you guys perform better? Seasoned professional athletes would, in all likelihood, shrug off such a question and mutter something about being able to perform in any setting. But this group is refreshingly willing to consider the hypothesis with the utmost seriousness. "I've always been the type of guy that likes, and even kind of needs, there to be big-time situations. Having all these fans creates that and makes everybody want to work even harder and play even better," says Blake McGinley definitively. "If you only have a few fans here, you're probably not going to care as much. 'Why am I here?' It's just not going to be as fun or as easy to win."

Adds the pitcher Eckert, "When I'm out there pitching, I have to say it doesn't really make a difference, 'cause you have to shut all that out. But I'd be lying—and any of these guys on the team would be lying—if I didn't say that in the back of my head, I have an unconscious feeling that there's so many people here, behind us. Our home record is great. We know the fans are behind us, and I have that feeling when I'm pitching. It does make it a whole lot better."

Portobanco is too serious or too proud to give the crowd credit for his performance, but at the same time he acknowledges that the KeySpan Park scene may hurt opponents. "I think that if you're a pitcher, you have to able to pitch whether there's a crowd or not. It's cool and it's fun, but these fans are not what can take you to the Major Leagues. Only your arm can do that," Portobanco says. Still, the twenty-one-year-old fireballer admits that "all the other teams, even the Yankees, are probably jealous of what we have here."

Anthony, who has no problem imagining himself on the field at KeySpan, is not at all surprised when I tell him the guys on the team really enjoy the yelling that kids such as he and his friends help provide when they come to games. "I'd think they like it," he says firmly. "I know I'll want people to cheer for me."

One player who Anthony is sure enjoys his presence is Vladimir Hernandez, a slick-fielding second baseman from Cuba who just recently joined the team by way of Mexico. "He's given me [sunflower] seeds and baseballs," Anthony says. "The second time I saw him and said 'what's up' he told me he remembered me."

The atmosphere inside KeySpan Park moves even the Cyclones' often stoic manager, Alfonzo. "The excitement here is amazing. From the first inning to the last, the fans are cheering," says the thirty-three-year-old Alfonzo, whose twelve-year Minor League playing career and three-year coaching career, including managing in Kingsport last year, has made him somewhat of an expert on the Minor League baseball experience. "I could tell it was going to be a special experience from the moment I got the job last December. The team scheduled a conference call with the press, and *twenty* reporters called in. Then when I arrived in Brooklyn before the season there were always people coming to talk to me. It's like being the manager of a big league team, and definitely different than any other Minor League team."

But it's not just that the ambiance is fun; Alfonzo believes it has a tangible effect on his team's performance. "I notice the biggest difference in pregame, because their concentration level—and mine—is so high," he says with a proud smile. "Usually guys at this level can't concentrate on the pregame drills, like when we work on bunting, bunt defense, and hitting the cutoff man. It's boring. But here in Brooklyn the guys are focused all the time. It's because of the fans. It affects me as well, helps me concentrate from beginning to end. When you play in front of fans like we have, you want to do well. These fans deserve it."

Leave it to Brett, who's simultaneously signing autographs and preparing for the game, to offer the most passionate response. "I'm dragging a little bit, and I've been losing a little weight since I've basically played baseball every day since the beginning of January [when the Cal State–Fullerton team began practicing], but every day I go out and play as hard as I can," he says. "I get the adrenaline to do that from our fans. If I was playing in front of ten fans, I'd be more lackluster. As a team, I think that we go out here and expect to win every home game, and at the same time we don't want to show anyone, like, a bad day. We could be horrible the day before, but if we're at home we got to play our best no matter what. It's like, the travel can be a real pain in the ass, but you get into this stadium, and there's 8,000 fans screaming. It's like playing in the big leagues whenever we're at home. I'm sure everyone loves playing in front of fans, but I *really* love it."

Campanaro, the media relations manager, who has had ample time to talk about the effects of KeySpan with the players, says, "I think most of the guys feed off the crowd."

Beyond the lift the KeySpan atmosphere gives the Cyclones is the deflation it must cause in other teams, unheralded outfits like the Spinners and Jammers (of Jamestown, New York), that are much more accustomed to crowds of 2,000 or 3,000 than 7,000 or 8,000. As Kay puts it, "My friend Aaron plays for the Staten Island Yankees, and another guy I played with is the third baseman from the Vermont Expos. This place isn't as big a deal to the guy from Staten Island because he's right over there and he's got a nice field, too. But he still says he likes it over here more," Kay says with a chuckle.

"And Murph [a.k.a. Shawn Norris, who got the nickname because his favorite player used to be Dale Murphy], the guy who plays for Vermont, he loves playing out here, and he hates playing in Vermont. It's exciting for all the guys on his team, and they'll ask us, 'Do you guys really get 8,000 every night?' and 'How is it to play in front of those type of crowds?' Some guys will just flat out tell me that they wish they could play here. In general, I think a lot of guys envy us and how lucky we are. And, well, the guys are also kind of in awe of this place and don't like it sometimes, just because they never win when they come here and because of the way the fans can get on you—especially against Staten Island. I mean, they just rip Rifkin here. I'm lucky because the fans love me, and I've never disliked any fan. It's just a godsend that I've been put here. This is the best place to play in the Minor Leagues right now."

While New York–Penn League teams such as the Mahoning Valley Scrappers, Lowell Spinners, and, of course, the Staten Island Yankees have sparkling new fields, albeit in less exciting areas than Coney Island, teams such as the Utica Blue Sox, Oneonta Tigers, and the Pittsfield Astros have facilities that are not on par with KeySpan Park. It's not unusual for games in these parks to be played in front of fewer than 1,000 people. These parks and their home markets, by the way, are in jeopardy of getting phased out of the New York–Penn League as it moves into bigger markets with newer stadiums. [*Indeed, by 2003, Utica and Pittsfield have lost their teams.*] The Cyclone players have said they think it's no coincidence that they, with their sellout crowds and state-of-the-art facilities, are playing the best baseball in the league. This acknowledgment that the players give the fans speaks to the difference between this level and the majors all by itself; at the ultimate level, players are often loathe to credit anyone but themselves (and maybe their teammates and coaches) for their successes.

As amusing, open, and pure as Brett is ("he is tremendous with the fans and the media," says Alfonzo), it isn't just frank talk and emotion that he brings to the team. Batting consistently in the third spot in the lineup, Kay has been an offensive juggernaut, using his wide batting stance and good eye for the strike zone to spray hits all over the field and maintain a batting average above .300 almost since his first appearance. On days that Alfonzo wants to give Kay's aching body a little rest by starting a backup at the catcher spot, Kay is often inserted into the designated hitter spot to make sure he still gets his swings. Kay's solid average and three home runs so far are impressive, considering that this is his first time using wooden bats in games that count. Brett, in a hitting groove that he can't totally explain, has said before that the offensive adjustment from college to the pros has been relatively easy. Even the bat switch isn't fazing him right now. "I remember the first batting practice I took here I hit the shit out of the ball, so I can't say it's been that hard for me," Brett says. "I had used wooden bats a little before I got here, in scout team leagues and stuff, so it isn't totally new to me."

And so far this season it's been established that if Brett is put at DH to keep his bat in the lineup, it's never for more than a brief rest, since his athleticism and his willingness to be a leader make him a potentially dominant defensive player. Alfonzo raves about Kay and feels he has as good a chance as anyone else on the team at making it to the majors. "He's very intelligent behind the plate, and he's got a great throwing arm and ability to block balls in the dirt," Alfonzo says. "Offensively he swings the bat good and can use the whole field. He's great too because he's a complete leader when he's behind the plate; he loves to take control of the game. His personality shows that he will be a great leader at the next levels, as well."

Of course, there's more to making the majors than just having the skills. Unless he's some sort of physical specimen with a "can't-miss" skill set, much of a player's future depends on circumstances. What round was he taken in? How much did he get paid? These are relevant questions because an organization is going to do what it can to make sure its top picks advance the furthest, lest the teams look stupid for picking them and giving them a million-dollars-plus deal in the first place. Brett, as an eighth-round choice who got $72,000, does not fit into that category, but it's not like he's a throwaway, either. Another crucial question is what the prospect's position looks like in the organization. With the Mets, catching has seemed fairly settled for a long time. In Mike Piazza, the Mets have arguably the best catcher (at least offensively) in the sport. It's ironic, too, because no position in baseball has as few stars as catcher, but, sure enough, the Mets have one of them. While Piazza's presence could be discouraging to Mets' organization catchers at the Double- and Triple-A level, Brett doesn't worry about it. Brett says he still looks at Mike Piazza as a fan would, and Brett knows that by the time he's ready for the majors, there's a good chance Piazza will have donned a first baseman's mitt or have left the Mets altogether. Besides Piazza and his backup, Vance Wilson, Jason Phillips is the organization's top caching prospect. Besides some older catchers in the organization who have picked up the unfortunate tag of "career Minor Leaguer," Brett is essentially competing with Mike Jacobs, Tyler Beuerlein, and Justin Huber to be next on the ladder. Jacobs, whom the Mets drafted in 1999, was the opening-night hero for the Cyclones. Scouts consider Jacobs a good left-handed hitter (lefty-hitting catchers are a rarity), but his defense is considered far behind Brett's, and if Jacobs ever makes it to the majors it would likely be as a first baseman. The Mets drafted Beuerlein one round ahead of Brett, out of a Division III college in Arizona, but Brett has already established himself as the superior talent. Huber, though currently behind Brett while playing for the Kingsport rookie team, is the catcher that the organization is buzzing about. Signed as an international free agent out of Australia, Huber is a bright hope for the team thanks to his hitting skills. "Huber is the one I hear about," says Brett. "He seems like a guy that I'd be sharing at-bats with in the future, maybe even later this season, or he may just fly right by me and there's nothing I can do about it. But it's always like that—there's always someone ready to take your spot, at every level. I just gotta keep plugging and working my ass off."

An observant young man who obviously knows the game well, Brett is honest about his chances. "I'm not your prototype catcher," he says. "I've got a decent arm and can hit a little bit, but that's it. That's why I'm not one of those guys you see getting a million dollars. It's all projections and stuff. To be seen like that, I need to change physically. I have to get stronger and gain some weight. But I do think I have the tools, and I know that when I'm going well, I'm [a legitimate Major League prospect]. And catcher is the best position to play to have a chance."

It isn't just a player's physical makeup that is studied when he's in the minors; playing professionally requires significant changes in a prospect's mental approach, which Brett is noticing and embracing. "In college, there's pressure because you're constantly worried about how you're doing and if it's going to affect you getting drafted, and if you'll get drafted; plus you're in school. Here, everything is just thrown at you, and there's not so much time to think about it. Just straight baseball," he says. "I think for the most part I'm doing well with that here."

Besides Brett, whom scouts think could make the majors around 2005, and Danny Garcia, who is about to get promoted, the Cyclone players that Alfonzo believes have the best shot at making it there are Angel Pagan, Jay Caliguiri, Joe Jiannetti, and the team's dominant pitching duo, Peeples and Portobanco. Pagan is a twenty-year-old from Puerto Rico who stands 6'1", runs like the wind, and plays all three outfield positions well. As Brett says, "Angel Pagan is a speed guy that can always put the ball in play. That's important." Pagan's chances are not, as far as anyone knows, enhanced by his fascinating name.

Caliguiri is a six-foot infielder who hits for average and can play first or third. His height might be a little iffy for the majors, but he can hit for power, and Alfonzo likes how hard he plays. Jiannetti is also a "corner" infielder (meaning he plays first, third, or both and will be expected throughout his career to live up to certain offensive numbers that a team expects to get from its corners). At 6'0", 190 pounds, Jiannetti is built like Caliguiri and is also a great contact hitter who's been red-hot ever since he joined the team two weeks ago.

The two pitching prospects that Alfonzo considers the team's most promising are the team's two aces, Peeples and Portobanco. Peeples is the Georgia native who is still amazed by big-city New York, while Portobanco is the street-smart Nicaraguan who played a couple of years of college ball in Miami. Different as their backgrounds may be, Peeples and Portobanco share some traits that help make them good prospects. First and foremost is their size. Peeples is listed at 6'4", 196, while Portobanco goes 6'3", 205. As a recent *Sports Illustrated* article explained, short pitchers are a dying breed in the big leagues, so Peeples and Portobanco warrant instant attention. An obvious bonus is their ability to throw hard, with both able to push ninety miles per hour on their fastballs while maintaining their control. So far this year, the two have harnessed their abilities quite well; Peeples is 5–0 with an ERA under 1.00, while Portobanco is 3–2 with an ERA of 1.14. These are dominant numbers. "Ross Peeples can pitch with the best of them," says Brett. "He has great stuff and, just as important, a great mentality for pitching." Adds Frank Corr, the Cyclones' first baseman, "I'd say Ross is the best pitcher

I've seen this year. He works fast, he goes right after the hitters. He's fun to watch as a player, and the fans, too—they love him."

Of Portobanco, Alfonzo says, "I like his attitude. He's been living with me all year, so I see it all the time—he wants to go hard, and he don't care about anything else. I'm sure you noticed that just from interviewing him. He's here to make the big leagues, and with a ninety-three-mile-per-hour fastball, I think he's on the right track."

Talking to Brett and his Brooklyn teammates about what it takes, combined with the greater focus on players' builds and abilities among Major League teams, you realize that Anthony Otero, a relatively little kid, faces almost insurmountable odds against ever playing an inning of professional baseball. But that will be for him to learn in due time or, even better, to disprove.

In my opinion, besides Garcia and the big-time pitchers, Kay has the best chance of any 2001 Cyclone to make it to the Bigs, if only because his size is a little more in line with what's required in the Major Leagues. Odds dictate that only three or four of these guys will ever make it to one of the Major League's thirty teams, and at most positions the average size is a bias that will be tough for guys to overcome. In an earlier chapter I mentioned Troy Glaus and Mo Vaughn as big corner guys. But almost every premiere corner player—Jason Giambi, Todd Helton, Scott Rolen, Mike Sweeney, Jim Thome—would tower over his position mates if he were on the Cyclones. It's not a very encouraging set of numbers for guys like Caliguiri and Jiannetti, and it's not like they can just learn how to play shortstop or second, where size isn't at a premium but speed and foolproof fielding skills are. Add a little weight and the ability to hit a few more homers, however, and it's not hard to see Brett filling out a uniform of his hometown California Angels, for example. Plus, the intensity Brett is showing as he gets more and more comfortable with the team—as long as he doesn't let it go too far—is a trait that cannot be taught and that is sure to impress scouts, especially when it comes from a catcher, whose job is to be the leader on the field and have good rapport with his pitchers. "Catching is such an integral part of the game; you need to be a quarterback and leader out there, and I think I have those qualities," Brett says.

Pitchers have always liked throwing to me, and I've always had good relationships with my pitchers. If a pitcher doesn't like throwing to you, that's no good. I think I'm considered a guy who calls a good game, and has a strong arm, and can hit a little bit. You have got Major League catchers like that, you know? A Brad Ausmus [currently with the Houston Astros, Ausmus is a 5'11", 200-pound veteran who went to Dartmouth], who seems to get credit for calling and catching a good game. He's not a great hitter but he gets the job done with his pitchers, and sometimes that's all you need. I'm not going to be like Mike Piazza or Pudge Rodriguez with the bat, but I'll always play the game the way it's supposed to be played, hitting it the other way, moving runners.

For sure, Brett possesses some unique offensive skills for a catcher. As he did in college, Brett has shown the ability to get on base via bunt base hits. He also has the speed to steal bases on occasion, and, as he notes himself, his strong bat control prevents him from striking out too much and gives him the ability to hit the ball to all fields.

As far as his interaction with the pitchers and calling pitches, Brett has been pleasantly surprised by how smooth everything is going. "In high school I called the pitches, and I loved it. But when I got to college, I didn't have a clue until my last year," Brett recalls. "I learned what the guys here like to throw mostly catching them in the bullpen that first week when I wasn't playing. There was still an adjustment when I got on the field for real—in my first two games I caught Harold Eckert and Matt Peterson, and I must have had eight or nine passed balls—but I learned after that. Nobody here ever acts like a jerk on the mound, which made it easy for us to jell."

Even given the fact that the odds are against these guys making it, it's not impossible. The New York–Penn League, in which the Cyclones play, has been at least a semiconsistent source of Major League talent since its inception, and on the website of the New York–Penn League historian and Auburn Doubleday employee Charlie Wride, there is a list of the more than 150 players on Major League rosters this season who played in the New York–Penn League earlier in their careers. With approximately

750 Major Leaguers altogether, that's not a bad percentage. There are also numerous big league coaches who played in the New York–Penn League. Famous current New York–based big leaguers include the Mets' Edgardo Alfonzo (whose brother Edgar is the Cyclones' manager) and Al Leiter and the Yankees' Bernie Williams, Andy Pettitte, and Jorge Posada (the latter two were batterymates at Oneonta in 1991). The list also includes the Arizona Diamondbacks' phenomenal pitching duo, Randy Johnson and Curt Schilling, a sort of Major League version of Peeples and Portobanco, as it were. Some of the all-time baseball greats who put in time in the New York–Penn League are Wade Boggs, Jerry Koosman, Don Mattingly, Tug McGraw, Tony Perez, Jim Rice, Pete Rose, Mel Stottlemyre, Robin Yount, and Maury Wills.

Few players, good or bad, spend more than a season and a half at this level. In the case of guys like the ones listed, the stay at the short-season A-level can be as short as a couple of weeks. It's not quite halfway through this summer's twelve-week season, and already the Cyclones have sent up, sent down, or simply released more than ten players, including Mike Jacobs, the catcher whose departure opened the door for Brett. The transient nature of this level of pro baseball is illustrated by thinking back to opening night. On the field, the biggest star was Jacobs, who drove in the game-winning run and is now playing for Capital City. Off the field, the biggest stars (i.e., the guys who did well in front of the many cameras and mics) were three guys with unique characteristics: the Australian Matt Gahan, the twenty-four-year-old Michael Piercy, and the Yalie Tony Coyne. The last two of these three were released on the same day in early July, well before the season reached the halfway point.

The fact that few fans made a stink about the players' departures, if they noticed at all, speaks to the fact that this team is succeeding as a concept more than anything. As fans have said on more than one occasion this summer, "We cheer for Brooklyn!" The winning hasn't hurt attendance, either, though the team has yet to be covered the way a Met or Yankee team is covered in relation to its on-field performance. Media coverage of the Cyclones, even during their twelve-game winning streak, is still focusing more on the Brooklyn baseball angle than on what the team has been accomplishing on the field. If the Cyclones can get into the playoffs and perhaps win the league championship at the same time that the novelty begins to wear off, the coverage will probably begin to change.

The player movement also helps to contribute to the occasional shoddy play fans are subjected to at KeySpan Park. Another reason for mistakes can be the uneven talent level; these players are in either their first or second year of professional baseball, and their experience levels can often be quite different. On the mound, the telling factor is the lack—the Cyclones' two aces notwithstanding—of guys who can hit 90 mph on the radar gun or, even rarer, throw in the 90s while still throwing strikes. Even so, at this level it's largely a pitchers' game. Most of the players are in only their first or second year of using a wooden bat on a full-time basis. Many talented players throughout the world pick up a wooden bat to practice and may even play on an occasional "wooden-bat" summer team, but high school and college teams in America use aluminum bats in games. When guys get up here, the adjustment can slow them down, and smart pitchers capitalize on that. Home runs are far less frequent than in the big leagues, and outfielders sometimes play so shallow that they look like extra infielders. In addition, bonehead moves—throwing to the wrong base, letting bloopers drop between fielders—are to be expected. One other thing that adds to the Minor League quality is that there are only two umpires, as opposed to four in the majors. This can lead to some poor calls. That said, these guys playing at KeySpan Park tonight and throughout the summer—well, at least a select few of them—represent the future of baseball.

There figure to be seasons when a "can't miss" prospect plays for the Cyclones, though there are none here this year. The Mets' highest draft picks of 2001 either went right to high-A ball (such as the first-round pick the Mets just signed, the pitcher Aaron Heilman, out of Notre Dame) or to rookie ball at Kingsport (e.g., the highly regarded high school products David Wright, Alhaji Turay, and Corey Ragsdale). There are guys like

Brett, Caliguiri, Jiannetti, and Peeples, but no bona fide future stars. According to Brett, this lack of big-money, hyped stars helps make guys "put the team first." At the same time, Caliguiri says it is still a very talented bunch. "I was actually told that the organization wanted to give all these fans the best team possible, so I consider it an honor to be on this team."

Asked how he thinks the overall play, which as we have seen is affected by player movement, varying talent levels, and spotty umpiring, compares to what he saw in the more structured college environment, Brett thinks for a minute. "This team, we play so well together and don't really get affected by everything else," Brett says. "I can't really speak for the other teams, but we have a great manager, great coaches, and a bunch of guys that get along. Plus, the amount of really good players on this team makes it a better team than I had in college."

And this good play and positive, team-first attitudes are being delivered at a time when, even Brett admits, paradoxically, guys who want to make the majors have no choice but to hope that they can continually move up through the Mets' system as quickly as possible. Well, almost as quickly as possible. "We know we're here to get better and then move up," Brett begins thoughtfully. "But it's so awesome to be here on this team that I've been saying that, like, a promotion is really almost like a demotion because you'd have to leave this place and the whole atmosphere. Still, even if I could finish this year here, which would be great, this is not a place that I want to stay beyond this year. I mean, in a way I could see it being fun to spend a fifteen-year career here, and I'm definitely going to miss this place when I'm gone, but, like I said, hopefully in the next couple of years I'll see places like St. Lucie and Binghamton [home of the Double-A Mets]."

No other player I speak to gives me such a strong endorsement of life as a Cyclone, though many admit that leaving this team, this season, would be one of the few promotions in professional baseball that would be sad for the advancing player. Even Alfonzo, the manager, says that, "baseball-wise, I know it's best to keep moving up to coach at higher levels, but it will be hard to leave here."

Alfonzo thinks the guys—especially the ones who have never played professionally anywhere else—will miss it even more than they realize. "I tell them, do not get used to this [type of support]," the manager says. "You'll go somewhere else where there will be no fans, and you still have to play hard. I tell them that Brooklyn is different from the rest of the Minor Leagues—everybody in Brooklyn loves baseball."

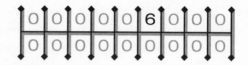

Brett Kay Moves to the BIG City,
Anthony Stays in Coney Island

Brett Kay has been given something that is making his magical summer even more special. It's a gift, of sorts. Since mid-July, he's been in possession of something every New Yorker wants—a Manhattan apartment. "The guy Bob who helped me with my contract, he's like my dad in a way, you know?" begins Brett, whom I've asked to explain his current living situation. "And his son used to be a model out here, and so the son has a place in the Chelsea part of Manhattan that no one lives in now because he's back in L.A. Normally he just rents it out to his buddies, but two or three weeks ago I had called Bob to talk about how crappy the living situation was. I guess whoever was staying in the apartment owed Bob's son a favor, so they asked him to move out for the rest of the summer. Then Bob called me and said, 'Go ahead and live in there.'"

Before I can even explain to this California native how lucky he is to live in such a neighborhood, and presumably for free, Brett continues happily, his pregame energy pushing his sentences out in excited bursts. "He's never there, you understand? They sent me the keys, and I was hooked up. So now I've got my own place in Manhattan, twenty blocks away from Times Square. It's on, um, like, 24th [Street] and 7th [Avenue]," Brett says, clearly not even totally sure where in this new city he lives. He is clear on the fact that he doesn't have to fight for rides in the team van anymore. "Now I take the subway to the field, which is an experience in itself. The N train or the F train are both near the apartment. I'm just trying to figure out which one is faster. It's not like I really know my way around yet, and I still get lost sometimes. I usually leave, like, four hours before I need to be here. I'll just be walking around 7th Avenue or whatever, somewhere in Chelsea. I mean, I get lost all the time."

In future conversations, more details come out about the apartment. "It's just a studio apartment. Not that big, but I don't need anything big," Brett says a couple of days later. "It has a bed, a TV, a computer that I can check my emails on. Everything is sweet. I'm making the best of it. There's a food market right outside my door where I can get my healthy stuff. I think Manhattan food is really good. There's also a liquor store nearby if I want. The whole setup is awesome."

Not that Brett is living wildly. "Nah, I'm still not there that much—I don't even go back there every single night. But at this age I've become a little more of an antisocial guy, so I do like being alone when I can. I know that some of the guys in the dorms [at St. John's University] like to go out at night, but I'm not a party guy. Even back home, I only like to go out if it's with my girlfriend or if everyone is going out. Besides, I didn't want to give the wrong impression by coming back to the dorms drunk. Some people can go out, drink, and play the next day, no problem, but my body is just not meant for that. When they'd do that I'd just be sitting in my room, alone. That's why this apartment is such a hook-up—as amazing as things are with this team in Brooklyn, lodging is a problem. Now I don't have to deal with that."

Besides, according to Brett, there is more than enough wild stuff going on in his neighbors' apartment. "I probably shouldn't say this, but, you know, the apartments are really close together in Manhattan. So one of the first days I was there, about ten in the morning, I'm eating my breakfast, and I look up and there's people having sex in the middle of the apartment. Then they're walking around—the guy had a dirty mullet and a big beard and he was just walking around the apartment. Since then I've seen 'em do drugs. They have to know I'm right there, because it's only about five feet to their window. I'm just like, 'Oh, my God.' It's a man and woman couple, but sometimes they bring more people over. This stuff is going on all the time. I don't think my teammates believe me, so I'm going to bring some of them over to my place to see for themselves."

As great as Brett's apartment is for morning entertainment and for some time away from his teammates, it's not necessarily a commute he likes to make after late nights of either home games or road trips that end with a bus dropping the guys at KeySpan at four in the morning. "When it's late and I'm really tired, I stay with the guys in Staten Island," Brett says. "Sometimes I get freaked out by the subway late at night. Nothing bad has happened to me on it, but there are some shady, weird people on those subways late at night. I just feel a little iffy riding it at that time of night."

The place in Staten Island is a home that belongs to a guy Brett knows only as "Raymond," who is a big Cyclones booster and let the team know his place was available. "He's got a car that he lets us use sometimes with a Mets' sticker on it, and that's all I know. The other guys living out there are David [Byard], [Ross] Peeples, Forrest Lawson, Mike Cox, and [Jay] Caliguiri. If I do go there, it's usually just to sleep. When I get up, I like to go back to the apartment, you know? Just have time to check my emails and be by myself."

So here he is, a California kid living the life as a subway-riding baseball player. No one finds the scenario funnier than the Cyclones' Dave Campanaro, who had told me the story about how scared Brett was of the subway when he had to take it back to Brooklyn after the guys were on MTV's *TRL*. "Now Brett is more accustomed to the city than anyone else on the team. He's got the studio in Manhattan, and he's taking those shaky subways [that scared him so much when he took his first ride] to the ballpark every day. It has been a hysterical transformation."

It's also been a transformation that has made Brett a favorite of the team's off-field staff and is one of the reasons he's a fan favorite. "Brett is willing to help out any way he can, from school visits to interviews," Campanaro says. "He's the first guy at the park [since he moved and can get there on his own], usually walking through the offices, saying hello to everyone and eating lunch at my desk. He is a really genuine guy, who I think is truly enjoying and appreciating his time in Brooklyn."

While most of the guys' dress choices—backwards caps, big jeans, t-shirts—make them look like they just fell off a college quad, Brett, whose postgame getup usually includes hipster black glasses and some nice sandals, actually looks the part of a guy with his own place in Manhattan. Just a month or so into the arrangement, Brett chuckles at the metamorphosis. "It is pretty crazy. I mean, I'm from southern California. Being near L.A. gives you some idea of what a big-city atmosphere might be like, but New York is a *way* different place. Things here are much more up-tempo and high-intensity. Before I got here, I didn't know what to expect or how I'd like it. Well, I love it."

Brett can't say whether this setup is making him perform better, but he certainly has few complaints about his lifestyle or his performance. His comfort level within the team has also been enhanced recently, thanks to the arrival of David Bacani, an infielder promoted from Kingsport. Bacani was a teammate of Brett's at Cal State–Fullerton who got sent to Rookie League upon signing. "That's *my* second baseman," Brett says. "One of my best friends from college; having him here is great."

By the way, Brett is the only Cyclone player in possession of such lodging, and there can't be many other Minor League players in America with such a setup. And even the Staten Island arrangement is pretty fortunate. Either way, Brett has been removed from the bizarre and chaotic lodging that many Cyclone players are still enduring.

Included in the relatively unlucky group of seven or eight still living at Xaverian High School is Rylie Ogle, a tall and lanky relief pitcher with an amusing disposition. For one thing, the 6'3" Ogle, a rookie from UC–Santa Barbara (a rival of Fullerton's), is a basketball fanatic and revels in the stories I tell him about Stephon Marbury, Coney Island's famous basketball export. "Man," he says, "I wish I had time to go check out the hoops down there [gesturing at the projects]. I'm not saying I'd go get in a game, but it would be fun to watch. Even in California you hear a lot about New York City basketball and the guys that came out of there."

Ogle is even more animated when talking about the lodging he's endured since he too got called up from Kingsport. "I'm staying in Xaverian, and it is pretty rough over there." Asked to explain, he says, "Well, we're staying in *classrooms*. Just regular classrooms that have sort of been converted. I guess the school is just letting the team use them. I have no idea what happens when school starts, like if these are classrooms they still use for school and will need us out of them. All that's set up in there are beds. And we haven't had any hot water for a little while. I mean, we have it here in the stadium, which is obviously where I shower after games, but sometimes I like to shower when I wake up, but I can't do it over there now. See, I usually stay up until like four or five in the morning and sleep 'til 1 p.m., so I like to take a shower to wake up then."

I ask him whether there's a TV to help pass the time. "We've got a little shitty one that we can use, but only if we use some paper clips and rig it just right. Even then we only get, like, three channels on it. I did hook it up to catch some *Baywatch: Hawaii Edition* the other night. And we do have a Sony PlayStation that works without a problem, so I've been playing a lot of that. When I was in school I'd have time to play video games like that maybe twice a semester. Now I'm playing all the time."

Compared to Kingsport, Rylie says, "the living here is worse. I had a nice homestay down there. But I can't complain about the baseball here. I mean, this facility and all the amazing fans? It really raises our level of play. And I've had people stop me outside the stadium just to say 'Thank you' for what we're doing in Brooklyn. That's a good feeling."

Listening to Rylie bemoan the Cyclones' living accommodations reminds me of how fortunate Brett was to have a friend that could hook up a free Manhattan apartment for him. But the "connections" that Brett has in baseball go far beyond just Bob Sporrer, the former Little League coach who let Brett stay in the Manhattan apartment and who will serve as Brett's de facto agent as long as he's in the Minor Leagues. Regarding this agent business, Brett explains, "If I make it to the majors, I'll get an agent. Until that time, all an agent—who you have to pay—is good for is getting you free stuff. And I can get pretty much all the bats, batting gloves, and regular gloves I need for free, anyway."

"How's that?" I ask Brett.

"Oh, my mom, after she and my dad got divorced, she was dating a rep for Rawlings [the huge baseball equipment company]. They almost got married, and me and him became pretty close," Brett says. "So he gives me all the stuff I need."

There's more. "So the guy Bob I keep telling you about, the one that's like my dad, his college roommate was Art Howe," says Brett, speaking about the Oakland A's [and future New York Mets] manager. "It's not like Bob is going to call Art to talk about me or anything, but it's a pretty cool thing, and it shows how connected he is to the baseball world. It's a part of why he's so knowledgeable about the game."

Brett goes on to explain that his older brother, Eric Kay, works in the media relations department for the Anaheim Angels, who were in New York City to play the Yankees August 3–6. "Eric was an athlete in high school, so I sort of followed him, but he didn't play pro ball or anything. He got into media relations, and he's been doing that for the Angels for a couple of years now," Brett explains. "When the Angels were playing the Yankees, he came and visited me one game—got a police escort from Yankee Stadium down to us after his game. Too bad I didn't play well while he was here."

One more baseball connection in Brett's life tops perhaps all the others in ironic value. When Brett's dad, Rick Kay, was playing football at Colorado University, his roommate was John Stearns, who was a standout football and baseball player at CU. Stearns's nickname was "Bad Dude," and he lived up to it with his aggressive approach to the game. For those who aren't big on their Mets' history, Stearns went on to become one of the best and most popular Mets in franchise history. After being taken with the second overall pick in the 1973 draft, Stearns reached the majors with the Phillies in 1974, then got traded to the Mets before the next season. Between 1977 and 1982, Stearns was the Mets' starting catcher, and he earned a spot in the All-Star Game in '77, '79, '80, and '82. The Mets were truly awful in that era, losing more than ninety games every year that Stearns was a regular in the lineup, but he was a rare bright spot and a consistent fan favorite. And it wasn't just his production—which peaked in 1978 with fifteen home runs, seventy-three RBIs, and twenty-five stolen bases—that made Stearns so popular with the New York faithful. It was also his style of play. Brett obviously wasn't old enough to see any of Stearns's exploits in person, but he's heard enough stories to understand what made Stearns a star. "From what I know about him, he was a real aggressive player," says Brett about the similarly built, 6'0", 185-pound Stearns. "He was a catcher who could run, he could bunt, he'd get hit by pitches. I mean, I *love* to bunt. And I think I can run a little bit. It's ironic because the way he played is, like, a model for how I want to play."

Without going into much detail, Brett makes it clear that, as close as Stearns was to his father and mother back in the '70s, the former Mets' All-Star has not been a big part of Brett's life. "I had sort of met him a couple of years ago, when I think he was working with the Orioles," Brett recalls. "I was with my brother and we went up to him, but he kind of shoved us away and didn't talk to us. We didn't know the history of him and my dad; maybe my dad was part of the whole 'Bad Dude' thing."

Fittingly for Brett's life, he should have a chance to interact with Stearns again soon; Stearns is the New York Mets' third-base coach, and the Cyclone players say they hope to go to a Mets' game on their off day at the end of this month.

As of August 16, the Cyclones have a record of 40–15. The team destroyed the New York–Penn League competition in the month of July, going 25–5 with a .284 team batting average and a 2.20 ERA, and the guys are playing nearly as well in August. Some recent highlights include a road win over the Hudson Valley Renegades on the eleventh in which Brett had three hits, and a rematch at home the next night, which, despite ending in a loss, was still a historic date—that evening's packed crowd pushed the season total to 208,377, which gave the Cyclones the biggest single-season attendance in New York–Penn League history (with eleven home games left!). The thirteenth brought a rain-delayed game against the Yankees that still needs to be completed. That date, which was delayed with yet another packed house waiting, featured one of Brett's most enjoyable fan moments of the season. Rather than spend the rain delay wrestling with teammates (as some did) or hiding back in the clubhouse (as others did), Brett took advantage of the rain delay to forge even deeper connections with the fans. Sitting at the end of the dugout, Brett called some spectators over and engaged them in a baseball trivia contest. Those who answered correctly got gifts from Brett, adding to his team-high total of fan donations. "I like to have trivia quizzes with the fans and give away stuff when they get my questions right," he says. "If we want to interact with the fans, we have a lot of chances to do that. I know I'm doing it a lot."

First place belongs to Brooklyn right now, but Brett and his teammates are not content with what they've accomplished this far. Before this evening's game, I walk outside the stadium along the first-base line. Where the main seating area stops, there's a fence that separates the bullpen from the parking lot, with the concourse one level up, stretching over part of the bullpen. The breeze is blowing as usual, but that does little to cool off this oppressively hot and humid late afternoon, particularly in this corner of the stadium. People are not just idling inside the bullpen, however. What's visible through the fence is a catcher, in full equipment, working on blocking balls in the dirt. There's a coach—a big fellow—throwing the balls in the dirt and imploring the catcher to block them. "Slide your feet!" "Get down!" For catchers, no drill is less pleasant than this one. Think about it: not only are you hot and sweaty in the catcher's gear, rolling around in the dirt to *practice* keeping bad pitches in front of you. If you do the job correctly, the reward is some nice, fat bruises, usually on the inside of your forearm biceps.

It doesn't take long to figure out that the catcher is Brett, judging from the outline of his size and his athletic technique in blocking balls. The figure throwing the balls in the dirt is a little harder to figure. It's not Alfonzo, HoJo, or Ojeda, to be sure. But hasn't another ex-Met been coming around to work with the guys a little? The answer is yes, and when Brett talks about this person later it goes a long way to help me understand why he didn't have any problems working on ball blocking on a scorching day before a game. "That was Gary Carter out there," Brett says with a grin, talking about the ex-Met catcher whose World Series–winning stint with the Mets dwarfs even what the excellent John Stearns had accomplished as Met catcher. "I've been getting to work out with him when he comes by here. I like to pick his brain a little, too. He seems like a great guy, and he obviously had a great career. You have to want to learn as much as you can from him."

This has been the unbelievable bonus to being a Cyclone. As if the stadium, the history, the adulation from the fans, and all the winning haven't been enough, the Brooklyn players are learning the game from guys they grew up watching. Besides Carter's occasional appearances, the Cyclones have also been joined sometimes by one of the Mets' roving Minor League coaches, the former Mets' infielder Tim Teufel. Teufel and Carter combine with Howard Johnson and Ojeda to make every day with this team a 1986 reunion of some sort. "Pretty amazing, huh? I mean, the '86 Mets were my favorite team of all-time," Brett says. "Darryl [Strawberry] was always my favorite player, but when I found out that HoJo and Bobby O were here, I was, like, 'cool!' And Gary Carter, too."

It's not all laughter and memories with these guys, however. "I'd say Bobby O is the most intimidating. He's really good at being a jokester and having a good time, but when he's serious, he is *serious*. He's really laid into me a couple of times, about pitch calls or whatever. Other than that, everyone has gotten along well; all these coaches are great guys, and it's easy to see that they know the ins and outs of the game."

While the dream-living guys on the Cyclones are going on to suffer a rare home loss to the New Jersey Cardinals (5–3, in thirteen innings), Anthony Otero is blocks away, chilling out in his apartment, blissfully unaware how long the odds are that his own dreams will come true.

The Oteros live in a modest third-floor apartment. Left of the front door is the living room/dining room, with the living room furniture covered in plastic. Adjacent to this big room is the kitchen, a narrow space with a TV at one end that blares out the evening news. To the right of the front door is a hallway that runs to the back of the apartment. At the end of the hallway are two bedrooms (James and Anthony share one, the parents the other) and the bathroom. The parents' bedroom looks out toward the city, and, like the bleachers at KeySpan, offers a view of the Twin Towers in downtown Manhattan, the nearby borough that the Oteros rarely visit.

Though they didn't feel like coming to the stadium tonight, Anthony and his friends are regulars at KeySpan these days. Asked again whether he'd ever be interested in working at the stadium as a vendor or something, perhaps as a summer job in a year or two, Anthony shakes his head no. "I told you, I want to *play* for the Cyclones some day," he says. The presence of the Cyclones in Brooklyn, in Coney Island, in Anthony's life, has only enhanced his wishes. "Yeah, seeing them play so much gets me more interested in baseball," Anthony confirms. "It makes me want to develop my skills, get older, probably try out for them one day in the future. But I don't care what stadium or team I go to, I just want to play the game I love."

Brett Kay, who is playing the game he loves, was born on October 31, 1979, into a middle-class family with some lucky connections, and he's used his talent and hard work to meet other influential people. "The biggest thing for me was to have [his youth baseball coaches] Bob and Mike in my life after my father," Brett says. These guys were part of Brett's greater baseball life; in Orange County, California, Little Leagues are plentiful.

His family helped a lot, as well. "My brother was an influence with baseball," shares Brett. "We had been to a couple of Dodger and Angel games when I was younger, but when my brother started working for the Angels he'd let me go all the time. The Angels sucked then, but it was still a baseball game."

Brett adds that his mother "has always been behind me 100 percent. She'll offer input about my future sometimes, but for the most part she just offers support. She knows that playing baseball is something I've worked my ass off to do, and as long as I decide to play, she'll be behind me."

If things don't work out on the diamond, the study-averse Brett will still be relatively close to having a college degree thanks to the credits he picked up during his three years at Fullerton. "Besides baseball, what I focused on in college was criminal justice," Brett explains. "That's what I majored in. If baseball doesn't work out, I'll go back to school, get my degree, get married, and start a new life. If that happens and you want to see me playing baseball, you can catch me at the [Cal State–Fullerton] alumni game every year."

Anthony, born on December 31, 1986, may come from a warm, two-parent home, but his family lacks the money to move out of the projects or explore the city he lives in. Anthony has never traveled, never been to summer camp, and never seen his beloved Yankees in person. Not that he feels the least bit neglected. For one thing, he's got his loving parents, Puerto Ricans who grew up in the Red Hook neighborhood and have been married for sixteen years. "My mom is great, and I've got my dad around. It's good to have a father," says Anthony, who admits this is pretty rare in the Coney Island Houses. "Yeah. Of all my friends, Freddie don't got a dad, Anthony don't got a dad, Derrick don't got a dad; almost everybody I hang out with don't have a dad. I feel lucky to have him around. He always plays with me and really with all of them, too. He'll play with all the kids, and they like him. They always say hello to him. My mom, too. She talks to them, he teaches them handball. It's good."

There are scattered Babe Ruth and Gil Hodges League baseball programs in Brooklyn that Anthony could look into if he and his family did some research and were really motivated, but there are no options right here in Coney Island. Part of the Cyclones' master plan is to change all that and to help provide a baseball league for youngsters in the community, but as of now such a setup does not exist. Therefore, Anthony is the ultimate self-made player.

"I just got good at baseball from being so active," Anthony begins. "From ever since I was young, my mother used to tell me, 'Go outside and play, play whatever sports you want.' And we did, we played everything. Basketball, football, handball. Baseball came from me watching the Yankees. She watched them all the time and got me into the Yankees, and from watching them I decided I'd try to play."

By this Anthony doesn't mean he went and found some league that would take him; he means he introduced the game to his 'hood. "I'd watch the games on TV and then say, 'Let's try this.' I learned to throw and field from watching on TV, and I started to get good. I showed the other kids and then we started playing in that park you always see us in. All the young kids started to play, and I like to help them get better, too."

It's not that Anthony thinks any of this is all that special, but I keep asking questions, so he keeps telling. So there was never even baseball in the playground here? "No. I think I would have played [Little League] if I could have, or played with other people here, but no one played. I think this is really just the second summer of baseball. This block is usually about basketball. But I learned how to play and I taught the young kids, and now they like it. Now people watch the games—they come down and watch, or they watch out the window. Most of the older people around here play basketball, but sometimes when we're playing baseball, they'll come watch us."

In other words, Anthony brought baseball to Coney Island Houses. It occurs to me that he should get a stipend for serving as the project's recreation director.

Of course, two or three summers of playground baseball does not a tradition make—certainly not one that can generate a professional baseball player. While playground basketball translates decently enough to the organized high school, college and even professional levels—especially in New York, where there are often some seriously talented players involved—the differences between playground baseball and the real thing are enormous. Combine Anthony's lack of baseball training with his smallish stature, and his making the Cyclones seems like an impossible goal. Whereas the thirteen-year-old Brett Kay had been invited onto an All-Star team with coaches who knew Major Leaguers and who treated him like a son, Anthony is serving as a player, umpire, and coach for anyone interested in baseball in an entire housing project.

The major opportunity for baseball instruction beyond a mentor or a Cyclone-sponsored neighborhood team, which the Oteros have heard nothing about at this point, is high school baseball. For baseball and academic reasons, the Oteros had hoped to get Anthony into a high school other than Lincoln. The New York City Board of Education allows the top public high schools—in Brooklyn, these are Brooklyn Tech, Midwood, and Edward R. Murrow—to admit students from all over, but the kids need either exceptional grades or a special talent (art, theater, sports) to be accepted. His playground prowess notwithstanding, Anthony has neither. "Anthony wants to play in school, but they have to give him a chance. He applied to a lot of high schools that would have been better schools and been a better place to play baseball, but he didn't get accepted," Mrs. Otero says dejectedly. "So he has to go to Lincoln, which is the neighborhood school. I'm a little worried that the only concern at Lincoln is the [nationally known] basketball team, flying them around the country. If you want to play basketball, they take care of you. I don't know about baseball. Anthony doesn't communicate with me that much, but I think he's eager to play baseball and I just hope that he can."

At this point, Mr. Otero interjects, worried that Anthony may not do what it takes to play as a freshman, anyway. "He's lazy in school," Mr. Otero says. "I mean, he's a smart kid, but it usually takes him, like, three months into the school year before he wakes up and realizes that he needs to get some work done if he wants to pass his classes. . . . When he was in the lower grades, he always got by on being the 'cute kid.' The teachers thought he was cute, and they'd let him slide. The teachers are not going to be like that in high school, so Anthony is going to need to learn how to be serious about school."

Later, Anthony confirms, "Basketball is definitely the top thing at Lincoln, and I think football is second. I don't think Lincoln has had a good baseball team for years."

Indeed, even if Anthony keeps his grades up and somehow shows enough polish, or at least raw ability, to make the Lincoln High baseball team, his experience will be a far cry from Brett's at lush Mater Dei High School. For one thing, though plans for a complex are in place at this point (2001), Lincoln doesn't even have a field of its own, and proper equipment is hard to come by. The team plays—and practices—at Six

Diamonds, part of a nearby park used by many local teams that is reached from Lincoln by public bus or coach-driven van.

Furthermore, while Mater Dei is a prestigious Catholic school that sends more than 95 percent of its students off to college, America's universities aren't exactly tripping over themselves to attend "college fairs" at Lincoln, which has fallen on hard times since the days when Joseph Heller and Arthur Miller walked its halls. With a burgeoning population divided mostly among blacks, Latinos, and Russians, few of whom come from money or from college-educated parents, and with the best and the brightest kids from the area heading off to Midwood or Murrow, Lincoln is fighting an uphill battle with regard to both its academic and its safety standards. According to the New York City Board of Ed's annual school report, just 61.5 percent of the students who began with the class of 2001 actually graduated in 2001, with some 80 percent of those students pursuing some sort of college afterward. While these numbers pale in comparison to those for a Mater Dei, or even with Midwood and Murrow, they are actually better than the New York City average. The one aspect of Lincoln that has consistently overcome the malaise that surrounds the school is the basketball program, which has been churning out Division I prospects for years, even if few of them have the academic skills to succeed at the high-quality universities they get accepted to.

Of course, Anthony is no hoops star. When pressed on what he will do when he gets older if baseball doesn't work out, Anthony actually sounds a lot like Brett. "My dream is definitely to play baseball, but if sports don't work out I'd want to be a cop." In many respects, if Anthony can just graduate high school he will have accomplished something, and any professional opportunities that follow would be gravy.

While New York playground respect is a badge of honor in basketball, in baseball it's a dubious claim. New York City is a far cry from the Dominican Republic, or even from American states such as Florida or California, where so many kids are playing baseball on their own that even the small percentage who make it end up constituting a large group of professional players. New York City, as well as most other urban areas in the United States, has largely deserted the game, which means that being the best kid in a project, on a block, or in a neighborhood is basically worthless. According to a recent article in the *Village Voice*, six players from Florida's Seminole High School team were selected in June's draft out of a total enrollment of fewer than 2,500 students. New York City high schools, on the other hand, have a total enrollment of about 350,000 students; yet, only two (both from the Bronx's private Mount St. Michael Academy) were drafted this year.

The nationwide phenomenon of inner-city kids—particularly African Americans—deserting baseball is doubly ironic in Brooklyn, since this is where Jackie Robinson made history when he broke baseball's color line and further added to the Dodgers' universal appeal.

Today, Jackie Robinson is ironically commemorated at the middle school that bears his name, I.S. 230, which sits across the street from the plot of land that he helped make famous. It is there, about seven miles from KeySpan Park, that Ebbets Field once stood. Now, facing out onto Bedford Avenue, where the famous right-field fence used to be, is a monstrous housing complex that would dwarf even the Coney Island Houses if stacked next to them. The Ebbets Field Apartments, as they're known, stand twenty-five stories high and contain 1,318 low- and middle-income apartments, with one-bedroom apartments going for about $700 a month for those who get in after spending upward of a year on a waiting list. The apartments sit in Flatbush, right on the edge of the fractious black and Jewish neighborhood of Crown Heights, just blocks from Prospect Park (how nice it must have been to walk to Dodger games in the old days) and the street that Mayor Giuliani recently renamed Gil Hodges Way in honor of Jackie's teammate. Truthfully, on a muggy, mid-August afternoon in 2001, the complex is pretty depressing. This monstrosity's courtyard sits empty and quiet, while some teens roll marijuana blunts in the parking lot.

Inside the management office that sits adjacent to the parking lot, some friendly black women offer a knowing nod when I tell them why I'm here—I'm hardly the first person to come looking for history. The women show off the nice collection of black-and-white photos and paintings of the old ball yard that the office has amassed over the years, but they don't seem all that impressed with what they've got. "This place should have a lot more that shows what was here. Next year they say we may get a Jackie Robinson statue, which would be a start," one of the women laments. With that, they send me outside to see the other, paltry evidence of what was here before. There is a plaque, with "1962" engraved inside a baseball, that says, "This is the former site of Ebbets Field." Besides the minor memorabilia in the office, the plaque, and the complex's name, these buildings might as well be in Canarsie or East New York. Or, for that matter, upper Manhattan, where the New York Giants' own classic stadium, the Polo Grounds, was torn down in 1964 to make way for 155th Street and 8th Avenue's own set of hideous apartments, the Polo Ground Houses.

A lot of media members came to this location in 1997, as New York and Major League Baseball were celebrating the fiftieth anniversary of Robinson's breaking the color line. What the reporters found, and what is just as true today, is that the kids here don't care about baseball, Jackie Robinson legacy or not. If any sport holds the interest of current residents, particularly young ones, it's basketball, which speaks to the racial and cultural changes that have taken place in Flatbush and throughout Brooklyn. And why shouldn't local kids love hoops? After all, not only is basketball marketed as a cool, street-influenced game with a hip-hop feel, but the NBA is dotted with players who came up on the city's hardcourts, such as Kenny Anderson, Ron Artest, Mark Jackson, Stephon Marbury, Lamar Odom, and Rod Strickland, not to mention Michael Jordan, who was born in Brooklyn before moving to North Carolina at a young age. What's more, many of the NBA stars not from New York grew up in project-style, urban housing, so kids feel they can relate to them. Professional basketball is starting to take in talented players from Europe, but the sport—as is proved in any NBA locker room before a game—is still played to a city-based, hip-hop soundtrack. Meanwhile, last month's baseball All-Star Game was largely played by Dominicans, Puerto Ricans, and guys from warm-weather states such as Florida (about fifty current Major Leaguers) and California (depending on the day, and who's been called up or sent down, there are sometimes more than 200 big-league players who hail from California). As such, the most common music in baseball locker rooms is salsa or country. There are pockets of inner cities—such as Dominican-dominated Washington Heights in upper Manhattan—that have taken to baseball the way that most modern-day housing projects take to basketball, but it doesn't have the same impact because it's not like there are baseball diamonds in the middle of the 'hood like there are basketball hoops. The only Brooklynites who come to mind among the current crop of Major Leaguers are the shortstop Rich Aurilia, who attended the same Xaverian High that Cyclones players now live in, the reliever John Franco, and the veteran utilityman Shawon Dunston, an anomaly who attended the public Thomas Jefferson High School in Brooklyn and was the first pick in the 1982 draft. Needless to say, you're a lot more likely to see a kid in a Marbury jersey than in an Aurilia, Dunston, or Franco jersey on the project playgrounds of Brooklyn. The borough of Queens has produced the occasional big-league player over the years, but most of them are products of the borough's outer, Long Island–type reaches, and they learn the game at private parochial high schools, the likes of which Anthony will not ever attend.

All of this background information on New York City and baseball is in the back of my mind when I visit Anthony and his friends a couple of days later. At 3 p.m., like clockwork, they're outside, playing a sport. It's usually baseball, but today it's handball. With Anthony and crew, it's almost never basketball. Again, this is the neighborhood that spawned Marbury, whose life has been fictionalized in the Spike Lee movie *He Got Game,* as well as in the nonfiction retelling of his freshman year in high school in *The Last Shot,* by Darcy Frey, which covers a year in the life of the Lincoln basketball team, of which Marbury was a member. For years, as *The Last Shot* explains in great detail, kids around here grew up on nothing but a steady diet of hoops. But the kids in the Coney Island Houses are changing that. The only basketball being played there consists of a couple of out-of-shape kids throwing an out-of-shape ball at the rim, while baseball or handball games run constantly, at least as long as Anthony Otero is here to organize them. The next Stephon is nowhere to be found. As Anthony's friend Josimar says, the kids in this group "done left basketball. I haven't touched a ball in God knows how long."

Anthony, proudly wearing his Derek Jeter replica Yankee jersey, is not willing to make blanket statements for the entire neighborhood. "The basketball [in this complex] isn't all that, but I know they play a lot of ball over at O'Dwyer [a.k.a. Surfside Gardens]. Stephon grew up over there. And do you know Sebastian, Stephon's cousin? He still lives there," Anthony says, referring first to the famous Surfside basketball court— a.k.a. "The Garden"—that centers a row of housing projects across Surf Avenue and then to the latest prodigy of the Marbury clan, Sebastian Telfair, who is already being touted as the next, well, Stephon Marbury. Telfair will be just a sophomore at Lincoln this year, but he's already known to basketball fans nationwide, thanks in part to his dominant performance at Adidas's summer camp last month. As a freshman, he, like his cousin, started at point guard for Lincoln. Since he's about 6'0", 165 pounds, Telfair will probably not be able to go right to the NBA like Kobe Bryant and Tracy McGrady, but he'll be a big-time college recruit, and all signs—even at this early stage—point to a successful career in the NBA before long. Brooklyn, and Coney Island, will have produced another hoop star. "I've known that kid my whole life," says Anthony of Sebastian, without even a hint of awe. "He's been playing ball every day as long as I could remember, and he's still doing it. My mom knows him, too. She's looked out for him, telling him to stay out of trouble and all that. We all know he's going to make it professional."

NCAA basketball coaches are seen regularly in the neighborhood, recruiting kids like Sebastian and many others for college. Baseball coaches are never here. It's obviously a very different situation from the one Kay grew up in. Suburban California, like Florida, is a breeding ground for professional baseball players. These are facts that Kay is starting to realize as his world widens but that Anthony has not realized.

For now, there's been enough discussion of baseball versus basketball, and the conversation shifts back to the Cyclones and what their presence has meant for these kids. During a break in their handball game, Anthony

De Los Santos says the greatest thing about the Cyclones playing in Coney Island is that "it gives us something to do. There never used to be anything for us to do at night in the summer. All we could do around here was watch stupid TV."

"Exactly," pipes in Josimar. "This stadium helps us keep busy with fun things to do." Anthony and his friends grew up with little disposable income, and, to be sure, they are not the ones that Coney Island business leaders see as the key to an economically viable future for the amusement zone. What's more, growing up on the beach and taking buses past the rides for their entire lives has dimmed any enthusiasm they might have felt had they landed here today. The Cyclones, on the other hand, are new, and they represent a dream to Anthony, which is a big part of why they've "changed his summer."

While it took a new team to spice up the summer of Anthony and his friends, who had long since tired of their neighborhood's amusements, even the most tunnel-visioned, baseball-obsessed players on the Cyclones (of whom there actually aren't many) have realized they're playing in the backyard of an amusement park the likes of which they've never seen. The players can eyeball the rides from their perch in the dugout, and a short walk before or after a game can provide an up-close look. Some of the players have taken walks through the arcade area, but except Angel Pagan, the only Brooklyn Cyclone on record as saying he's ridden the real Cyclone, few appear to have actually ridden anything. And Brett is not going to break that trend. "It's cool to look at the Cyclone, but there is no way I'm going on that thing. I hate roller coasters," he says. "I have been wanting to go to the Aquarium for awhile, since I'm a big, like, fish and animal guy, but I haven't had the chance to get over there yet. I've been out on the boardwalk a couple of times, but I haven't really checked out Coney Island the way I would like."

And, if they mean what they say, Anthony and his friends are even less frequent customers of the amusement parks than the players. Luckily for the area businessmen and ride operators, however, plenty of outsiders are curious.

As the inaugural season continues, most local amusement operators say that the Cyclones have driven up business, with both the Aquarium and the Wonder Wheel crediting the team's presence with increasing business more than 10 percent. None of those customers, alas, have been baseball players who hit the Wonder Wheel billboard in left center field inside KeySpan—the ad is in too tough a spot. Also, the Cyclone organization says it's had a big role in doubling the crowds at Astroland's Friday night fireworks, from 17,000 to sometimes 35,000. The Cyclones' presence has also improved law enforcement, for better or worse. The positive result is that the numerous cops walking everywhere from the boardwalk to the old-fashioned Bowery have helped make people who had written this area off—or who never even thought about it—feel safe. The downside is the sterilization that can come with an increased police presence. As the guy at the piña colada stand across from the batting cage says when I ask for some rum with my frozen drink, "I gotta be real careful with that stuff. They've been sending undercover cops to bust me for selling that stuff. Ever since the stadium opened, it seems like things are really changing around here. They're trying to make it real clean, maybe too clean."

Speaking with a *New York Times Magazine* writer for a recent story (this team has remained a media sensation all summer), Fred Wilpon spoke about what he was trying to accomplish by putting his Class-A team here in Coney Island, in the midst of a reduced but still magical wonderland. "I used to come here with my father," Wilpon told the *Times*'s Nicholas Dawidoff. "We've tried to integrate the Coney Island we knew and what we know Coney Island will be. The reason for this location, aside from the fact that it's beautiful, was the need for a first-class attraction people could come to with the family at reasonable prices and have safe, attractive fun. It has all the infrastructure. It'll become a vital community again. When the redevelopment of 42nd Street [Times Square] was conceived, they said it couldn't be done. Look at 42nd Street now! I know this area, and I know the potential."

And, speaking with a reporter for CNN Financial News, Wilpon's son Jeffrey said the team is "putting the neighborhood back on the map, and

I really believe that people in Coney Island and throughout Brooklyn are feeling good about it again. To bring 250,000 people back to this neighborhood that maybe haven't been here or wouldn't have come here is something that will show them that the neighborhood is good and there'll be some more development here."

Left unsaid by both Wilpons is the fact that they stand to make millions off the scenario, particularly since they didn't have to pay for any of the improvements. In fact, later in the *Times Magazine* story, Fred Wilpon admits that he believes so much in the idea of baseball in Coney Island that he "would have done it if I knew we'd break even. . . . If I knew we'd lose money, would I have done it? Probably. Yes." Too bad for the city's residents that Giuliani never even made such a request.

The junior Wilpon's statement is a little flawed; at least some of the Cyclone fans are locals (more than just Anthony and his friends). But his greater point, as proved by the reactions and numbers being produced by many local business operators, remains true. And, if there are many people, such as Robert Lederman, who remain unhappy with the arrival of the team and the questionable funding it received, most of them are griping quietly.

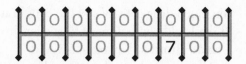

The Last Home Game of the Regular Season

September 2 is another brilliant day in a summer that has been filled with them. New York has a reputation for sticky, humid days, but, except for a few of those in the dog days of August, there's been little rain or humidity. Most days, like this one, have been perfect for hanging around outside. Especially down here, on Nautilus Playground in the middle of the Coney Island Houses, where the breeze is never further away than the next laughing child.

It's a Sunday, but that doesn't change the afternoon vibe around here, only some of the participants and the clothes they're wearing. The spirited game du jour is again handball, as Anthony and a kid named Pepe are taking on Anthony Sr. and another younger kid whom I've never seen around. Pepe wears a shiny new watch, leading Anthony to joke with him: "You got the ice, man. That's the ice."

When Anthony smiles and jokes, as he does with regularity, it only enhances what a healthy kid he is. The summer of playing outside has left his body fit and his skin tanned dark, and the Cyclones—not to mention his project's burgeoning baseball and handball abilities—have given him plenty of reasons to smile.

Mr. Otero is nearly as chipper as Junior this afternoon. A hard-working car mechanic who grew up in the project-dominated neighborhood of Red Hook, isolated from the bulk of Brooklyn by the Brooklyn-Queens Expressway, Mr. Otero finds comfort in the oceanfront isolation of Coney Island. "I really don't mind it here, except for the fact that there's a little too much drug activity and the cops don't come around enough," he says. "Like I told you before, if they ever turn these buildings into co-ops and I could afford to buy ours, I would."

All summer long, the Oteros have stuck to a company line about their big, new neighbor to the east—baseball. Anthony loves it and all other sports. James enjoys it. Mrs. Otero is an avowed Yankee lover and Mets' hater who still refuses to visit KeySpan Park but who insists on watching every Yankee game when it comes on TV. Even though she hasn't gone to the Park, Mrs. Otero still has feelings about the games. "It seems like it's mainly white people at the games," she says almost dismissively. The Oteros' skin is about as dark as that of many Americans of Mediterranean ancestry, but this isn't about skin color per se—it's about an attitude: "I've heard some complaints that the people down here aren't supportive, but it doesn't seem like the team is for us." There's a black-owned clothing company based in Manhattan called FUBU, which is a shortened version of For Us By Us. Lots of kids in the Coney Island Houses sport FUBU gear, and the irony hits me all of a sudden. That mantra is not being lived up to by the Cyclones, though again, the politics that surround the team do not seem to faze Anthony.

Today is the Brooklyn Cyclones' regular-season home finale, and nothing could seem more obvious to Anthony, James, Anthony De Los Santos, and Josimar than to head over to the stadium. An added bonus on this day is that Anthony's dad, by far the least interested in baseball of anyone in the family, is coming along. "My dad is coming with us today," says Anthony, who hasn't had any cousins or anyone else visit that he could bring to a game for the first time. "I can't wait for him to see what it's like inside the stadium."

Scanning the playground, crowded with young black and Latino kids scurrying around, I also notice a couple of Starbury t-shirts, though I wonder how long these will be en vogue. Earlier this summer, there was a shocking NBA trade—the nearby New Jersey Nets traded Marbury to the Phoenix Suns. It figures that Marbury, who is known for his impromptu visits back to his old stomping grounds, won't be coming around these parts nearly as often any more. Besides FUBU and Starbury gear, I also notice, for the first time all summer, that there are kids wearing Cyclone gear. The sports universe for these kids has grown exponentially over the past two months. About all they knew two months ago was that a big-time basketball star had grown up the same way they were growing up and that the Yankees played on TV, the Bronx seeming as far away as Canada for all the traveling Anthony and most of his pals had done. Now they were living with professional baseball right in their neighborhood. Besides Kaiser Park, the closest big patch of green to their apartments is KeySpan Park's outfield. And on this, the penultimate day of "unofficial summer" (Labor Day is tomorrow and school beckons after that), these kids are surely going to honor their new heroes and that patch of green. Though the game does not start until 5 p.m., the posse, with Mr. Otero cheerily accompanying Anthony, James, and three of their friends, rolls out of the Coney Island Houses at 4 p.m., eager to grab some more autographs and cheer on the new neighborhood team.

For Anthony, the first day of school Tuesday will be his first day at Lincoln High School. But, as his dad has observed, Anthony is not about to let on that he's worried about it. "Nah, it shouldn't be bad," Anthony says with a shrug. "Almost every kid that grows up here, or the projects across the street or whatever, they all go to Lincoln. So I'm gonna know a lot of people."

It's not like there's much of a back-to-school vibe anywhere in the area today, and how could there be? Yes, this end of Surf Avenue is gray and rundown, but on a late afternoon, as we take the boardwalk route back to the stadium, things look lovely—and not at all conducive to going to a classroom for the first day of school.

The scene on the boardwalk as we head back to KeySpan is as spectacular as ever. Sunbathers fill the beach at a seemingly one-to-one ratio with the grains of sand, and the ocean is a panoply of sailboats. At various times during the fifteen-minute walk from the Houses to the bleacher entrance to the stadium, we spot Cyclone hats on fans speaking Spanish, Russian, and English. Steeplechase pier, jutting out behind the bleacher entrance, is more crowded than usual with chattering *pescadores,* while seagulls swoop above. If Rudy Giuliani had begun this project with the goal of making Coney Island a desired destination for people of all ages, races, and socioeconomic levels, he had pretty much achieved his goal— and pretty quickly. Unfortunately, this type of thinking doesn't seem to be part of his public vernacular. He speaks in terms of dollars and sense, even if what he's saying about the former doesn't always come out sounding like the latter. The fact that this place is presenting, on summer's unofficial last Sunday, one of the most diverse and crowded beach scenes you could find on the entire planet is as much thanks to the resiliency, diversity, and curiosity of all New Yorkers as to any mission of the mayor.

Leaving the Otero crew to enter through the back of the stadium with their customary bleacher tickets, I head to the front of the stadium before entering through the press entrance off the parking lot. The area in front and to the east of the stadium, on Surf Avenue, is crowded today, as well. Rainbow Village, the ramshackle flea market area on Surf that is in jeopardy of being closed by the city, is actually crammed with people perusing the aisles of bizarre baubles. And Nathan's is jammed, including the now-complete outdoor seating area that is drawing serious praise from visitors who haven't been here in the past month; the customers are biting into their hot dogs as if they contained the power to extend summer.

Inside the stadium, the players are eagerly preparing for the final regular-season game, the finale of a four-game series against the Batavia Muckdogs (property of the Philadelphia Phillies). A season of thrills and memorable moments continued throughout August. First, the beginning of the month brought the famous Brooklyn-bred filmmaker (and sports fan) Spike Lee out to KeySpan Park to shine his directorial light on some Cyclones. This wasn't a movie, though; it was a fashion photo shoot that *Harper's Bazaar* magazine had hired Lee to coordinate. Not surprisingly, along with Tyler Beuerlein, David Byard, Mike Cox, Forrest Lawson, Robert McIntyre, Angel Pagan, and Ross Peeples, Brett Kay was chosen to be part of the shoot. And he remembers the experience fondly. "So, yeah, Spike was doing a shoot for the magazine *Harper's Bazaar* after a game," begins Brett. "And, you know, Dave Campanaro and I were already real close, and I was always willing to do whatever he needed me to do. So when he asked me to be a part of it, I thought, yeah, why not?

Spike had some models down there with him, he took some pictures of us. It was cool!"

Continuing the story of his day as a model, Brett turns into a fan, not unlike the kids who have been approaching him for treats all summer. "I made sure I got a signed ball from him. I was sitting with Spike Lee! This is a guy who has done movies that I loved—*Do the Right Thing, Summer of Sam*. I mean, I really like this guy's movies. You don't always realize it when you're in the presence of powerful people, people that make a difference, and I didn't exactly when he was there. But once he left I thought about how cool it was."

Monday, August 20, a day off for the big-league New York Mets, brought another Met out to KeySpan, only this time it wasn't for a rehab stint. It was "John Franco Night" at KeySpan, as the Cyclones honored the long-time Mets' reliever who came out of Bensonhurst, in Brooklyn, and later starred at St. John's University and with the Cincinnati Reds before joining the Mets in 1990 and quickly becoming a fan favorite. The event brought Giuliani back to the ballpark, as well as the Mets' second baseman Edgardo Alfonzo (who got to check in with his brother, the Cyclones' manager) and the mercurial sports announcer Keith Olbermann, who was covering the game for local cable. The Cyclones sent their special guests home happy with a comeback win over the New Jersey Cardinals, 5–3.

Five days after Johnny Franco got his props from the Brooklyn fans, a whole different kind of excitement hit KeySpan when the Cyclones hosted the Renegades in their very next home game. The Cyclones, who had out-hit the rest of the league all season, were bashing the Renegades' pitchers all night, culminating with a three-home-run explosion in their half of the eighth inning. There were solo homers by Leandro Arias and Forrest Lawson and then, after the bases had loaded, a grand slam by the New York–Penn home-run leader, Frank Corr. Baseball's code dictates that so many round-trippers usually get rewarded with a brushback pitch, which theoretically puts the confident and free-swinging hitters back in their place. Sure enough, the Renegades' pitcher threw a fastball that looked like it was headed for backup catcher Francisco Sosa's head. The ball ended up hitting Sosa's bat when he ducked and ironically caromed into the field of play, forcing Sosa to run to first base, where he was forced out. But that did little to change Sosa's—and his teammates'—impression that the Renegades' pitcher had thrown a dirty brushback pitch. Next thing you knew, Sosa, joined shortly thereafter by a number of his teammates, including Joe Jiannetti, was going at the Renegades' first baseman; Jiannetti had a feeling a brushback pitch was coming. Some other Cyclones joined the melee, for which they paid the price. The fight's fallout included three-day suspensions and $75 fines for the six players who were involved, while Jiannetti, who was the most active, got a four-day suspension and a $100 fine. Brett was amused by the whole thing—that there was a fight, and that he didn't have to lose any games or money for having played too big of a role in it.

Two days after the fight game, the Cyclones videographer Vic Christopher showed up to show the guys how they had fared as small-time pugilists. With his copy of the game video and his portable camera in tow, Christopher walked around the dugout, laughingly showing the guys how they looked in action. The team was unquestionably bonding over this incident, and the players didn't mind looking together at the female fan shots that Christopher had snuck in, either. Babes and (home-run) bombs: what more would these guys all want to talk about? The suspensions and the video distraction may have been too much for the Cyclones, who lost on August 27, 9–2.

The next night they beat Pittsfield, 7–5, locking up Brooklyn's first playoff berth since the Dodgers were in the World Series in 1956.

The team is on a high, and it's lasted all week. On Wednesday, August 29, just the third off day of the season, many of the guys on the team went to a spa for hair changes and dye jobs—hence the freshly buzzed and fake-blonde hairstyles around the dugout. After the spa trip, most of the Cyclones went over to Shea Stadium for the Mets' game. Going to the Mets' game induced giddy reactions from most of these players, who are still essentially young kids who love baseball and still look up to big leaguers.

John Stearns's presence, as well as Brett's well-documented connections to baseball, meant that going to a big-league locker room wasn't quite as big a deal to Brett as it was to other guys on the team.

"It'll be my first Mets' game, so that should be cool. Hopefully, I'll get to meet some players and everything," said Blake McGinley beforehand.

"We had good seats, and then we got to go in the clubhouse," says Luz Portobanco. "I knew a couple of players already, but going to the game I met some more. It was a lot of fun."

Brett says that "the trip to Shea was cool. We had a suite, we got free food, and we got to go to the clubhouse. I didn't know how John [Stearns, the Mets' third-base coach and the former roommate of his father] would be, but he was real cool. He's the one that brought all of us into the clubhouse, and he was saying to everyone how he knew my dad and they used to be roommates and do this or that together."

The team is more relaxed than any game-day baseball team I've ever seen or heard of. First pitch for this twilight affair is at 5 p.m., and guys are just getting onto the field to stretch at 4:20 (on opening day, by way of contrast, some guys were here at 1 p.m. for a 7 p.m. start). They know that a long grind is winding down and that time with loved ones is not far off. But, more immediately, they are looking forward to the playoffs and a chance to bring Brooklyn its first title since 1955!

Many players, some of whom are heard croaking, "Water, water, can someone bring some water?" are also nursing some nasty hangovers today. Last night, the Cyclones won their fiftieth game of the season (against just twenty-two losses), and it was a historic night. The team clinched the McNamara Division title, giving all the players something to tell their grandkids about. After the game, a 7–6 come-from-behind victory over Batavia in which the Cyclones scored in each of the last four innings, champagne was sprayed in the locker room. And then the partying really began. While his teammates meander around the field to stretch and sign the requisite autographs with only about thirty minutes left until gametime, Rylie Ogle gives a recap of the previous night's activities. "We went to that bar Peggy O'Neill's," he says, mentioning a Bay

Ridge bar whose sign is splashed across the left-field wall. "They took care of us there. *Real* good care of us. I think I was double-fisted with beers most of the night. I'd finish one and be handed another. That went on until about 5:30 this morning, and you know nothing good happens then. I'm used to bars and clubs in California, which close at 2 a.m. When I looked at my watch and saw what time it was, I was pretty thrown. It was ugly. A bunch of us just ended up talking trash about who's the better basketball player."

Listening in, Ogle's bullpen mate McGinley confirms the account with a simple "I'm definitely done with beers for a while."

"Yep, you're right," Ogle replies. "I'm good, too."

Brett Kay is one of the few Cyclones who didn't take part in the all-night drinkfest. "I've got Bob and some other people in town, so I wanted to spend time with them," he says, putting on a game face that seems out of place next to his joking teammates. One of the most interesting things about Brett is the range of his emotions. In talking to Campanaro and watching the team interact during my time in the dugout and the locker room, I've seen proof that Brett can be the most personable, and at times the goofiest, guy on the team. But, when it comes time to get to work and think about the game at hand, Brett is arguably the most serious Cyclone, as his stern look today indicates. Given his lack of a hangover, Kay figures he's got a good shot to have a good game. I'm amazed he even cares, since the games don't count the way they did a couple of days ago. Then it hits me—these guys didn't get to become professional baseball players by taking days off, mentally or physically. If some guys let go last night, fine, they have an excuse to be out of it today, but for the most part they approach this job with a devotion that would shame 95 percent of the workers in America.

Brett's serious demeanor is further challenged this afternoon by the presence in the dugout of the team's "Cyclones for the Day," youngsters Mitchell Rappaport and Emily Izzo, both of whom are hanging out in the dugout with wide grins on their faces, talking most of all with the pitcher Harold Eckert, who has spoken in the past about his interest in kids and being a teacher someday. Mitchell is a roly-poly ten-year-old from

Midwood who answers my questions more seriously than most of the players do. The brief Q and As I give the kids reveal how many kids throughout the borough feel about the team.

How'd you get this job for tonight?

"I won it in a contest. I wrote something in a paper about the team, put it in a box, and they picked me."

Have you been to games before?

"Yeah, pretty many. I love coming here."

Where do you live?

"Avenue J."

Did you used to go to Met or Yankee games?

"Yeah. I've been to maybe three or four, and one Staten Island Yankee game. My father works for Brooklyn Skyline newspapers and he gets free tickets and stuff."

Do you like coming here better than Shea or Yankee stadiums because it's so close to where you live?

"Yeah. Of course."

Do you have a favorite player?

"No. Well, not really," Mitchell says sheepishly. "Do you know who Robert McIntyre is? It's him. I really want to get his autograph."

Last question—are the Cyclones your favorite team?

"Minor League they are. The Mets are my favorite Major League team. I think I'd rather the Mets win a title."

Mitchell's partner for the day is Emily Izzo, a cute and precocious twelve-year-old from nearby on 3rd Street.

You won this award the same way as Mitchell?

"Yeah, my dad filled something out for me at the bank."

Had you been to some games before tonight?

"Yeah, about ten or twelve."

Did you used to go to Met or Yankee games?

"Yeah. All the time. I prefer the Mets' games because I don't really like the Yankees. I guess that's one of the main reasons that I like the Cyclones. Not just that I like the Cyclones but because I like the Mets."

Who would you rather see win a championship—Mets or Cyclones?

"I think, maybe, the Cyclones, because they represent just Brooklyn. I like the Mets, but they are New York. I'm for whoever represents just Brooklyn."

At about 4:50, the kids leave the dugout for their first-row seats, while the writers and reporters head to the press box. When the game begins, Kay's professionalism doesn't exactly produce much excitement, for him or the team, as the game is a boring affair with all the offensive firepower of a college fast-pitch softball game. Watching the game brings back flashbacks to opening night, when the outfielders played so shallow they looked like extra infielders and the hitters looked as though they'd never picked up a wooden bat before.

As espn.com's gifted baseball writer Rob Neyer put it after a trip that brought him to games at KeySpan Park and Richmond County Ballpark, the sport, at this level, is played at a much "smaller" level than its big-league parent.

Would you like to guess how many bunts we saw in [one] game? Seven. Three sacrifice hits, two bunts for base hits, one bunt designed as a base hit that became an out, and a foul bunt (also designed as a base hit) that presaged a strikeout. Meanwhile—and I regret that I didn't keep precise track of this—most of the hitters on both teams acted like their biggest regret in life is that there's nothing to swing at *before* the first pitch. I know that it's important to teach the kids all those nifty fundamentals, but don't you think it's a little strange that teams would be stressing one of the *least* important skills (bunting) while apparently completely disregarding one of the *most* important skills (plate discipline)? As a fan, I love the combination because bunts and first-pitch swinging results in a fast-paced, entertaining game. But minor-league teams aren't there to entertain fans, they're there to develop baseball players. And this seems a strange way to go about it.

Not that the fans mind the style of play. As most of the fans I speak to put it, they know what they're here for. Neyer, who hails from Kansas, would later write, "There's a big difference in the fans [in Brooklyn], too.

The people in the Ballpark at St. George didn't strike me as a whole lot different from the fans you might see in, say, Kane County (IL.) or Bakersfield (CA.). You watch a game with the fans in Brooklyn, though, and you *know* that you're in Brooklyn. I was inside the gates for less than a minute before I heard one Brooklynite cuss out another Brooklynite, and while the fans were generally a well-behaved lot, they were a bit rowdy and not at all self-conscious about it, in that way that distinguishes native northeasterners from the rest of us."

If there's any day when the fans should feel free to be their Brooklyn selves it's today, which has been christened "Fan Appreciation Day" by the organization. Everyone got a poster, there are further giveaways throughout the game, and as usual hordes of kids are on the scene. Afterward, as per Sunday custom, the kids will be allowed on the field to run the bases, an adventure that Anthony has happily taken part in several times this summer—and will today as well.

Incidentally, if any fans deserve appreciation, it's this record-setting bunch. The crowd for today is announced as a record: "Eight thousand, two hundred, and forty-eight people," the press box is told. That's 8,248, in a stadium thought days before this season began to have a capacity of 6,500. The opening-night program, in fact, had explained and diagramed the capacity in detail. There was, of course, no mention of the bleachers in that program, which had been printed a week before the first game. "It looks really full today," agrees Dave Campanaro, "They released about as many tickets as they can, and we had all the luxury boxes filled. I think it looks great in here."

This is yet another overcapacity crowd in a summer that's been filled with them. For the season, the Cyclones are averaging 7,821 per game. This number shatters the previous New York–Penn League record and puts the team well ahead of the other league attendance leaders, who must all be proud themselves. Going into the last three days of the regular season, Mahoning Valley, Staten Island, and Lowell are all averaging better than 5,000 fans per game. The Cyclones even came *this close* to surpassing the average attendance of one Major League team (the Montreal Expos, who are last in the majors with a well-below-capacity average of 7,900 fans per game, albeit while playing eighty-one home games).

Campanaro explains how the team can keep packing fans in, even when "capacity" has been met. "The 7,500 number does not include the luxury boxes, which hold a couple hundred people when they're filled, or the maximum number of people we can get in the bleachers. Since there's no actual seats in the bleachers [the tickets for out there are all general admission] and those tickets are only available during the day of the game, sometimes when the demand is high enough they'll release some more tickets."

There's also enough elbow room in the concourses for the team to sell standing-room tickets, which it has started to do. And on some days season-ticket holders don't show up—not really a surprise since they put out such a small amount relatively on each game—so the team can sell upward of 8,000 tickets but have closer to 7,000 fans in the stadium. "Attendance" always refers to tickets sold, which helps the Cyclones. Today looks like one of those "everyone with a ticket is here" kind of days, however, which is a pleasure for anyone who likes the look of a sold-out ballpark.

The whole vista is more than even Cyclone execs expected or even hoped for. "[When the team was created], we thought we'd be doing very well if our attendance averaged three to four thousand a game," the team's general manager, Steve Cohen, told the *Daily News*. "But the longer we were here the more enthusiasm we saw."

While "supply" has become a somewhat nebulous term as it relates to tickets, one place the supply is finite—and therefore out—is Cyclone City, the ballpark's classy souvenir store. This afternoon it looks like a college dorm the day a kid goes home for the summer—cleaned out and not all that clean. About all that is on the rack are some Ebbets Field t-shirts. I ask one of the employees what happened. "Man, we've sold out of like every Cyclone thing we've got." Two days later, in the *New York Times,* the Cyclones' senior vice president for business affairs, R. C. Reuteman, will say that the team has sold more merchandise than "any team in the minor leagues save one," and that, by the end of playoffs, the Cyclones are "expected to pass the reigning champions," the Triple-A Pacific Coast League Sacramento River Cats, "whose season is twice as long."

One person who can't act too surprised by the Cyclones' runaway success is Mayor Giuliani, who strong-armed the team into existence with promises that went far beyond big crowds inside the stadium. There's little proof all the "development" that Giuliani mentioned will get done outside the stadium, but as for what has happened inside its walls, the mayor considers this season a success. And, as with much of what he's been involved in over the years—the plunging crime rates, achieved with a "By Any Means Necessary" tactic, for example—Giuliani will say that the ends justify the means. As much money as the city spent on his advice, the fact is the project came out beautifully and Brooklyn residents have a fun new activity with which to occupy their summer evenings. As Giuliani readily acknowledges in Dawidoff's article in the *New York Times Magazine,* there was no referendum in which people could vote on whether they wanted to foot the bill for either the Cyclones' park or the Yankees' new stadium in Staten Island. The reason, he says firmly, is that "they would have voted it down. That's why you need a leader. Somebody who has some vision." And, well beyond the robust attendance figures the teams are pulling in, Giuliani reiterates his heretofore unproven promise that the impact will extend outside the stadium. In the same story, he says his legacy will be the creation of "the anchor of the economic redevelopment of two neighborhoods that desperately need it."

In the same article, Dick Zigun, the artistic director of Coney Island USA, says, "Financially, we haven't seen any change yet. But in terms of people's impression of Coney Island, there is already a significant change."

There is no sign of a hotel yet and, according to the Cyclones, no guarantee that one is coming. But still, Michael Carey, head of the New York City Economic Development Corporation, which helped Giuliani push this stadium plan through, tells the *Daily News* that this is just the beginning of Coney Island's revitalization. "There is going to be more private investment and development. [And there is still] money in the budget [and land between the stadium and the amusement area] for some type of sports facility, which could be built in lieu of the SportsPlex."

Of course, what has happened this summer by no means satisfies all those who objected to the way this team was created. After all, Howard Golden, the outgoing borough president and father of the SportsPlex idea, had predicted that a Minor League team in Coney Island could probably plan on attracting almost twice as many fans as the Cyclones have averaged, and on twice as many dates, to boot. Given that the Cyclones have almost outdrawn the Major League Expos, it seems inarguable that Coney Island could support at least a Double-A team in a slightly expanded KeySpan Park. Golden has, for the most part, let his silence on the subject all summer speak louder than anything he could say. About the most that came out of his office was a terse statement, made before one of the Cyclone-Yankee match-ups earlier this summer: "Although the competition between the Brooklyn Cyclones and Staten Island Yankees cannot replace the rivalries of old, I am certain the borough looks forward to many heated contests between the two teams."

As has been the case all year, the larger civic issues surrounding this team's genesis could not be further from the minds of the fans packed into KeySpan Park this evening. Judging from the cross-section of fans selected for the various in-game contests, this crowd is not quite as big-city as the one on opening day. The fans who streamed in from Long Island, New Jersey, and Manhattan in their SUVs aren't as prevalent today. Instead, it's a pan-Brooklyn experience. There are four fans who get introduced to the crowd by Party Marty, the Cyclones' human mascot, for trivia questions and the like that get played on the video scoreboard; one is from Mill Basin, the next from Prospect Heights, the third from Marine Park, and the fourth from Sheepshead Bay. And, if their telling of their home neighborhood didn't give it away, their accents surely would have. "Party Marty" is pug-faced Marty Haber, who spends his days selling group tickets to see the Cyclones, but his true calling seems to be entertaining Brooklyn baseball fans, which he's done quite well all season by appealing to the Brooklyn pride in the average Cyclone fan.

Party Marty is just one of many diversions presented to the fans, just in case the action on the field or the views one can see aren't enough. This is a trend that has been happening, for better or worse, at ballparks across the country. And, since the research dictates that Minor League fans are younger and there less for the game than for the atmosphere, teams have taken it upon themselves to assault fans with distractions of all sorts. Besides the microphone-wielding Marty, the team also presents Sandy the Seagull on a nightly basis. Sandy is a costume seagull who does a good job of entertaining the fans subtly, in the spirit of old-school baseball mascots like the Phillie Phanatic and Mr. Met. At some games, Sandy is joined by some other costume animals with baseball themes—the "Zooperstars," with names such as "Shark McGwire" and "Clammy Sosa"—for further between-inning hijinks. There is also loud music and nonstop contests, from the trivia questions to games on the field, where fans have to do things like spin around, blindfolded, with their head on a bat pointed at the ground and then find an object. The whole onslaught comes off as overbearing to fans who find the game and the stadium to be entertainment enough, but the thinking is that obviously many people enjoy this chaos, or else they wouldn't all be here.

Anthony and his friends get a kick out of the between-inning entertainment, and they definitely enjoy cruising the concourse during the game, eyeing the snack bar and often running into classmates who don't live in their complex. But when he's in a seat and the game is in progress, Anthony watches the game as closely as any scout. "I watch real close so I could learn," he says during the game, wearing an uncharacteristically serious expression. "I learn a lot at these games. I watch how they throw—there's a way they do it that doesn't hurt your arm. I learn how to play the outfield, like what the guys do when the ball bounces off the wall. I can learn a lot by watching in person. How they bat, how they stand when they're at bat, how they lead off the base and steal bases." Anthony adds that, because he still considers himself a Yankee fan more than anything, he's not going to spend his time at the game cheering wildly. "I'd rather just chill and watch the game," he states.

Anthony's whole crew is in heaven—even Mr. Otero. "I've bought tickets a couple of times this season, but I've always let them come and have fun," says Anthony Sr. "So this is my first time inside here. I think it's amazing. They really needed something like this in the neighborhood. It used to be a ghost town in this part, you know, once you got past where the rides are. Now you've got the team and all the people it's bringing, it's great. And these kids love it."

The sluggish Cyclones end up losing the game, 1–0, with Peeples turning in a great performance on the mound but the offense managing just four hits, none by Brett. Brett actually came to bat with two outs in the ninth, took his wide stance, and tried to tie the game with one swing. Instead, he grounded out, ending a frustrating game in frustrating fashion. Still, with the game—and the regular home season—over, the Cyclone players go on a gift-giving extravaganza. Brett is one of the most active givers, as he and his teammates literally dig into their bags and pull out anything they can find, from t-shirts to sunflower seeds to sweaty old batting gloves, and hand them out to their fervent supporters. The players are also autographing anything waved in their face, and they seem nearly as happy as those doing the waving. Among the autograph hunters is the group from the Coney Island Houses. While Mr. Otero looks on with a smile, Anthony, James, and Josimar are hanging out around the autograph hunters, several rows up the first-base side above the Cyclones dugout, like they're almost too cool to be fighting for goodies now that they've been here so many times—and already possess the autographs, balls, and sunflower seeds to prove it. The kids are also laughing and joking with some of the ushers and vendors who know who the kids are because they've been here so often. "That's our man Ray," says Anthony, gesturing at one of the ushers while slapping five with an ice-cream vendor. "He's the one that usually looks out for us and lets us sit where we want."

As on the playground back home, Anthony is a leader here, helping determine when the kids watch and when they walk around. He's also the one who usually decided when the guys will come to the games. Still, his involvement with the team this summer doesn't lend itself to any in-depth analysis of how he thinks it happened, given the lack of enthusiasm Anthony possessed for the Cyclones just months ago. Anthony says he "remembers" that he didn't care about the Cyclones at first, but he can't elaborate on what changed. After some prodding, Anthony says, "I guess I'm just happy about the stadium because otherwise it really is boring around here. We wanted to care at first, but it didn't seem like we could get tickets. Once we realized we could, we went all the time. We been to at least ten games. It gives us something to do."

Now Anthony is turning his attention to tomorrow, wondering whether he'll try to get playoff tickets, which will go on sale tomorrow at 9 a.m. People are already lining up to spend the night out here. Unsure of his ticket plans, Anthony gives a great answer to my final question of the day: What will you write about if they give you that assignment kids always get in school, "What did you do over the summer?" "Oh, they'll definitely ask us to do that. School always asks for that. I'm going to tell them about the Cyclones," says Anthony, beaming, "'cause that was the biggest thing for me."

With that, Anthony and his boys jog down the few rows to the field and hop the short fence down the right-field line from the dugout. They're on the field, joining scores of other kids for the weekly Sunday promotion, "Modell's Kids Run the Bases."

Out of gifts and with their hand muscles fatigued from signing so much stuff, the Cyclone players, most of whom are completely exhausted from last night's festivities, retire to the locker room, where the scene is completely mellow. The opening-night media throng seems years ago, as does the opening-night sense of nerves that gripped most of these young guys, many of whom were just beginning their careers. Despite the growth he's enjoyed since that night, not to mention the relaxed atmosphere, the division title that was clinched last night, and the twenty minutes of joy he just provided for kids with his autograph signing and gift giving, Brett is in a pretty bad mood as he strips off his uniform. "I've got people visiting me that came to this game, and I don't think they had a very good time today because I had a horseshit game," Kay says sharply. "I didn't think that pitcher was good at all, but he shut me down. The other guys might have been flat because they went out last night, but I shouldn't have been; I wasn't with them."

Brett also looks ahead a little, to a time when a season that's been tremendously fun but physically grueling will come to an end. In the process, he helps explain why he might've had a bad game, especially since there was nothing at stake. "Man, I'm tired as shit. I've always been skinny, but I started to lose even more weight recently. I can feel my body deteriorating. And as a catcher that's already skinny, I don't have much more I can afford to lose. Being in the apartment in Manhattan helps me try and eat as well as I can, but it's been a long haul. This 'season,' if you want to call it that, started for me in January, working out like nine hours a day with my college team and catching almost every game for them. Then I come here, catch almost every day, and we have like three days off out of seventy-nine, or something like that. The physical part has been tough. I can't wait to get home."

Before California, however, Brett's going to Florida for Instructional League, an optional, invitation-only session that most organizations hold for their prospects through September and part of October. As he says, "It's really, really good that the team wants to keep working with me after the season, and I'm going to go. . . . I think the organization likes me and is happy with the season I've had. I think I have enough to make it. And if not, not. But if I do, well, what a great life that would be. And to do that I need to go to Instructional League. But [Instructional League] kind of sucks because that's another month away from home, away from my girlfriend, away from my dogs. I can't wait to get back there, hang out with everyone, eat, drink, and put some weight back on. As soon as Instructional League ends, I'm not playing again until next spring training."

Getting back to the big picture, I remind Brett that the 1–0 loss was a meaningless game and ask him to consider all that's happened in the past ten weeks, including the visit by his man Bob, who surely wasn't that upset that he saw Brett have a poor day at the plate. Brett gets the picture and smiles. "Having Bob here now, and my brother a couple weeks ago, has been great, because I don't think my family and friends back home realize just how cool it is, that we're playing on this field, that I'm playing for the Brooklyn Cyclones. I tell them what I can, and everyone thinks it's awesome and everything, but it's more than that. Actually playing here, I think it's been the best experience possible."

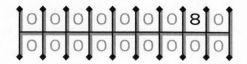

The Postseason

The playoffs have brought a new intensity level to KeySpan Park, and Brett is in the middle of the excitement. But before he gets ready for the decisive Game Three of the playoffs, he recalls another highlight of his Brooklyn summer, which took place the morning after the final home game of the regular season.

The night after the 1–0 loss to the Muckdogs, Brett said farewell to his out-of-town visitors and actually did go out, having some drinks with his teammates and staying out extremely late for the first time this summer. Without question, it was a night for crashing in Staten Island, as opposed to taking the late-night subway to Manhattan. The next morning, a Monday, the team was to meet at KeySpan for a bus to Batavia, New York (like Jamestown, where the Cyclones began their season, the 16,000-person Batavia, outside Rochester, is a far cry from Brooklyn), where the team would play its final series of the regular season.

With the playoff berth clinched, people were on line to buy playoff tickets when the players straggled up to the ballpark Monday morning. Recalls Brett,

When they put the tickets on sale before we played Batavia, there was a huge line that morning for tickets. I had stayed out late the night before and ended up staying up all night, but I got to the stadium and all these fans were there already. The tickets were going on sale at 9 a.m. or something, but people had been there since the night before! It was amazing.

So, after I dropped my stuff in the locker room and before our bus left, I went out there where people were waiting. I went up to the first person in line and said, "Hey, here's a bat just for being so loyal." There were a couple news cameras there, and they put me on TV with one of the kids I was talking to on line. It's, like, seven in the morning, I'd gotten no sleep, and here I am, talking to the reporter, all "This is great, look at how happy these people are. What a great opportunity for them to be part of this." We were just meeting to take the bus, and even that turned into something. It was so cool to be out there and realize how many fans we have. I was running back into the clubhouse to get 'em whatever stuff we hadn't given away after the game the night before. The fans were loving that.

Although the playoff pairings weren't completely set when the tickets went on sale, it took only a little imagination to figure out who the Cyclones would be playing . . . the Staten Island Yankees. The *Daily News* even lent its level of legitimacy to the best-of-three series by printing up a special section before the series began on Thursday, September 6.

The regular season ended with the Cyclones owning a division- and league-best record of 52–24; Williamsport, of the Pinckney-Stedler division, had the second-best mark at 48–26 (the games-played differential resulted from rainouts that were never made up). The Cyclones ended the regular season with their names all over the New York–Penn League leaderboards, including Frank Corr, with thirteen home runs, Angel Pagan, with thirty stolen bases, Jay Caliguiri, with a .328 batting average, and Ross Peeples and Harold Eckert, with nine wins each. Peeples also led the league in ERA with a minuscule 1.34 mark. Brett had a batting average of .311 and an on-base average of .380 in 201 plate appearances, with five home runs and eighteen RBIs. Brett's stats don't jump off the page, but, considering they come from a catcher who did not join the team until the season was a week old and the lineup until it was a week older, the numbers are good enough, especially when combined with his athleticism, defense, and the emotional intangibles he brings to a team, to maintain people's impression of Brett as a legitimate pro prospect. And his best moment is yet to come.

New York–Penn League rules dictate that the first two teams in each division have a playoff to see which will advance to the championship series. In the Cyclones' case, second place in the McNamara Division belonged, of course, to the Yankees, whose debut season has been pretty special in its own right. On the field, the "Baby Bombers" went 48–28, while prospects such as John-Ford Griffin and Aaron Rifkin excelled at the plate. Rifkin, Brett's good buddy from Fullerton, was the league's Most Valuable Player, in fact, hitting .318 with ten home runs and forty-nine RBIs.

Staten Island's season was considered a big hit at the box office, as well; the team averaged just under 5,000 fans per game all season. And, as the organization's chief operating officer, Josh Getzler, told the *News*, something about these teams' seasons seemed fated to involve a playoff match-up. "I have believed, since I knew the Cyclones were coming and we'd both be playing in beautiful new stadiums, that it would be shocking if both teams didn't meet in the playoffs."

After losing the first game of the series on the road, 6–1, the Cyclones took care of their home field advantage, winning a sloppy Game Two 8–4 on Friday night (with Brett scoring the go-ahead run), to set up tonight's decisive Game Three. It's a crisp, late-summer evening, with the ocean breeze less a relief to the heat than an element that is making fans thankful they have an extra layer on tonight.

There are more than 8,000 fans crammed into KeySpan Park, Fox Sports New York is televising a Cyclone game live for the first time all season, and the mayor is on hand again, beaming throughout. How could he not be happy? One of the teams he brought to life is going to make the New York–Penn League championship series in the first year of their rivalry.

Luckily for the Cyclones, their manager, Alfonzo, had set up the pitching rotation so that the team's star, Peeples, would get the start. Peeples is up to the challenge, pitching brilliantly and shutting the visiting Yankees out through six full innings. The Cyclones, meanwhile, get a run in the bottom of the fifth when the speedy Angel Pagan drives in a run on an infield single. Nursing a 1–0 lead in the top of the seventh, Peeples allows runners to reach first and second base with no outs. This is Brett Kay's turn to assert himself. Trying to get the runners into scoring position, the visitors try a sacrifice bunt, which is dropped in front of home plate. The athletic Brett is not going for it, barehanding the bad bunt and whipping the ball to third to get the lead runner. The next Yankee batter hits a line drive to left. By all indications, the tying run will score, and the groan that's emitted from this 95-percent Cyclone, 5-percent Yankee crowd seemingly proves it. In fact, all one has to do is look at Brett, who's got his hands placed dejectedly on his hip as the game-tying runner, Jason Turner, cruises around third and heads home. But wait! Brett is pulling a trick out of Little League. As the Cyclone left fielder John Toner chases down the ball and unloads a bullet throw right to home plate, Kay rapidly snaps to attention and, in one slick motion, catches the throw and tags out the duped Turner, who had slowed when he saw Brett standing as if there was no shot at getting him out. The Cyclones' tenuous lead preserved through Brett's remarkable defense, the team gets the last out of the inning and whoops their way into the dugout for the bottom of the seventh.

Pagan drives in another run in the seventh to make it 2–0, although that lead doesn't appear that safe when McGinley, relieving Peeples, allows a run in the top of the eighth. As if his brilliant defensive play weren't enough, Brett comes up in the bottom of the eighth and smacks a towering two-run homer to left field, raising his arms into the air as he rounds the bases and pushing the lead to 4–1. Blake McGinley strikes out the side in the ninth, then serves as the foundation for a huge pile-up at the mound, which is how the series ends for the championship-bound Brooklyn Cyclones.

With his trademark-able cackle/laugh and ear-to-ear grin, Kay explains his trick in the boisterous postgame locker room. "I call it 'The Dead Man.' I've been doing it since Little League," he says.

Later, he recaps the absurdity of helping win a game with the "Dead Man." "Well, that's the biggest memory of the greatest game of my life," Brett says with a wide smile.

I had never used that play all season. Bob and Mike had taught me that, and I remember when they showed me being like, "That's never gonna work." I did use it a couple times in high school, but not since then. That game, man, by far was the greatest game I've ever played in my life. It was like something above just said, Hey, it's your turn to shine. My teammates were great that game, too. First I made the play on the bunt. Then the Yankee guy hit it to the right place, Toner made a perfect throw, and for some reason I just thought of it. I was feeling kind of mellow about it, saying to myself, "I hope this guy doesn't score. I should try the Dead Man play." He was out—for sure—and I don't even know if he touched home plate. I just said to myself, "Wow. *That* was a cool play." Then I came up the next inning and hit the home run. I remember because the first pitch was an outside fastball and I checked my swing. I thought I went, but the ump said no and called it a ball. So that would've changed the whole at-bat if I had been 0–1. The next pitch was a fastball that he left in a good spot to hit. I don't know what happened after I hit it—I was just in a zone. I remember rounding the bases, and the place was just pumped. I threw off my helmet, everyone was pumped.

One of the men in the stands for Brett's heroics, though presumably not waving his arms madly, was Steve Phillips, the Mets' general manager. When Brett finds this out—that the Mets' boss, more or less, watched him be the star—he beams. "I did perform well, so maybe that caught their eye or whatever. I performed well all season, and I gave my all every game, because that's how I play," says Brett, lapsing into motivational speak that sounds hokey when delivered by an established pro but perfectly believable coming from Brett. "As a competitor, you have to give all you have every day, or else you're cheating yourself and your teammates. That game I think signified the way I played all year, and I just think someone, somewhere, said, 'You've played your ass off and you deserve this game.' It was just a huge game. My early at-bats [against the Yankees' highly touted starter Javier Ortiz] made me look silly. But they put the other guy in to relieve, and it was just hoopla from there."

Brett's joyousness in the wake of the dramatic Game Three victory over the Yankees carried outside the stadium. "Walking outside, I was so happy after that game. Fans didn't want autographs, they just wanted hugs. People were just like, 'You guys are awesome.' The first person I called was Bob, who was home in San Diego, and I said, 'You won't believe what I just did—the Dead Man play!' And he said, 'I saw it. It was on TV on the satellite, and it was the most unbelievable game I've ever seen you play.' I was in the right place at the right time."

Not everyone who cares about the Cyclones is in the stands, however. Anthony and his friends were shut out of the stadium, but there was no bitterness this time. "We went over there, but that game was sold out. We weren't surprised, though, because it's the playoffs and all," Anthony says on the phone the day after the Cyclones had advanced. "But my mom put in on TV, and me and my boys watched it. That was a great game!"

The Cyclones' storybook—really, you couldn't make this season up—victory over the Yankees advanced them into the New York–Penn League championship series. Their opponent will be the Pinckney-Stedler regular-season and playoff champion Williamsport (PA) Crosscutters, the Pittsburgh Pirates' affiliate, which reached the finals by beating the Jamestown Jammers two games to one. Because of a New York–Penn League system that rotates home field for the championship on an annual basis, Williamsport has home field, even though the Cyclones have the better record. Not that the Cyclone players have any doubt that the title will be theirs. "We know we need to win two more games, and I know we'll get 'em," says Brett.

There's championship fever in Brooklyn in 2001, and that's a welcome idea to a lot of fans. With all the excitement that the idea of baseball in Coney Island has provided this summer, one can forget that simply the existence of professional baseball in Brooklyn is enough to bring tears of joy to some long-time Brooklynites. To begin with, the Cyclones' birth brought up memories galore, from personal family recollections to ones focused on Brooklyn's rich baseball history, thanks almost entirely to the lovable Brooklyn Dodgers and their earlier incarnations.

◆

Hy Bueller is a seventy-nine-year-old baseball fan and Coney Island resident. Hy and his late wife moved into the Warbass Co-Ops at Neptune Avenue and Ocean Parkway within a year of their being built, in January 1965. He was born on the Lower East Side of Manhattan, then moved out to Brooklyn as a teen, then back to the Lower East Side, then back to Brooklyn. Hy lived in Brooklyn during the Dodgers' heyday and went to many games, "riding the trolley" to Bedford Avenue. Hy was at the first night game in Ebbets Field history, in June 1938, when Johnny Vander Meer pitched the second of his consecutive no-hitters, a feat that has never been matched. "I was sixteen at the time, and it was an amazing game to see," Bueller says excitedly. "Can you believe it—two straight no-hitters! And at night!"

Ebbets Field in this era of baseball in Brooklyn—which continued after Durocher left, thanks to the Dodgers' continued success and the awesome rivalry with the Yankees—was the place to be. Earlier this season, the *New York Times*'s long-time columnist Dave Anderson was moved by the Cyclones' birth to think back on his Dodger experiences.

> If you were a kid in Brooklyn during the 1942 pennant race, which the Cardinals won, heaven was sitting in the upper center-field bleachers for 55 cents with a bag of bologna sandwiches and enough nickels to buy Cokes during a Sunday doubleheader with the Cardinals. . . . By the seventh inning of the second game, when most of the ushers had left, you sneaked down through the stands and sat behind third base. You got to Ebbets Field on the subway, getting off at the Prospect Park station on the BMT, and you went home on the subway.

As a former resident of a home just blocks from Ebbets Field, the New York City businessman Steve Asch recalls "*living* at Ebbets Field. From as soon as school ended in June until it started in September—and even some days when I should have been in school—my best friend and I would be going to games."

The high point in Brooklyn Dodger history came with the 1955 World Series victory over the Yankees, Brooklyn's first and only World Series in nine tries. But the glory of 1955 was short-lived, for baseball in Brooklyn evaporated faster than any fan could have imagined. Reports of today show that the Dodgers' owner, Walter O'Malley, was growing increasingly frustrated with Ebbets Field and was in talks with Robert Moses about finding an appropriate place in Brooklyn to build a new park for the Dodgers. Working behind the scenes, Moses and O'Malley negotiated but couldn't find a suitable solution. So, with a healthy offer on the table to move to Los Angeles, O'Malley took the money and ran after the 1957 season ended. Just like that, the Dodgers were gone, and three years later Ebbets Field was, as well. But the public was caught totally unaware by this turn of events and ultimately blamed O'Malley, who remained public enemy number one in the borough until his death in 1979. The fact that the general public didn't know anything was amiss is proven by the far-from-capacity crowd (fewer than 7,000 total) that showed up on September 24, 1957, for the last game at Ebbets Field. Nowadays, when a stadium closes, it's a marketing scheme that's milked all year, with fans buying souvenir t-shirts, stadium chairs, whatever, and coming out in droves to see the final game. But no one in Brooklyn knew to consider that game the last one. "There was no talk like that," recalls Asch, almost still in shock. "That announcement that they were leaving, it came like a bolt of lightning. It was like someone had taken my right arm from me."

That year, 1957, seems ages ago, but there are many residents of the borough who can still describe their favorite Dodger moment or list the starting lineup from the 1955 World Series. The Dodgers and their fans had a love affair that few teams can equal. Perhaps it was the players' involvement in the community (from signing autographs to eating at the same diner as their fans) or their status as lovable losers (despite their regular season prowess, the Brooklyns won just that single World Series). Whatever it was, the team had a following that is still loyal today and that has been immortalized in many books and countless pop culture references. For the Cyclones, a Class-A Minor League team, to hope to replicate this type of popularity is obviously absurd, but people seem willing to embrace the team on their own terms. When you get into questions of whether it's the same, however, the fans who were in Brooklyn for the Dodgers are not ready to make that type of statement.

Asch made his first visit to KeySpan toward the end of the regular season. "I went from work one night, and we had a good time," Asch says. "It's definitely cool. But it does not mean that the glory days of baseball have been restored in Brooklyn."

Bueller agrees. "I was supposed to go to a game a couple of weeks ago," he says in early September. "But I ended up not going. I understand there's a lot of excitement about the team, but it is just a Minor League team, and it doesn't really feel like professional baseball. It's very novel, a good idea more for the youngsters than people who were Dodger fans."

Even the fans who are fully supporting the Cyclones aren't ready to go all the way with their praise. Richard Kissell, of Westchester County, a forty-five-year-old with New York City roots and a Cyclones miniseason-ticket, was interviewed by the *Journal News* earlier in the season. "There's no way there's ever going to be [Major League baseball] back in Brooklyn. Maybe a Triple-A team. There is a symmetry in the fact that baseball is being played in Brooklyn. I do enjoy that, but I don't look at it as a replacement."

Still, as has been said before, many of the things that made the Dodgers popular—among which were winning and accessibility—are as true of the Cyclones as they were of the Dodgers. Bumping into Rylie Ogle on the street can't be as thrilling as bumping into the Dodger pitcher Don Newcombe, but the reaction from the player is similar—a handshake and an autograph. The fans here appreciate that. And Ogle says it happens all the time. "In the last couple weeks I've had all sorts of people just stop me and say 'thank you' for what we're doing," he says.

The appreciation for the Cyclones has also remained extremely visible on the team's website. A good example of the unabashed love many fans have for the concept of baseball in Brooklyn comes from a poster named Josh Siegel, who writes, "Brooklyn baseball has more heart and character

than the Mets and Yanks combined, even if it's only the minor league
now. Go Cyclones!" Or, from another message poster, Mike Stephens,
"Baseball in Brooklyn? It's like something out of a dream . . . like mythol-
ogy come to life. For those who are too young to have seen it the first
time; for those who remember the days long gone, and for my grand-
mother, who loved Duke Snider until the day she died . . . Play Ball! Let's
go Cyclones!"

Smartly, the Cyclone organization has certainly milked the Dodgers'
past while building up its own image. The VIP/Will Call entrance to the
stadium is through a doorway with a sign that reads "Brooklyn Baseball
Club." No Mets' reference, no "Cyclones," just Brooklyn. As the Dodgers
used to do it. And in Cyclone City, the team's massive souvenir store, no
team is better represented than the Brooklyn Dodgers. There are replica
hats and t-shirts and countless Brooklyn Dodger baubles that allow the
fans to enjoy today while recognizing the past. The blast from the past,
"Hit Sign, Win Suit" billboard has even come into play. It was back in the
season's first homestand, in fact, when the Cyclone slugger Jay Caliguiri
rapped a double off the sign. Weeks later, Caliguiri accepted his just
reward from Garage Clothing, saying, "I'm glad I hit that sign, because I
definitely needed a new suit. It's a good tradition."

Caliguiri is not the only Cyclone who realizes what history is being
lived out. "Everything that happened with the Brooklyn Dodgers was
before I was born, so I had never experienced anything like that, nor did
I know what a big deal they were," says Blake McGinley. "But it didn't
take long to learn. Now that I'm here and everyone is excited about us,
and comparing the Brooklyn Cyclones to the Brooklyn Dodgers, I'm
happy to be a part of it."

Kay figured it out quickly, as well. "What I knew about this team
before I got here is that Bob had told me it was a nice ballpark, and I
thought it sounded sweet. But I didn't really know what to expect or what
was going to go on here. I figured the key was just to come to New York
and enjoy myself. Next thing I knew I was having the time of my life. . . .
It's just been a great, unforgettable season. The fans love it here, we love

it here. It's already a win-win situation for everyone, no matter how our season ends."

Game One of the championship series was played in Williamsport on Monday night, September 10. The Cyclones defeated the Crosscutters, 7–4, and drove back to Brooklyn happily, knowing a league championship was just one win away (with long-awaited time with the family and friends to follow). And, with Portobanco and Peeples due up in the rotation, winning one more game should not have been a difficult task. "Winning Game One was easy, so we knew they had no chance against us back at home," Brett would recall later. "It was like a three-hour bus ride back to the stadium. They dropped us off around 2 a.m., and I just went to Staten Island with the guys. I was planning to wake up the next day [an off day, with Game Two scheduled for September 12 and Game Three, if necessary, scheduled for the thirteenth] and go back to my apartment and hang out."

He never made it, and Games Two and Three never happened.

This book, more than anything else, is told by Brett Kay and Anthony Otero. And this is how they experienced September 11. "So we woke up in Staten Island at about eight in the morning, we're watching TV, and we just don't know what's going on," recalls Brett.

We went out to the Staten Island pier and saw the second building crumble and it was just like, "Dude, what's going on?" All the terrorist stuff starts coming out, and you don't know how to feel. My family was frantic. My family and friends back home were freaking out, they knew that it was a plan of mine to go to the World Trade Center on a day off, and even if I didn't do that, for all they knew about New York my apartment was right next to the World Trade Center. And I had been on the subway underneath the World Trade Center a bunch of times. I had my cell phone, but nobody could get through to me. When they eventually did, my mom was crying, and my girlfriend was crying. It turns out that even if I was in Chelsea I would've been far enough away, but what if I had chosen that day to go down and enjoy the Trade Center? You don't know what could have happened. It was shocking, and it was a bummer things had to end that way. Obviously, the championship was the furthest thing from my mind when I thought about all the people that died. This was something that is going to be on people's minds for at least the next five or ten years, and probably forever.

Anthony had been in high school for one week. "I was in class at Lincoln when it happened," he says somberly.

My teacher said that both of the Twin Towers blew up. She brung in a TV so we could watch it. They kept showing the planes crashing and everybody was shocked, everybody was crying. The school has kids whose parents worked in the Trade Center. There was a girl in my class, and both her parents worked there or were there for business that day, and she just said, "My parents just died," and she was saying that nobody else in her family cares about her. It was sad.

They sent everybody home from school because they didn't know what was happening. They thought there were going to be terrorist attacks everywhere. They said, "We're going to cut this day short. Go home, everybody, be safe." And they let us go. So we went outside, and I could see the smoke and everything from the flagpole at school. Back home, the view from my mom's room was different. It was a lot of smoke then, and when it cleared, there was no more Twin Towers.

Lincoln reopened its doors to students the next day, but the Cyclones' season was closed. The New York–Penn League announced on September 12 that it was canceling the Cyclone-Crosscutter series, and the teams were declared co-champions. Brooklyn had its title, but not the way anyone wanted. As Jeff Wilpon said, "We would have liked to jump around in the soda or champagne, but I don't think anybody would be in the mood for baseball."

Brett: "I went back into Manhattan late on the eleventh and stayed at my apartment. The next couple days some of the guys got a chance to come see my place—they hated it, said it was too small—and then a couple days later we had like a lunch for the team, especially for the guys going to Instructional. A lot of teams had canceled Instructional, but the Mets didn't. So we went down to the stadium—pretty much the whole team except for a few guys that had left for home and got in deep crap for doing that—got our stuff and went to lunch at a place next to the field. We talked about how it was a great, miracle season, but we were reminded not to let go of what had happened. We all understood. And from there it was over."

Anthony stopped by the stadium on the thirteenth on his way home from school. "I went by the stadium, and they were giving out papers saying that they gave the Cyclones the championship, or I guess half the championship. I guess the tragedy of 9/11 just ended the season. I'm sure they would have won it all, but 9/11 was more important."

September 11 brought the season that baseball returned to Brooklyn to a jarring end, but there is no question that the Brooklyn Cyclones will come back as strong as ever. This is a team that brought life and passion to people, from vendors to barmen, cops to councilmen, and, most of all, to its neighbors and its players.

Anthony Otero needed something special to get him out of his project shell; Brett Kay needed something intense to snap him out of his SoCal reverie. The Brooklyn Cyclones provided this something for both of them, and their lives will never be the same.

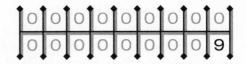

Epilogue September 15, 2003

While New York City was mourning the second anniversary of the tragedy of 9/11/01, the Cyclone organization and its fans were dealing with a more minor sadness—the team's championship series loss to the Williamsport Crosscutters. Two years after Brett Kay's Cyclones had been a game away from winning the New York–Penn League title over the Crosscutters when 9/11 ended the season, and one year after the Year Two Cyclones suffered through a 37–37 season, the new Brett Kays and Ross Peeples, with names like Rashad Parker and Matthew Lindstrom, were trying to gain a measure of redemption. It was not to be, as the Cyclones were swept out of the Williamsport series on September 10.

While none of the 2001 Cyclones were a part of this year's 47–28 regular season and championship runner-up effort, in many ways the scene at KeySpan Park was the same as ever. . . .

Despite their mediocre performance on the field, the 2002 Cyclones topped their own 2001 showing and set the short-season Class-A attendance record with 317,124 fans for thirty-eight dates—an average of 8,345 per game. KeySpan remained an ultrapopular place to watch baseball during the successful 2003 season, as 307,383 paying customers attended the thirty-seven dates (rainouts and double-headers affect the number of open dates). KeySpan Park was voted "Best New Ballpark" at the close of 2001 by Ballparks.com, and it remains one of the gems of the entire Minor League baseball universe. KeySpan also now has the Brooklyn Baseball Gallery, a well-designed, one-room museum, housed in the ground floor of the stadium, that has some beautiful old memorabilia. The museum opened during the 2002 season in a ceremony attended by former Brooklyn Dodgers Duke Snider, Ralph Branca, Gene Hermanski, Al Gionfriddo, Tommy Holmes and Johnny Podres, as well as Joan Hodges (Gil's wife) and Rachel Robinson (Jackie's wife). There is talk of further embracing the past by putting up a statue of Jackie Robinson and Pee Wee Reese with Reese's arm around Robinson's in the famous pose, honoring their efforts of teamwork and friendship that struck a blow against racism when Robinson broke into the big leagues in 1947. A statue would look good outside the stadium, which has another monument that's been built since the 2001 season ended—a statue/wall on the west side of the stadium that honors the Brooklyn-based firemen who died on September 11.

On the Surf Avenue side of KeySpan, Peggy O'Neill's bar, which has the location in Bay Ridge where Cyclone players were known to get "taken care of," has a bar built into the stadium, with a seating area that stretches out onto the sidewalk. On nice days—which are frequent in a Coney Island summer—the pre- and postgame crowd at Peggy O'Neill's is substantial. This probably isn't doing much for good old Ruby's Bar on the boardwalk, but the folks who work at that drinking hole maintain that their business is not at all predicated on the baseball team.

Fans that can't make it to the stadium can still follow the Cyclones on the airwaves. The Cyclones had ten games televised on Fox Sports New York in 2002 and 2003, and they had a brief stint in 2002 on Sporting News AM-Radio (though 2003 found them back on Kingsborough Community College's pitifully weak 90.9 FM). The stadium itself is also getting busier, as the organization is doing a better job of renting it out when the Cyclones aren't using it. Since the middle of the 2001 season, KeySpan has become the home of the "Borough Baseball Challenge" which pits New York City college teams against one another, city high school championships, several boxing matches, and music concerts. KeySpan also welcomed the big-league New York Mets for an open workout at the end of March 2003 (which drew thousands of fans despite nasty weather that mostly kept the players in the dugout). The workout was being heavily hyped by the Cyclones' website, because it represented, in the organization's own words, "Major Leaguers taking the field in Brooklyn for the first time in forty-six years."

The Cyclones have maintained their close Mets' ties with the coaching staff as well. Howard Johnson, the batting coach in 2001, was the manager in 2002, and the 2001 "roving" instructor, Tim Teufel, was the manager in 2003.

The area around KeySpan Park that is unaffiliated with the team or stadium has changed slightly since the first season ended, but not the way then-mayor Rudolph Giuliani had predicted. As a *Daily News* article in the summer of 2003 put it, "the promised economic benefit to the neighborhood has yet to materialize," citing merely modest gains at local restaurants and at the Aquarium.

The same article makes a valid excuse as well: the Stillwell Avenue station is still in the midst of the massive renovation project that was planned in tune with the Cyclones' arrival. Of the trains that used to go all the way to Stillwell, only the W still does; the others stop earlier now and offer bus service to the area. When construction is complete, hopefully before the 2004 Cyclones (and beach) season hits its stride, the station will be a state-of-the-art hub, whisking passengers from multiple lines in and out of the neighborhood. The completed station may be what really helps the development torch pick up, because, as of now, the changes spurred by the building of KeySpan Park seem a lot closer to what my real estate source predicted (a nice neighborhood amenity) than what Rudy Giuliani or Robert Lederman did (a massive force that will change the entire neighborhood and bring in corporations, for better—Giuliani—or for worse—Lederman). We're also living in a different time now. The September 11 tragedy and fears of subsequent terrorist attacks have changed the city's focus greatly, and there aren't gobs of money sitting around that people can use to gamble on Coney Island investment. It's probably safe to say that if KeySpan hadn't been built when it was, not even Giuliani would have been able to force the construction of KeySpan Park if he were still in office. Regardless, the Cyclone organization—which always seemed more in tune with what the team's effect could be than the bombastic mayor—is pleased with its modest but real influence on the neighborhood. "Clearly, it's not the kind of thing that will happen overnight, but we think we're making a positive impact, and it's definitely one of our areas of focus," says the Cyclones' media relations manager, Dave Campanaro. "In addition to winning games and selling tickets, the effect we have on the community is one of the major factors in determining our success. Fred Wilpon targeted Coney Island because of his emotional attachment to the area, and our impact is very important to him, and to the entire organization."

The man who thought that baseball in Brooklyn could have an even bigger impact if it played a full season, former Brooklyn borough president Howard Golden, has fallen further out of the picture than he was in 2001, even if his argument for a bigger stadium and longer season in Coney Island has greater merit today than it did back then. Golden was forced out of the Brooklyn borough president's office by term limits at the end of 2001 and was replaced by energetic Democrat Marty Markowitz. Golden maintains office space in a downtown Brooklyn law firm, but in the spring of 2003 he ignored numerous calls for comment while a secretary told me Golden has had some health concerns and would not talk to the media. Golden's beloved SportsPlex is likely dead unless it is built as part of a massive, citywide Olympic construction process in the event that New York City is "rewarded" with the 2012 Olympic Games. A former representative of Golden's who had worked on the SportsPlex says he doesn't think it's happening, and he added that Golden remains extremely bitter about how everything went with the birth of the Cyclones. "Why do you want to speak to Golden?" I'm asked. "He didn't do much with the Cyclones, and when he was involved it was controversial." While Golden's borough hall had a Dodger flag raised above it that the borough president said would fly until the Dodgers returned to Brooklyn, in June 2002 Markowitz took down that flag, presented it to Golden as a gift, and then raised a Cyclones flag.

Golden's polar opposite on Cyclone matters, the former New York City mayor Rudolph Giuliani, is now running a consulting firm in New York City. His national profile received a tremendous boost because of the way he handled the aftereffects of 9/11, and whispers persist that Giuliani will be a vice presidential candidate before long. Giuliani also took the time to cowrite one of the best-selling books of 2002, *Leadership*, which surprisingly barely mentions the Cyclones.

Giuliani's successor as mayor is Michael Bloomberg, the financial mogul with a softer image than Giuliani but perhaps even more divisive policy changes (banning smoking in bars and disbanding the Board of Education, for starters). Without making the grandiose statements about Minor League baseball and its effect on the city that his predecessor did, the Republican Bloomberg has continued the mayor's office's strong support of the city's teams, attending the home openers for the Cyclones as well as the Staten Island Yankees in 2002 and 2003.

In residential Coney Island, Mrs. Janet Otero is still being the best mother she can be, and the best Yankee fan, too. A cable TV dispute about money largely kept the Yankees off TV in 2002, but she remains devoted to the team and continues to maintain that Yankee Stadium will be the first stadium she ever goes to. "I'll wake up in the middle of the night to go to the bathroom or get some water or whatever, and I'll hear the radio on the Yankees, like whenever they're playing a late-night game," says Anthony. "And she'll be right next to the radio, listening to the game."

Mr. Otero remains unmoved by baseball. He followed up his regular-season finale in 2001 by attending the exact same end-of-season game in 2002, but that was it. He's still okay with the neighborhood, though during the area's off-season he still doesn't see all that much charm in Coney Island. "Besides the crowds in the season—when the neighborhood was already pretty busy, not much has changed. As far as the stuff they built into the stadium, it still seems like it's only open when the team is there," Mr. Otero says while waiting for a pizza order to be ready from the small, pre-Cyclone pizza shop around the corner from KeySpan.

Both Otero parents still bring up the specter of Disney, which, according to a *Crains' Business* story in the summer of 2002 was restarting talks to bring its style of amusement to Coney Island. "When it came out last summer it was on the news and everything, and people were worried," says Mrs. Otero. "I think there was even some people that took a bus to protest against Disney, but we didn't go."

James Otero, while not quite the athlete or sports fan that his older brother is (his Mom says he "gets bored by sports real easily"), is an excellent student, and, like they did with Anthony, the Oteros helped him apply to many high schools with better reputations than Lincoln's. James was accepted into Edward R. Murrow High School in the Midwood section of Brooklyn. "It's one of the best schools in Brooklyn, and we're proud he's going there," says Mrs. Otero. Mr. Otero adds, "I gotta drive him every day because it's a pain to get there, but it's important that he do well in school."

Anthony's baseball life, while still not likely to involve the pros, has gotten slightly more organized than it was in the summer of 2001, in part thanks to the Cyclones. After not playing for the Lincoln team as a freshman due to bad grades, during the summer of 2002 Anthony did get involved in a summer team that was based at Kaiser Park, a sprawling complex near the Coney Island Houses that stretches between Neptune Avenue and Gravesend Bay. Besides the handball courts it's known for (where Mr. Otero goes when he wants some real competition), Kaiser has four ballfields that, with the Cyclones' money and grounds-crew assistance, were made usable for kids like Anthony. The organized play and coaching, Anthony says, helped him "get real better at baseball." Anthony did so well playing at Kaiser that he was chosen for a Police Athletic League–sponsored traveling All-Star Team that got to play in Shea Stadium on August 8, 2002. Even the thought of seeing her son and his 60th precinct team play in a big-league stadium wasn't enough to induce Mrs. Otero to set foot in Shea before she went to Yankee Stadium, but she was awfully proud of Anthony just the same. "I wanted her to come, but I understand because it still has to be Yankee Stadium first," Anthony says. "Besides, some of my friends came to cheer for me, and that was really nice of them."

Galvanized by his PAL experience and momentarily passing his classes in school, Anthony made the junior varsity team at Lincoln in 2003, but the spring's horrendous weather limited the team to just seven games, while the varsity went 1–11 and did not even qualify for the thirty-two-team playoffs. If he can keep his grades at a passing level, Anthony figures to have a good shot at making the varsity team as a high school junior. But, as he and his family bemoaned from the moment he started at Lincoln, it is a high school without much of a baseball program. Even more depressing, despite decent equipment that Anthony was left in charge of and a couple of volunteer coaches, the Kaiser Park league never really got off the ground in 2003 because, despite Anthony's best efforts, not enough kids wanted to play.

Anthony remains devoted as ever to attending Cyclone games. "I've gone to lots of games [in the 2002 and 2003 seasons]. I see a lot of kids from school there, too. Sometimes me and my friends still buy the $5 bleacher tickets and then sit wherever. But the guy who is in charge of the league at Kaiser, Bob, he gave us tickets to go to the games also. If we went with him, or if we had our own tickets but we'd see him at the game, we'd sit with him. If the people tried to move us he'd say, 'no, these are the kids from my Little League.' He was proud to say that. He was telling everybody, which made us feel important."

Seeing Anthony beaming at KeySpan in the summer of 2002, I ask if he thinks he'll be going to games in the future as well. "I'll go all the time. As long as I live here, I'm going to games," he says with a smile.

In the summer of 2003, I bring Anthony, his girlfriend of six months, his brother James, and their old friend Josimar Aleman to a Yankee game. While still impressed with KeySpan, the kids' first visit to The Stadium truly blows them away. The trip also highlights Anthony's appropriately shrinking confidence that he might ever play for the Yankees. Seeing the likes of Hideki Matsui and Bernie Williams up close (our seats were in the upper deck, but Anthony and his boys are masters of sneaking into the first row, apparently no matter what stadium they're in) highlights what an amazing level big leaguers play at. Despite my invitation and the potentially historic implications for her personal baseball history, Mrs. Otero chooses not to join us at the game we attend, an August match-up with the Kansas City Royals. "I just want my kids to go and have fun," she tells me. Seemingly as always, they do just that.

The players who made up the beloved 2001 Cyclones team have generally been scattered around the Minor League map, with a concentration of them in Port St. Lucie, home of the Mets' high Class-A team, which they led to the 2003 Florida State League title.

On September 1, 2003, the very first Brooklyn Cyclone reached the Major Leagues, but it was not one that people ever really linked with the team back in 2001. It was Danny Garcia, a 6'1", 180-pound infielder who had been drafted in the fifth round of the 2001 draft out of Pepperdine University. Garcia's problem with the Cyclones was that he was too good. After hitting .321 and helping the team to a 14–1 mark in the fifteen games he played in Brooklyn during the 2001 season, Garcia was promoted to Capital City. Since then, he marched through the Mets' system, having successful stints at Capital City (low, full-season Class-A ball), Port St. Lucie (High-A), Binghamton (Double-A), and Norfolk (Triple-A). While Garcia became somewhat famous in his September stint with the Mets (earning front-page sports coverage in the *Daily News* by getting two hits in a game at Shea on September 2), other inaugural Cyclones struggled to recapture their 2001 magic.

After mediocre 2002 seasons, the original Cyclones' top starting pitchers, Luz Portobanco and Ross Peeples, arguably had even worse 2003 seasons. Portobanco was 2–5 with a 5.69 ERA at Port St. Lucie (Florida), while Peeples was so bad in a brief stint at Port St. Lucie that he was sent back to Capital City (Columbia, South Carolina), where he finished 1–4 with a 6.35 ERA. Meanwhile, Harold Eckert, the kid-friendly starting pitcher who says he'll be a teacher if he doesn't make it in baseball, put together an excellent 2003 season in Port St. Lucie (7–3 with a 2.93 ERA).

Like they did in 2001, David Byard and Blake McGinley helped those guys out of the bullpen in 2003, each pitching regularly for Port St. Lucie. Byard went 1–1 with four saves and a 1.46 ERA, while McGinley was a spectacular 9–1 with seven saves and a 1.02 ERA.

The outfielder Angel Pagan, whose ability so impressed Brett, played just about every day for Port St. Lucie in 2003, hitting .249 with one homer, thirty-three RBIs, and thirty-five stolen bases. Brett's favorite opponent, former college teammate and close friend Aaron Rifkin, who spent the summer of 2001 starring for the Staten Island Yankees, has moved impressively up the Yankee system. After splitting 2002 between the Yankees High Single-A and Double-A teams, Rifkin spent all of 2003 at Double-A Trenton, hitting .269 with nineteen home runs and ninety RBIs. It's rare that a Yankee moves all the way through that system because George Steinbrenner is so impatient to import superstars from other teams, but it would not be the least bit surprising to see Rifkin traded and make the Bigs elsewhere by the end of 2004 or beginning of 2005.

Mike Jacobs, the opening-night hero whom Brett replaced in the starting lineup when Jacobs got called up to Capital City in 2001, was with Double-A Binghamton for all of 2003, starring for the "B Mets" by catching and leading the team with seventeen home runs and eighty-one RBIs. At this point, Jacobs, along with the Australian Justin Huber, who spent about half of the 2003 season in Binghamton, are probably the best catching prospects in the Mets' organization. Both of them spent the summer of 2003 in the right place to learn how to be a big-league catcher. The Binghamton Mets' manager in 2003 was none other than John Stearns, the former Mets' All-Star who once roomed with Brett Kay's father at Colorado University.

Assuming the Mets' organization brings Stearns back to Binghamton in 2004, will Brett get the chance to play for him, too? Heading into the 2003 season, Brett placed his goals pretty squarely on getting to Binghamton by the beginning of 2004, but as of September '03, Brett has little way to know if that's going to happen.

In both 2002 and 2003, Brett had good spring trainings in the Mets' big-league camp. The fact that the Mets' organization wanted him in big-league camp is a good sign for Brett. Young guys don't get invited to that camp with the hope they'll make the team, but it means the organization thinks highly of him and wants to see him in the company of the big lea-guers. Brett is still wowed by the company he gets to keep in camp. A highlight of his first big-league camp, in 2002, came when Brett saw, from across the room, the Mets' first baseman, Mo Vaughn, reaching into Brett's chewing tobacco supply and taking a pinch. Not wanting to ruffle any feathers, Brett watched the apparent theft silently. When he returned to his locker and picked up his tobacco, there was a $50 bill there. "So that's how these guys operate," he thought to himself. The highlight of big-league camp in 2003 was serving as Mike Piazza's tossing partner when the players warm up. "I'm playing catch with Mike Piazza every day," Brett says during 2003 spring training in Port St. Lucie. "You know what he calls me? Mary Kay, like the cosmetic line. How cool is it that I'm hanging out with him?!"

Brett also spent a large portion of his time in 2003 spring training working out with Stearns, who is taking on a fairly large role with the catchers in the Mets' organization. "He's our catching coach right now," says Brett. "It's amazing how things work out. It's funny, 'cause he'll ask about my mom, speak to me about my dad a little. He's a great guy, but I don't know him like my parents did. And I can't really get underneath that shell right now, because the focus is on baseball. But I'd like to someday."

While Stearns managed the Mets' Double-A team in 2003, he was joined by some of Brett's old friends—Bobby Ojeda (who worked as pitching coach) and Edgar Alfonzo (hitting coach).

And speaking of Brett's coincidental connections, Art Howe, the for-mer roommate of Brett's "father figure," Bob Sporrer, is now the manag-er of the big-league Mets. When Brett Kay is involved, it is a small world after all.

The biggest problem for Brett, who showed talent and an ability to perform under pressure during the 2001 Cyclones' season, is that he has not had very impressive regular seasons over the last two summers.

In 2002, Brett spent a brief stint with Capital City and then hit .222 in sixty-four games at Port St. Lucie. "I was really happy with the [2001] season that I had, and I had a good Instructional League, as well. I went home thinking, I had a great year and everything's going to be all right next year. But then [the 2002 season] was nothing I wanted. I think I put too much pressure on myself and tried to play through a couple injuries, a wrist injury, my back flared up, and that was a mistake."

I just think that mentally—I'm really big into the mental part of the game—I just beat myself up too much. I was leading my league in hitting at one point, and then it was a pitfall from there. I tore myself up after that, and I couldn't get out of it and let it bother me. I thought I was ready for the higher level but obviously I wasn't. Me going to big-league camp my second year out, not that it wasn't a great experience for me, and not that I came out cocky, but I thought that overall things would be as easy as they were in Brooklyn, but they weren't. It was just a bad year. After that season, I skipped Instructional League—I just wanted to get home. When I came home, I stayed in a shell for a month or two because I didn't want to talk to anybody. There's a lot of people around Orange County that are naysayers. There's some guys that are your buddies but then there's guys that are just pricks. So I stayed in my little shell.

By the spring of 2003, Brett was feeling better. "Now that I'm back in camp, everything looks good again. I'm in great shape, and I think I'm prepared mentally and physically. The mindset is, it's my third year. I had a great first year, a bad second year, and if this year's mediocre, that's no good. You gotta set high goals for yourself. I expect to do well this year— I always expect that—but if not, then it's not to be. We'll see. I'll go in prepared, and I'll enjoy it. I may be behind [Justin] Huber, and if that's the case I'll make the best of it. I'm not going to whine and cry about it. It's baseball, and it's a business. Whatever happens, happens."

Speaking before the 2003 season, Alfonzo, who managed Brett at Port St. Lucie in 2002, still feels like Brett has a good shot to make the big leagues. "He did not have a good second year," Alfonzo says. "That was his first year playing a full season [rather than the short-season format the Cyclones play], and the jump is not easy. Plus he had come in early for big-league camp. That's a lot of baseball the first time you do it. He seemed tired. But it's okay. I still think he can make it because now his mind is prepared for what it takes to make it at the next levels. And he's still a great leader."

The 2003 season brought more frustrating inconsistency to Brett's game. Playing only for Port St. Lucie, Brett appeared in sixty-four games (at catcher, DH, and first base, hitting .251 with three home runs, nineteen RBIs, and five stolen bases). Ironically, Huber wasn't even that much of a barrier; the majority of the catching time went to the light-hitting Joe Hietpas, who was a sixteenth-round pick in 2001 and didn't even make the Cyclones until 2002. "Justin was here for a little, but the team actually started to win when he got promoted, which was a little awkward," says Brett, waiting in Port St. Lucie for his girlfriend to fly in so they can drive back to California for the winter (remember, Brett doesn't do commercial flights). "I think maybe Joe and I were a little better with the pitchers. But the team must have liked Joe's defense even more than mine, because even though I hit okay, they didn't play me all that much."

The bubbly Brett Kay of 2001, and even of spring training 2003, is nowhere to be found right now. Even though catchers usually take the longest to develop of any position, Brett feels the clock ticking on his career if he doesn't make some serious progress soon. "Playing baseball is still my dream," he says seriously. "But I believe that we each have our own destiny. Maybe I reached my peak already. I had such a great season in Brooklyn, but then I had a so-so year last season and a so-so year this season. I just played so inconsistently. I was also a little banged up. I think I may have arm surgery this off-season."

The surgery, which would be paid for by the Mets because his pain has been spurred by baseball, will keep Brett in touch with the Mets' organization through this off-season. Not like they'll be giving him updates on where he fits into their future plans, however. "They really don't communicate with you about where you stand," Brett mutters. "I just need to see what kind of off-season I have. If my arm turns out okay and I have a good winter of working out, I think I'll try again next year. It also depends if I can get a job with my brother (who works for the Anaheim Angels) this winter. I'm sorry to be so vague, but I really don't know what to say after the season I had."

Brett's offensive struggles and the minimal fan support (two rungs higher than Brooklyn, the Port St. Lucie Mets average about 1,200 a game—Brett says "there are good fans here, but it never seems like more than a thousand") hammer home the point that what happened in Brooklyn in the summer of 2001 was a dream. Still, Brett tries to enjoy himself. "In Port St. Lucie me and some of my buddies from the Cyclones rented a house on the bay. We're right next to a Pitch N Putt golf course. We'd go fishing every night, golf whenever we could. We had a great time."

In all, Brett's last two seasons could hardly have been more unlike 2001, when, as Dave Campanaro says, "Brett made sure he'd always be remembered as a Cyclone because of how he was with the fans and the plays he made against the Yankees in the deciding game of the playoff series."

"Oh, yeah, it's different. I still watch the tape of that Yankee playoff game all the time. There's been nothing like that [since then]," says Brett, who catches his breath a bit when reminded that it was his last game in KeySpan Park. "Weird, huh?"

Brett has not been in New York since he left for Florida Instructional League several days after 9/11. "I'd love to go back there. I miss it. I loved that place. Everything about that year: living in Manhattan, having all these girls think I'm a god or something—even though I have a girl back home, it was still a good feeling. And playing in the best stadium you could ever imagine, like a true mini big leagues. It was awesome, and I was in a zone the whole year. That season in Brooklyn was something that I'll never experience again."

2001 Statistics and Standings

Cyclones Final Batting Statistics, 2001

PLAYER	AVG	G	AB	R	H	2B	HR	RBI	BB	SO	SB	SLG	OBP
Abreu, Dave, 2B	.182	4	11	1	2	0	1	1	0	2	0	.455	.182
Arias, Leandro, 2B	.241	36	112	12	27	7	3	11	10	31	2	.402	.303
Bacani, David, 2B	.295	23	95	13	28	6	0	9	5	12	5	.358	.340
Beuerlein, Tyler, C	.253	21	75	10	19	5	0	6	8	26	0	.320	.341
Caligiuri, Jay, 1B	.328	66	238	38	78	14	5	34	26	31	4	.475	.403
Corr, Frank, OF	.302	61	212	38	64	21	13	46	14	32	6	.594	.365
Coyne, Tony, IF	.000	1	2	0	0	0	0	0	0	1	0	.000	.000
Devarez, Noel, OF	.250	54	188	30	47	10	10	33	10	63	3	.463	.296
Garcia, Danny, 2B	.321	15	56	10	18	2	1	6	4	10	3	.411	.387
Hernandez, Vladimir, 2B	.245	15	49	2	12	1	0	4	2	7	2	.306	.269
Huber, Justin, C	.000	3	9	0	0	0	0	0	0	4	0	.000	.000
Jacobs, Mike, C	.288	19	66	12	19	5	1	15	6	11	1	.409	.364
Jiannetti, Joe, 3B	.348	41	158	24	55	13	3	29	18	29	8	.487	.420
Kay, Brett, C	**.311**	**49**	**180**	**28**	**56**	**13**	**5**	**18**	**16**	**28**	**2**	**.467**	**.380**
Lawson, Forrest, OF	.280	49	164	18	46	6	1	15	6	23	7	.360	.314
Lydon, Wayne, OF	.246	21	57	12	14	1	0	1	7	18	10	.298	.348
McIntyre, Robert, SS	.197	67	233	35	46	10	8	35	18	67	7	.352	.263
Pagan, Angel, OF	.315	62	238	46	75	10	0	15	22	30	30	.374	.388
Piercy, Michael, PH	.000	3	1	0	0	0	0	1	1	0	1	.000	.500
Pittman, Richard, SS	.333	5	12	0	4	0	0	0	1	5	0	.333	.385
Rodriguez, Edgar, 3B	.239	27	92	8	22	5	5	13	4	23	0	.457	.287
Shinjo, Tsuyoshi, OF	.286	2	7	0	2	0	0	1	1	2	0	.286	.375
Sosa, Francisco, C	.389	24	72	12	28	3	1	8	2	7	2	.500	.421
Todd, Jeremy, 1B	.182	17	44	4	8	1	0	3	7	13	0	.205	.291
Toner, John, OF	.258	38	124	10	32	8	1	16	8	33	3	.363	.326
Zaragoza, Joel, 3B	.170	28	53	5	9	2	0	1	3	16	1	.208	.228
Team Totals	.279		2548	368	711	143	58	321	199	524	97	.414	.343

Cyclones Final Pitching Statistics, 2001

PLAYER	W–L	ERA	G	GS	SV	IP	H	R	ER	BB	SO	OPPAVG
Bowen, Chad	1–2	4.82	3	2	0	9.1	14	5	5	3	11	.359
Braswell, Bryan	1–0	2.08	5	2	0	13	12	3	3	2	13	.235
Byard, David	3–1	1.46	22	0	9	37	21	7	6	11	32	.164
Cabrera, Yunior	0–0	3.00	1	0	0	3	4	1	1	2	4	.308
Cox, Mike	6–1	2.91	13	7	0	52.2	40	25	17	41	73	.213
DiNardo, Lenny	1–2	2.00	9	5	0	36	26	10	8	17	40	.200
Eckert, Harold	9–1	3.34	13	11	0	70	51	31	26	21	75	.200
Gahan, Matthew	4–1	1.99	10	3	4	40.2	29	16	9	7	42	.187
Herbison, Brett	0–2	6.75	6	5	0	12	15	11	9	6	9	.294
Martin, Tom	0–0	0.00	1	1	0	1	2	0	0	0	0	.500
Mattox, David	1–0	0.90	2	2	0	10	5	2	1	3	12	.147
McGinley, Blake	5–0	1.94	18	0	4	46.1	30	12	10	11	59	.182
Ogle, Rylie	0–1	1.26	6	0	0	14.1	15	3	2	5	14	.278
Olson, Ryan	0–1	2.16	7	1	2	25	15	6	6	9	22	.169
Ough, Wayne	0–1	6.48	7	3	0	16.2	11	12	12	17	19	.180
Peeples, Ross	9–3	1.34	16	15	0	80.1	63	19	12	29	67	.214
Peterson, Matt	2–2	1.62	6	6	0	33.1	26	7	6	14	19	.217
Portobanco, Luz	5–3	2.04	13	12	0	70.2	51	20	16	29	52	.210
Roman, Orlando	1–1	5.03	9	0	2	19.2	14	13	11	8	18	.192
Scobie, Jason	3–0	0.89	18	0	7	40.1	22	4	4	8	32	.161
Sherman, Chris	0–0	3.72	3	0	1	9.2	10	4	4	5	6	.286
Walker, Brian	1–2	2.57	13	1	2	28	26	11	8	12	24	.236
Others	0–0	4.50	1	0	0	2	3	1	1	1	1	.375
Team Totals	52–24	2.37		76	31	671	505	223	177	261	644	.207

Final 2001 New York-Penn League Standings

McNAMARA DIVISION

Team (Affiliation)	W–L°	PCT	GB	LAST 10
Brooklyn Cyclones (Mets)	52–24	.684	—	5–5
Staten Island Yankees (Yankees)	48–28	.632	4	7–3
Pittsfield Astros (Astros)	45–30	.600	6.5	7–3
Hudson Valley Renegades (Devil Rays)	39–37	.513	13	3–7
New Jersey Cardinals (Cardinals)	35–41	.461	17	6–4
Lowell Spinners (Red Sox)	33–43	.434	19	7–3
Vermont Expos (Expos)	28–47	.373	23.5	1–9

PINCKNEY-STEDLER DIVISION

Team (Affiliation)	W–L°	PCT	GB	LAST 10
Williamsport Crosscutters (Pirates)	48–26	.649	—	6–4
Jamestown Jammers (Braves)	39–36	.520	9.5	6–4
Oneonta Tigers (Tigers)	37–37	.500	11	6–4
Batavia Muckdogs (Phillies)	37–39	.487	12	4–6
Auburn Doubledays (Blue Jays)	32–42	.432	16	3–7
Utica Blue Sox (Marlins)	27–47	.365	21	4–6
Mahoning Valley Scrappers (Indians)	26–49	.347	22.5	4–6

°Games played may differ from team to team due to cancelled games that were not made up

Acknowledgments

First and foremost, I have to thank the people who gave this book life beyond a simple historical recap: Brett Kay and the Otero family of Anthony Jr., James, Anthony Sr., and Janet. They allowed me into their lives not only during the magical summer of 2001, but for many months after, even up to today, as I would recheck dates and facts and just want to see how they were doing. I'm not certain we'll ever see Brett or Anthony make it to the Bigs, but I know they'll both lead contented lives because they are amazing guys who can derive pleasure from life's simple things.

For assistance with interviews, research, and advice, in varying degrees, I turned gratefully to Cal State–Fullerton's sports information director, Ryan Ermeling; the Cyclones' media relations manager, Dave Campanaro, and his colleague Gary Perone; the office of New York–Penn League commissioner Ben Hayes; *New York Daily News* managing editor Bill Boyle; and Michael Fabricant, the head of the Ph.D. Program in Social Welfare at New York's Hunter College School of Social Work. Mike made his biggest impact on me, however, when he introduced me to the woman who helped conceive this book in the first place, my excellent agent, Lane Zachary. Lane, in turn, helped bring the book to New York University Press, where Steve Maikowski, Charles Hames, Despina Papazoglou Gimbel, Stephen Magro, Melissa Scheld, Jennifer Yoon,

Nicholas Taylor, and others behind the scenes made it a reality. Big thanks to all of them.

Personally, I am grateful to my coworkers at *SLAM, KING,* and *XXL* magazines, especially E-i-C's Russ Bengtson and Datwon Thomas for being patient with me while I worked on this. I am also grateful to Justin Borucki, Andrea Buman, Patricia DeLuca, Ryan Jones, and Susan Price for assisting with the minutiae of book writing (and the art assistance it can call for). I also received support from my parents, Jeff and Nancy, my sisters, Emily and Samantha, and my brother-in-law, Ted Keating, as well as Sid and Frieda Bueller, Terry Quiros, and the Luis Quiros family— Luis, Martha, Julian, and Jeffrey. My friends, including Elena Perez with her connects, and Bo Ketner and Scott Potash, who constantly checked on my progress, were a big help as well.

And, finally, I'm honored to thank my beautiful wife, Laura Quiros, a smart and spiritual woman who is teaching me to dream while she keeps achieving her own dreams. And who knew she could help edit, too?

About the Author

Since starting his professional writing career at age twenty, Ben Osborne has had considerable success covering sports and urban affairs as a freelancer for major newspapers and magazines, including the *New York Times*, the *New York Daily News*, the *Village Voice*, and the *Washington Post*, and as a staff writer for the sibling magazines *SLAM, KING,* and *XXL*. He lives in Brooklyn with his wife. This is his second book.